Leaving

ROXANA
ROBINSON

MAGPIE
BOOKS

A MAGPIE BOOK

First published in the United Kingdom, Republic of Ireland and Australia
by Magpie, an imprint of Oneworld Publications Ltd, 2024
This paperback edition published 2024

Copyright © Roxana Robinson, 2024

The moral right of Roxana Robinson to be identified as the
Author of this work has been asserted by her in accordance
with the Copyright, Designs and Patents Act 1988

All rights reserved
Copyright under Berne Convention
A CIP record for this title is available from the British Library

ISBN 978-0-86154-775-3
eISBN 978-0-86154-776-0

Book design by Beth Steidle
Printed and bound in Great Britain by Clays Ltd, Elcograf S.p.A.

This book is a work of fiction. Names, characters, businesses,
organisations, places and events are either the product of the author's
imagination or are used fictitiously. Any resemblance to actual
persons, living or dead, events or locales is entirely coincidental.

Oneworld Publications Ltd
10 Bloomsbury Street
London WC1B 3SR
England

Stay up to date with the latest books,
special offers, and exclusive content from
Oneworld with our newsletter

Sign up on our website
oneworld-publications.com

Praise for *Leaving*

'Elegant... Robinson's storytelling is classic, page after page of swiftly moving scenes and writing as precise as rows of tilled earth... I'd read any story she has to tell.' Amity Gage, *New York Times*

'Robinson's finest work yet... A wondrous feat.'
Joan Frank, *Washington Post*

'Quietly compelling... Captures the aching pull of an all-consuming affair.'
New Yorker

'Robinson has captured all the sadness, poignancy and resignation of loss. Anyone who has ever been left, has ever left someone...will find in it an echo of their experience.' *Spectator*

'Robinson's smart, seductive writing style creates a sense of quiet menace that keeps the reader guessing until the book's shattering conclusion.'
Daily Mail Books to Look Forward to in 2024
pick by Christina Appleyard

'An impassioned portrayal of desire and loyalty, of romantic love and family duty, and an exploration into what we owe to each other—and to ourselves.'
Oprah Daily

'As absorbing as it is haunting... These two twined characters and their story will certainly stay with me for a long time.'
Meg Wolitzer, author of *The Wife*

'Compelling, heartstopping and all-too-believable, this is a marvelous read.'
Gish Jen, author of *The Resisters*

'A searing interrogation of honor and passion. It dissects the hidden cost of the choices we make, and the consequences with which we must endeavor to live.' Geraldine Brooks, author of *Horse*

'Roxana Robinson brings her wit, her beautiful sentences, and her compassionate clarity to this book about the price of love and the enduring need for it.' Amy Bloom, author of *In Love*

'These characters have such depth and this is an intense and heartbreaking story.'
Prima

'A remarkable novel—a quietly expansive story, in which elements of love and family coalesce and escalate into tragedy... A triumph of a book.'
Joan Silber, author of *Improvement*

'Robinson's captivating story of love, regret and the choices we make—or don't—is beautifully told, with two flawed and wonderfully drawn, nuanced characters at the heart of it.'
Julie Emery, *Heat* ★★★★

'The writing is beautiful; every sentence perfectly turned, and the settings are equally elegant.'
Daily Mail

'Examining responsibility and love, this is a beautifully written, honest account of the reality of experiencing deep passion late in life.'
Platinum

'Roxana Robinson demonstrates her trademark gifts as an intelligent, sensitive analyst of family life.'
Wendy Smith, *Chicago Tribune*

'As it navigates the chasm between responsibility and desire, this beautiful book will sweep you away.'
Marion Winik, *People*

'Elegantly structured and written, shimmering with feeling and truth. A triumph.'
Kirkus Reviews

'With searing perception and genuine empathy, Robinson...captures the fraught nuances of complicated family dynamics, treating the spurned-lover trope with gentleness and compassion.'
Carol Haggas, *Booklist* starred review

'Full of insights about the ambiguities, demands, and mysteries attached to passion, love, and commitment.'
Glenn C. Altschuler, *Psychology Today*

This book is for darling Tony

PART I

Chapter 1

"I NEVER THOUGHT I'D SEE YOU HERE," SARAH SAYS. THEN she adds, "But I never thought I'd see you anywhere."

They're at the opera house, on the second floor, near the head of the grand staircase. He's facing her, leaning his hips against the railing, hands set lightly on either side. Beyond him, in the high open space of the atrium, hang the glittering crystal chandeliers, frozen starbursts. Below, people move up and down the broad red-carpeted staircase, hurrying but stately. They are mostly over fifty, this is the second intermission, and there is only so much time left to meet someone, eat something, drink something, void, before the caped ushers begin playing their little xylophones, the bright tuneless melodies announcing the last act.

She had known him at once. His younger face is still visible within this older one, though this one is creased now, hollowed here, fuller there. The same square shape, same bright brown eyes and wide brow. The same thick light-brown hair, though now not so thick. The same fierce vitality in the gaze.

"I always thought I'd see you somewhere," he says. He looks directly into her eyes. He'd always done this, looked straight into her, as though she were important. It had always unnerved her. "You look just the same."

She smiles but shakes her head.

"You know what I mean," he says. "You do. Your eyes."

They had been close at one time.

AFTER THE LAST curtain call—the dark-haired soprano curtsying deeply and charmingly, kissing her fingertips to the audience as plastic-wrapped bouquets thud onto the stage, before the swirling gold curtain is finally drawn for good—Sarah stands, putting on her jacket. She buttons it as she inches her way across the row of seats to join the slow scrum in the aisle. She glances around for Warren, though he'd told her he was on the other side of the house. Almost as soon as they'd met, the little xylophones had begun their atonal melodies, and they'd had to part. He'd asked her to come out for a drink afterward but she'd said no. She'd said it would be too late.

Actually it had been too sudden. She couldn't decide, in that moment, if she wanted to sit across from him again, letting him look into her. He asked for her email address but he hadn't written it down; she thinks he'll forget it. It's so easy to forget those addresses, which seem in the moment so obvious, so unforgettable, clara38@whatever, but they're also obvious in all their other iterations, too, was it clara39@somewhereelse, or clarab38? Hers is simple and obvious. She thinks he'll forget it.

Out in the lower hall the crowd moves slowly toward the wide stairs up to the lobby. Near the base of the staircase is a small white-haired woman in a red coat. She stands stock-still, like a rock in the current. Her feet are slightly apart, braced against something. Anxiety fills her; Sarah can feel it as she approaches. She stops beside the woman.

"Would you like my arm going up the stairs?" Sarah asks.

The woman looks up. She has a pleasant lined face, withered cheeks, small bright blue eyes. Relief floods from her like mist from a mountain. "Oh yes," she says. "Thank you so much."

She takes Sarah's forearm and they begin the climb. The woman leans against her, clasping tight. She's desperate about something: pain, or fear. The panicked grip makes Sarah think of someone drowning, how you should never let them touch you, because they'll take you down with them. She's never known what you were supposed to do instead. You can't simply watch. But this tiny frail woman can't pull her down, Sarah is stable enough for them both. They go slowly, step by step.

"I had surgery on my foot," the woman explains, apologetic. "Weeks ago. I thought I was pretty much healed, so I didn't bring my cane. It wasn't so bad when I came, but now I can hardly walk. Stupid of me."

At the top of the stairs they continue; Sarah can't simply walk away from her. When they reach the heavy glass door Sarah holds it open and the woman shuffles through. The audience pushes past, bursting from the building, striding off quickly across the plaza, toward cabs, cars, subways. Sarah and the woman pause at the edge of the vast plain. It's clear that she can't manage this on her own.

"I'll take you to Broadway," says Sarah, "and put you in a cab."

"You're very kind." The woman takes Sarah's arm again and they begin the slow trek. "I should have brought my cane, but I was determined I'd be all right." She shakes her head. "Stubbornness," she says, "and vanity."

Sarah wonders if it's only women who apologize for everything. Would a man blame his physical helplessness on his own character flaws?

It's January. The night sky is dark and dense, bright with the reflected glow of the city. In the center of the plaza the fountain pulses, low illuminated jets moving to a mysterious rhythm. The woman grips her arm hard, shuffling fearfully. Sarah matches her steps to the woman's and wonders if this will happen to her: If you're hale it's hard to imagine being helpless. The worst of it must be being alone.

Sarah looks around again for Warren, but he must be long gone by now. The opera is still shimmering in her mind, the music surging behind her thoughts. Tosca's death lies within her like a single piercing note.

At Broadway they move slowly north until Sarah steps off the curb, her arm raised, to hail a cab. When it pulls over she comes back. The woman's feet are braced apart again, her face taut with anxiety.

Sarah helps her into the cab. Settling against the seat, the woman looks up at her. "I can't thank you enough," she says. "So stupid of me."

"Happy to do it." Sarah means it: a woman alone, near-helpless. She wonders if the woman has children, and where they are. When would you call your child for help? If you found yourself at the opera house after the last act, unable to climb the stairs? How bad would it have to be? Her mother would never have called her.

HE HADN'T FORGOTTEN her address.

His first message is short. I was glad to see you. She doesn't answer at once. It's the tone that concerns her. He's married, she knows that. What does she want? But she was glad to see him. She's allowed to be a friend. Finally she writes back, Yes. Me too.

He writes again. He's coming to New York on business next month; will she meet him for dinner? She thinks about it. The speed of email telescopes time, so that thinking about it for a few hours seems like days. Coming into the city for dinner is complicated for her: she lives in northern Westchester, over an hour away. It really means spending the night. She doesn't like driving home late, alone, her head fumed with wine. But she has a friend with a spare bedroom, who always offers it. She writes back, Yes.

They meet at the restaurant, a fancy one on the West Side. Along the street are big plate-glass windows. As Sarah walks along the sidewalk, her little suitcase trundling behind her, she sees him inside. He's at a table in the middle of the room, very upright. His elbows are set elegantly on the table, hands clasped. He's watching the door.

As she comes in he smiles at her, spreading open both hands in celebration.

The restaurant is modern and expensive. The latter is evident from the heightened awareness of everyone in the room, the slightly hostile deference of the headwaiter; the attentive, slightly condescending waiters, the sharp sidelong glances of the diners. The glitter of earrings and bracelets. Along the inner wall, more plate-glass windows give onto the kitchen, where chefs in white coats move swiftly, chopping and stirring and slicing, among white tile and stainless steel, pots and knives, steam and flame. The kitchen is like a silent movie, the workers framed, frenetic, soundless.

Warren stands to greet her, smiling.

"Thank you," she says, sliding onto the banquette. When he sits down their faces are close, and he looks directly into her eyes.

Unsettled, she speaks to break the silence.

"I don't think men stand up for women anymore," she says. "Do they? When we were kids, my father would say to my brother, 'Stand up when your mother comes into the room.' Do you remember? No one does that now."

"The culture of our youth," he says. "Gone."

"Good riddance, most of it," she says. "All those rules."

"It's good to see you," he says.

Thirty years, anyway. Nearly forty.

THEY'D GROWN UP IN the same community outside Philadelphia. The Main Line was a long suburban cluster of linked villages set along the commuter railroad that ran west of the city. It was a tribal place, everyone connected by kin or friendship. They weren't all rich; money wasn't the main thing. Philadelphia cared about a family's longevity, not its wealth. Ostentation was frowned upon, no flashy cars or grandiose houses. Everyone went somewhere else in the summer, some ramshackle shingle building, tiny or rambling, owned outright or shared among three generations and forty-five cousins, in the mountains or on a lake or on the New England shore. And everyone went to private schools, which were less expensive then. That was how the children became members of the tribe. The boys' and girls' schools were separate, but they all met at Glee Club concerts and dances and sports and birthday parties. Warren and Sarah had known each other since childhood. He'd taken out her sister Lynn before he'd taken out Sarah. He and Sarah started seeing each other during their junior year in college. All the rest of that year, and that summer, the last before graduation, they'd been a couple. She'd thought they might get married.

One evening at the end of August he arrived to pick her up at her parents' house in Villanova. She was upstairs getting dressed when she heard his car. It was an old green Austin-Healey that sounded like a motorboat. He wasn't rich; the car was secondhand, though still glamorous.

Sarah stood in front of the mirror, trying to zip up her dress, a pink linen sheath with a long side zipper. She heard the car come up the gravel driveway and stop in front of the house. The zipper was stuck just below the upper edge of her bra. She heard the car door shut, then Warren running up the flagstone path. He called up to her.

"Sarah Carson Blackwell, come down! I can see you up there, fussing. Come down! I have something to tell you!"

Sarah said nothing, tugging at the zipper. She heard the big front door open and shut: now he was inside the house. She could feel his presence, a little charge of electricity, the air lightening. She abandoned the zipper, leaving a racy little gap under her arm, and stepped into her heels.

When she reached the front hall Warren had gone into the library, where her parents were watching the news. They sat in dark red armchairs on either side of the little Chesterfield sofa. They each had a scotch and ice in a cut-glass tumbler.

Sarah's mother, Carola, came from an old Philadelphia family. During the eighteenth century the Wingates had been in the China trade, and also in government, senators and governors and diplomats. One of the Wingate houses was now open to the public—a big handsome stone Georgian, though its neighborhood was now seedy and run-down. Everyone knew that Sarah was a Wingate. But Sarah's father, George, was not from Philadelphia. He was from Minneapolis and a Catholic (the tribe was Episcopalian), so he was a double outsider. He was a partner in a good Philadelphia law firm, but it was Carola who had the tribal connection. Also the money. There was still quite a lot of it, through trusts and real estate. Her father resented the imbalance. Because of this, her mother always deferred to him.

"What are you all up to tonight?" asked Carola. She had square shoulders, thick gray hair, and heavy eyebrows. She swirled the ice in her glass.

"We're setting off on an adventure," Warren said.

"Jenna Davenport's birthday party," Sarah added.

"That will be fun." Her mother liked Warren.

George stared with animosity at the newscaster, who was talking about Vietnam. George hated the war, he hated hearing about it, and he hated Walter Cronkite, with his mustache and his earnest, avuncular manner.

"More idiocy," George said. He took a swallow of his drink.

"Are you driving that car?" Carola was smiling at Warren, almost flirting. "The one that sounds like a motorboat?"

"I am," said Warren. "Always ready to take you for a spin, Mrs. Blackwell."

Carola smiled a bit more and shook her head.

"You'd have to wear a scarf," Sarah said. "The wind ruins your hair."

"Your mother doesn't care about that," Warren said. "Your mother has always secretly longed to be a race-car driver. I'm always ready to help her realize that wish."

Carola laughed outright, twinkling.

George Blackwell looked at Warren. "What kind of car is it?"

"Austin-Healey," said Warren. "If you know the car you might think it's a bit lightweight, the steering a bit unresponsive, and you'd be right. Also that it sounds like a motorboat."

George stared at him, then took another swallow.

"You might also think it's beautiful," Warren finished. "Mine's not in perfect shape, which is why I could afford it."

"Shall we go?" Sarah didn't like all this sparring, her mother's twinkle, her father's veiled hostility.

"Have a good time." Carola raised her hand and waggled her fingers in a decorous farewell. George said nothing.

"Thanks," Sarah said. " 'Bye."

SARAH WAS NOT close to her parents. She would not have known how: her mother was cool and formal, her father brusque and cynical. Nor were their children close to each other. Alden kept to himself; Lynn resented Sarah. Sarah was the middle child, quiet and responsible.

As a treat Sarah was sometimes allowed into her parents' room while her mother was dressing to go out. Sarah chose the jewelry for her mother to wear. It was usually modest—a string of pearls, earrings made of seashells—unless the occasion was big and formal. Then Carola wore real jewelry, fancy things.

Sarah watched her mother standing before the mirror in her white slip. She raised her arms, holding the silk sheath above her, lightly bunched. She slid her hands through the armholes, then dropped the dress down over her head, wriggling her shoulders to get through. Her mother was tall, with a long waist and rounded arms. Her head reappeared, her dark smooth hair in its neat bob, emerging from the open neck. Her arms arose, bare and white. The dress slid down into place and she pulled it all the way down over her slip. Her movements were smooth and practiced. This was how it was to be a grown-up woman.

The sheath was watered green silk, which shimmered where the light fell on it. Sarah had found square-cut emerald earrings that matched the dress perfectly. She held them out to Carola, who was smoothing the sheath down over her hips, looking at herself in the tall mirror.

"Mama?" Sarah said.

Her mother turned to look. "Too obvious," she said. "Find some red ones."

Her mother's jewelry was kept in a little lacquered Japanese chest on the mirrored top of her dressing table. Sarah swiveled open the drawers one by one. She found a pair of oval rubies, rimmed with diamonds. They were small; her mother's jewelry was good but not showy.

"Those'll do," her mother said, taking them. She leaned over to put them before the mirror on the dressing table.

Sarah stood beside her and watched her mother's reflection. As Carola clipped on each earring, she grimaced.

"Why do you make that face?" Sarah asked.

"It hurts when you put them on," Carola said. "After a while you stop feeling the pain. Then when you take them off it hurts again."

"I'm sorry," said Sarah, awed and saddened by this knowledge.

Her mother shook her head. "It's just how it is."

"You look beautiful," Sarah said.

Her mother gave a small wry smile and turned away from the mirror. "Handsome is as handsome does," she said. "My mother used to say that."

Sarah didn't know what this meant. Though once, when she was five, she'd been standing in the front hall one afternoon. She had opened the door of the closet, which had a full-length mirror in the back of it. She was looking at herself and trying out poses. She set one hand on her hip and raised her chin, looking sideways in the silvery glass. She narrowed her eyes, the way a princess might. The front door opened, and her father came in from outside. He pulled the heavy door closed behind him. He saw her; she froze.

"Admiring yourself?"

She said nothing.

"What do you think?" he asked. "Think you're beautiful?"

She said nothing.

"Well, you're not," he said, with a little laugh. "You can put that right out of your mind." He walked on through the hall into the living room, and through that to the library.

Sarah didn't move. She didn't want to make the smallest gesture that would acknowledge that she was standing where she was, tilting her head and slanting her eyes as if she were somebody. She hadn't even thought about beautiful. Right then what she wanted was invisible, so she could leave the mirror, the hall, the ground floor, tiptoe up the big staircase, without anyone knowing what she'd done. Without anyone knowing her bottomless shame. She didn't understand what she'd done, but she felt the shame rise up and engulf her.

WARREN HAD TAKEN down the convertible top.

When she got in, Sarah took her scarf from her bag, tying it tightly under her chin. She knew she should like the idea of a convertible—speed and freedom—but it was so noisy, it made it impossible to talk, and the buffeting wind was like an attack, blowing her hair into a frenzy. Warren fired up the motorboat engine. As they started down the driveway, he turned and said something she couldn't hear; she shook her head. He put on the brakes abruptly, skidding slightly on the gravel. He got out and leaned into the back to tug up the top. It scissored slowly upward, then into an awkward arch over her head. Inside again, he locked it into place with little latches.

"Why did you do that?" she asked.

"I want to be able to hear you." He started the engine's low chortle. "We have to be able to talk."

"So what was it you said?" she asked. "That I couldn't hear."

"I said, 'Let's go around the world. Next summer, after graduation.'" He looked at her as he shifted gears, wrestling the stick into place.

"Great," Sarah said. "I want to go to Italy. I love Italy." She thought of the Tuscan landscape, the red-tiled roofs, the dark spires of the cypress trees. The cool dimness of cathedrals.

Warren went on. "We'll work our way from country to country. We'll get jobs wherever we go."

"Jobs?" Sarah said. "What kind of jobs?" She was thinking of a Eurail Pass and youth hostels.

"Any kind," he said. "We'll be waiters. Bus conductors. Street sweepers."

He looked at her again. She smiled. She didn't know if he was serious.

Warren was famously unconventional. When he was fifteen he'd taken his parents' car and driven into the city to see a concert. And he'd been fired from the tennis camp where he'd taught for doing something—drinking? He carried a sort of unsettling charge, a bad-boy attraction. But this trip sounded crazy.

"Street sweepers," she said. Warren wasn't rich, maybe he couldn't afford a Eurail Pass and youth hostels. But couldn't he get a job before they went, and save for it? If they had to spend all their time finding jobs, and then working at them, how would they see the museums?

"Any old jobs," he said, downshifting. The engine made its growling noise.

"My parents would love *that*," said Sarah.

"I'll take care of your parents. Come on," he said. "We'll leave right after graduation. You've never been to Bucharest."

He reached over and took her hand and tapped it on her thigh.

"Bucharest? Behind the Iron Curtain?" she said. "What country is it in?"

"Romania," he said, "and yes."

"We can't go to a Communist country," she said.

"We'll talk our way in," Warren said. "Right through Checkpoint Charlie." He whistled, to show how fast they'd go through.

But you couldn't travel in Communist countries, they didn't let you in. So what did he mean?

Sarah wanted to go to Europe to see cathedrals and museums. She wanted to walk along the Seine, to hear French in the air around her. She wanted to hear the church bells in Rome. She didn't want to wait on tables in a dingy café. Or be arrested as a spy by the KGB.

Sarah smiled at him, wondering if all this was a joke. Smiling was stalling for time: Often she didn't understand what they meant, men. She knew some of Warren, but not all. She knew the part he'd shown her, but there was a great mountain of him still in shadow, a part she didn't know yet. She had no idea what he meant about this trip. If he thought it would be fun to break the laws and flout the authorities, she didn't want it.

Sarah had gone to an all-girls' school, the one her mother had gone to, and was now at a women's college. She'd never spent much time with boys; she found them mysterious. What did they want to talk about? What were women allowed to say? Disagreement was not permissible with her father; he disliked it. And he disliked subjects that he found boring. During dinner, the rule was "general conversation," which meant things that interested him. Not personal things. If the children became earnest or emotional, their father turned mocking. Being emotional in general was frowned on; being emotional in public was forbidden. Don't make a scene, her mother would say. What was permissible to say to boys? Sarah wasn't sure.

Warren smiled at her, then turned to the road, still holding her hand. Was he serious? If he was, she had no idea who he was.

Jenna Davenport's party went on late. They ended up in the backyard, drinking beer and playing Ghost. Warren won, using words that sounded not quite plausible and yet that were. Sarah challenged him at P-R-O-P-R-I-O. She was thinking of propriety, but he was thinking of proprioception. He always came up with things no one else had thought of.

It was the end of the summer. Warren kept mentioning the trip to their friends. He made it sound like a joke, a romp. Sarah didn't want to make a fuss in front of other people (don't make a scene), and she didn't want to make a fuss when they were alone (don't disagree). But she didn't understand it. Something shifted inside her; her trust in him began to lessen. He had taken that car, he'd been fired for drinking, and what did that mean? Was he one of those boys who was always in trouble? Because she didn't want that. She could feel herself withdrawing from him. The night before he left for college they had a fight; they made up and she cried. They had sex at the end, so late it was starting to get light, and she kept falling asleep. They made up but the distance was still there. She still felt she didn't know him, what kind of person he was. During the year they'd see each other seldom—her college was just outside New York City, his was outside Brunswick, Maine, six hours away. Then in the fall of her senior year she met Rob.

He was a friend of her roommate Celia's boyfriend, Andy. A group of them came down from Cambridge for the weekend. Celia asked Sarah to come out with them. They walked around the campus, the boys horsing around, showing off, then went out for pizza. Rob pulled his chair up next to Sarah, pushing in, nosing out another boy already beside her. He leaned close to her and said, "I've been watching you. I've been watching you and I can tell you are smart!" He was smiling as he said it, teasing, but not.

Rob had electric-blue eyes and an intimate manner. He was going to become a journalist. "Long-form," he added, a phrase she'd never heard. "I'm going to write for *The New Yorker*," he said. "Or *The Atlantic*. Investigative pieces. I want to make things change." She was impressed: he'd not only chosen a field but a particular place in it.

The phone booth in her dormitory was at the other end of the hall from Sarah's room. When the phone rang, whoever was nearest would answer, shout out a name, and then leave the receiver dangling. Rob began calling Sarah nearly every night, his calls interspersed with Warren's. It irritated the girls who answered.

"Blackwell again!" they would yell. "BLACKWELL!"

Sarah would call, "Thank you!" and hurry down the hall.

As she talked, other girls walked past, peering into the booth, tapping their watches to show how long she'd been on. Sarah nodded in response; she said she had to go.

She had told Rob about Warren at once. "I have a boyfriend," she said. Rob smiled and lifted a strand of hair off her shoulder, smoothing it back, away from her face. "Lucky him!" he said. He must have known already, she thought.

She hadn't told Warren about Rob; she wasn't sure what to say. Just telling him that she'd met someone else would sound as though she were breaking up with him. And she wasn't, was she? She mentioned that she'd gone into the city to see an exhibition at MoMA.

"A bunch of us went," she said. "Celia's boyfriend, Andy, and some friends of his."

"That's great that you can go into the city so easily!" Warren said. His goodwill engulfed her, making her uneasy. Was she taking advantage of him? Was she deceiving him? He was planning to visit her for Columbus Day weekend.

Rob and Andy came down often. They stayed with Andy's aunt, two towns over. The four of them went into the city, or stayed on campus. When the weather was good they had picnics on the lawn. When it got cold they sat in the dorm and played Hearts. When Rob won a trick he slapped his card down on top of hers. "Dahhh!" he shouted. "I've got you! Submit!"

"Just one trick," she protested. "You've only taken one trick," but he grabbed her and tickled her. She collapsed, helpless. "Stop," she begged. Tickling drove her mad.

Rob acted as though he owned her. She sort of liked his presumption. She wouldn't kiss him, because of Warren. He acted as though Warren didn't matter. He said he was going to take her to

France. "In Paris, we'll stay at the Ritz," he said. "They have pink linen sheets."

Rob's family wasn't rich, either, but Rob was very clear about his future: he was going to be successful and important.

During that fall Warren seemed very far away. When he called, Sarah felt uncomfortable. She couldn't remember what they had talked about before. Once he mentioned Bucharest, as though this were something to look forward to. It seemed difficult to discuss on the phone, distance echoing between them. The idea expanded in her mind; it became the thing she thought of first when she thought of him—that awful trip. Who was he?

One night in the dorm she spent an hour on the phone with Rob. She was in fits of laughter: he was so silly. It made her feel loose and unguarded, light and happy. After they hung up Sarah went back to her room. When the phone rang again, a girl yelled, "Blackwell! My god, you've only been off for six minutes!"

"Sorry!" She hurried back to the booth. The girl who had answered was standing in her doorway, glaring.

Sarah sat down and picked up the phone.

"Finally!" Warren said. "Someone's been on for an hour. Glad I've finally got you!"

"Yeah," she said. "Hi."

The girl in the doorway did not move.

"So how are you?" he asked. "What's going on?"

"Not much," she said.

"On Columbus Day weekend I'll be able to leave on Thursday, and I can stay until Monday. What would you like to do?"

Last time Warren had come, the spring before, she'd found him a room in an awful B&B. The woman was cold and unfriendly. Sarah had had to sneak into the house, Warren coughing as they went up the stairs to disguise her footsteps. The bed was narrow and the sheets damp. The window looked onto a small backyard in which a hopeless black Lab lay chained to a kennel. Sarah didn't want to go there again. It reminded her of Bucharest. She never wanted to go to Bucharest and she never wanted to hear about it again. A wall rose up in her.

"I don't think you should come at Columbus Day," she said.

There was a pause.

"Okay," he said. "Why?"

"I don't think we should see each other anymore."

There was another pause.

"Sarah," he said. "What's going on?"

"That's what I think."

"Are you sure?"

"Yes." Now she'd said it.

He said, "I'm sorry."

She said, "I'm sorry, too."

He said, "But why?"

"We're too different." She had planned to say this, but as she said it, it made no sense.

There was a long silence.

"Too different," he said. "What do you mean?"

But she was past explaining. She couldn't bring up the trip; she was done. She didn't want someone so wild, so importunate, someone who threw her into such confusion. She thought of the awful B&B. She didn't want to stay on the phone with him for one more minute.

"Just that," she said. "We see the world differently."

"I'm sorry you think so," he said again.

She said, "Yes."

"Can I come down to talk about it? This is kind of sudden."

"No," she said, "I'm afraid that's not a good idea."

She didn't want to see him, she didn't want to see his face or hear his voice. She didn't know what to say to him: How could she see him? But she was shocked by her cruelty.

After she hung up and came out, the other girl was still standing in her doorway. "Sorry," Sarah said. "All yours." She went back down the hall, her hands deep in the pockets of her bathrobe. She felt ashamed of her unkindness toward Warren. She felt like throwing up. For a long time afterward, whenever she remembered this she felt ashamed. She felt as though she had lied, there was something dishonest about what she had said. Though the truth was that she didn't want to see him anymore. That was the truth; still, she felt ashamed. As though she had deceived herself.

She and Rob were married in June, after graduation. She wanted to get a degree in art history, but Rob didn't want her to apply. He was thinking then of the diplomatic corps. "What if I get a job in Washington, and you're in school in New York?" She'd withdrawn her application.

Now no one gets married right after college. (Her daughter Meg had waited until she was twenty-seven, which was so much smarter.) Later Warren had married Janet Cartwright, who was from Lake Forest. Or Saint Paul, somewhere like that. Sarah had met her later, on visits home. She was friendly and sociable, tall and long-limbed and distinctive. She was not quite a beauty, but appealing, with blond hair, big liquid brown eyes, and very white square teeth. A radiant smile. Sarah remembers that.

THE WAITRESS BRINGS them little white pots of foam topped with a dark slice of something.

"With the compliments of the chef." The waitress is stocky and authoritative. Her hair is pulled back in a complicated French braid. She wears a charcoal-gray jacket and speaks confidentially, describing what they are about to eat. It's a mousse, made from too many ingredients.

"Wonderful!" Warren says. "Give him our thanks."

They are in a row of banquettes bisecting the room. On one side of them is an animated foursome, two couples. On the other side is a trio, an older man and woman and a young woman in her twenties.

Sarah takes a spoonful of the foam. It leaves a high-tide mark along her upper lip.

"Briny." She licks it off. "Did you end up going around the world?"

"Not then," he says. "And never all at one go. But I travel a lot. I'm on the board of the MFA. We go on a lot of their trips."

We. But she doesn't want to hear about his marriage.

"What did you think of *Tosca*?" she asks. "That Bulgarian soprano?"

"I thought she was remarkable. What about you?"

"When I first started going to the opera," Sarah says, "I cried every time, because the stories are so heartbreaking. I thought people who didn't cry were callous. After a while, when I'd seen the same operas over and over, I stopped crying at the stories and began listening to the music. I could see how that was another way to watch it, as a student of the music, instead of as a kind of emotional sponge."

"And?"

"She did it to me all over again. It was like the first time."

It wasn't just her voice.

At the end, Tosca, betrayed, bereft, had moved to her death with shocking simplicity, merely stepping off the parapet into the emptiness. It was heartbreakingly offhand. There was no flourish, no attention drawn to the act. This made it more devastating. Wait, Sarah wanted to say. Is that it? Are you sure? That can't be all, it can't be over.

Other Toscas had used the moment for melodrama, gesturing, taking long flamboyant leaps. But this had been so modest, so private, so wrenching. Could a suicide be private? Wasn't it public by its nature? You were breaking the social contract. Don't we owe something to others? Haven't we all made a tacit agreement to see this through to the end? Suicide seemed like the breaking of a vow, one taken by every living creature. Tosca had broken the vow she'd made to Sarah, who was counting on her survival.

But Sarah doesn't want to talk about that part; she wants to keep it to herself. She changes the subject.

"Do you go to the opera often?" she asks.

"No," he says. "Janet doesn't like it. So I come alone when I'm on a trip. Especially here."

"What was your business meeting?" she asks. "That you came down for."

"It's tomorrow. For an architects' organization. I'm an architect."

"Really? What kind?"

"We're a small firm. We do mostly residential," Warren says. "Renovations, too. But it's like a jigsaw puzzle. Any project means working with everyone—the client, the building department, structural engineers."

She nods. "And what are your houses like? Modern? Classical? Who are your architect gods?"

"We have a lot of gods. We draw on a lot of different sources—modernist, beaux arts, neoclassical, shingle style. We do some purely modernist houses, glass and steel. But some clients want something more familiar, more conventional. We're pretty eclectic. There are a lot of possible design solutions to every problem."

"Sounds interesting," Sarah says.

"It is to me," he says, and smiles. "A lot of our projects are summer houses. Those are the clients' dream houses. The clients can be a bit more playful, a bit more expansive, than they would be with a year-round house. So that makes the projects really fun to work on. We're literally making dreams come true. I love it. And you?" he asks. "Did you get a degree in art history? I remember that's what you wanted to do."

"I got married," she says. "Rob didn't want me to go to graduate school."

He nods, taking that in. "What then?"

"Had children," she says. "After the kids were gone I did go back and get a degree. And I got a divorce. And I got a job as curator at the Aylesford Museum. It's on the Hudson. American Impressionists and Chinese export china. I was there for sixteen years. I retired two years ago and now I'm on the board of our local museum, which is small and has no collection."

"Art, after all."

"As it turned out." She tells him about the Tapp, which puts on exhibitions, some from elsewhere, some self-generated. She's on the exhibition committee, "The most interesting one."

"Because?"

"People bring us ideas and we choose. It's kind of an art smorgasbord." She tells him about her favorites: Buddhism, American modernists, William Morris.

"Very eclectic," he says. "Impressive."

"Once we choose an exhibition, I get to work on it." She smiles at him. She feels as though she's at a job interview: she wants to impress him.

He nods. "And what about your own family? What kids do you have?"

"Two," she says, "a son and a daughter."

"I have only a daughter," he says.

She nods. "How old?"

"Katrina's twenty-four," he says. "Yours?"

"Older. Meg, thirty-six, and Josh, thirty."

They smile at each other.

"It's funny," she says. "When we knew each other before, we were just ourselves. Before you have any kids the idea of them is so peripheral. Then it was just something to worry about—getting pregnant had nothing to do with children, it had to do with us. Even when I got married I put it off, having kids."

"And now they're central," he says. "I can't imagine things without them."

"But before you have them you have no idea what it means," she says. "The way they add to you as a person, how you become yourself plus the child. You can never become a single person again, you're always that joined thing, the parent of the child."

"There's no divorce from them," says Warren.

"No," Sarah agrees. "It's for life. And they take over your life eventually, their lives supersede yours. Because for a long time you think they're yours. I mean, when they're small you think you own them. You think they'll do what you want. You think they partly are you. Because they once were yours, they were inside you. Then they were helpless. They actually were your creatures."

"And then it turned out," says Warren, "they were not your creatures!"

They both laugh, because of course they had never thought they were owned by their parents. They had always known that they owned themselves.

"What does your daughter do?" asks Sarah. "This person who owns herself?"

His daughter Katrina works for a design firm in Brooklyn. Sarah's son Josh works for a tech company in Seattle and her daughter Meg is an editor at a publishing house in New York. Meg's married, with a daughter and a son; Josh is still single.

"An editor and a techie!" Warren says, grinning. "I love kids with big plans."

"You always had big plans," Sarah says. "Didn't you drive across Canada?"

He laughs. "I was going to break the record for driving coast-to-coast, but my car wouldn't have made it. I had an old Saab then. I decided not to be responsible for both its destruction and my own."

"The Austin-Healey was gone?" she says.

"Long gone."

"It was a great car," Sarah says.

What had made it great was Warren: people turned to look at whatever it was that was making that gurgling roar and he waved to them. If kids stared, he offered them rides. It was as though he'd bought the car for everyone.

Warren had been turned down by the draft. He'd had a spot on his lungs and was 4F, though later the spot had turned out to be nothing. After college he'd traveled through South America, then come back to get a degree in architecture. First he'd worked for a big firm, then later he'd started his own.

"Do you live right in Boston or outside?" she asks.

"Outside," he says, "Brookline."

"What's your house like?" Sarah asks.

"Neo-Colonial. Red brick, white trim," he says.

"I'm trying to picture your life," she says.

She likes looking at him, his square, weathered face, his dark eyes, friendly and intense. His hair is receding but his eyebrows seem thicker, wilder.

Sarah doesn't want to hear about his marriage; she doesn't want to see him turn discreetly proud, or intimate and confessional. She doesn't want to hear anything about his wife, not a single word. She feels some risk, some dangerous charge, in that direction.

She and Warren had once spent an afternoon in the room over her parents' garage. They had sex on an old rattan sofa, on big hard cushions that smelled of mildew. During their struggles the gap between the cushions had widened, and afterward Sarah lay with her back pressed into the divide. The edges dug into her back and she tried to shift. At once he reared up, away from her.

"Am I hurting you?" he asked. As he pulled away, their skins, slick with sweat, made a small smacking sound. She pulled him back onto her chest.

"Don't go," she said.

"But I don't want to hurt you. I'm always afraid you'll break or something."

"I won't," she said.

He settled down again carefully, lying partly on his side to keep his weight off. He lay on the outer edge of the sofa. He put his hand flat on her chest, between her breasts.

"You're so pale," he said. "So warm."

She smiled. It was he who was warm, electric.

By then it was evening, and the light outside was fading. The windows were dim with cobwebs, the room crowded with objects. An old ping-pong table without a net took up the center. Along the walls were stacks of cardboard boxes and a row of mahogany chairs banished from some dining room. A cluster of standing lamps occupied a corner, rows of pictures leaned against the walls.

Warren looked around the room.

"Your family never gets rid of things, does it?" he said.

"You have no idea," she said. "This is just the room over the garage. And just at this house."

"What's it like, the house in Maine?" he asked.

"You'll see it," she said. "Big, old. Shingled. We'll go there." She shifted beneath him.

"Am I hurting you?" he asked again. "How do people figure this out? Are you sure it doesn't hurt if I'm lying completely on top of you? All my weight?"

"I'm sure," she said. He was only the second boy she'd gone to bed with.

"I want to lie on you forever," he said. "You're so soft. But you have to tell me if I hurt you. I never want to hurt you."

As it turned out, he never did see the house in Maine. She didn't remember the rest of that day, only how it felt to have him lying on her, warm and solid, then asking if he was hurting her, trying to be careful. Tender. She remembered thinking that word. Tender.

FRENCH BRAID APPEARS to recite the specials. The menu is all seafood, complicated dishes with strange sauces and exotic vegetables. Sarah asks about a fish she'd never heard of, and French Braid says it is firm and white, with a subtle nutty flavor.

When she leaves, Sarah says, "Do you think they're given a list of adjectives? Would she say that about the salad?"

"I'm always amazed that they can memorize the specials every night. I think they're all actors, used to learning lines," Warren says. Then he adds, "It's good to see you again."

She smiles but says nothing. He gives off a kind of energetic charge, a tingle. It's exciting but not relaxing.

"What else?" he asks. "Now I want to picture your life. What's your house like? Where is it? Tell me everything."

She lives near the top of northern Westchester, in a newish house that they'd remodeled. It's on six acres, away from the road, and the land goes down to the reservoir.

"Is it the house you lived in with Rob?"

She nods. "But I've been there alone for nearly twenty years."

She's used to being single. She's past the grief, the guilt, her children's blame. She had destroyed the family, and they'd held her accountable. Mostly Meg. For a long time that blame had scalded her: It was like living in an acid bath. But now it was over, the tub drained. The children had forgiven her, or at least accepted it. Maybe they'd never forgive her. She doesn't forgive herself for causing them pain, but she had to do it.

She likes living alone, now that the children have launched into their own lives. When she comes home she is greeted by the dog, tall and elegant, her tail moving politely, her dark eyes alight. Sarah moves from room to room, turning on lights in the silent house. Solitude is a relief.

The fish is just as French Braid had said, white, firm, delicious. There are stiff little bits of herbs in the sauce; Sarah has to pick one from her teeth.

"What do you think is happening on your left?" Warren asks quietly.

At a nearby table sit a man and a woman, their backs to Warren and Sarah. Facing them is a young woman in her twenties. The woman with her back to them is talking to the young woman in a low and forceful voice.

"I think it's dad, daughter, and stepmom," Warren says. "I couldn't help listening while I was waiting for you. It's pretty dire."

The stepmother, if that's who she is, is furious.

"You had no right," she says to the daughter, "to send that email." Her voice is hushed and vindictive.

The daughter says, "I didn't mean to embarrass—"

"*You did not embarrass me*," hisses the woman. "But you had no right to send it. I don't know what you were thinking of." A cloud of invisible venom hangs in the air. No one is eating.

The daughter starts to speak. She has a round face, white skin, and dark eyes, dark shoulder-length hair. She wears a black dress, the scoop neck showing her collarbones. Her eyes are large and intent. She looks transfixed. "I'm sorry," she says, "I didn't mean—"

"You should be sorry," interrupts the stepmother, speaking fast, stabbing her finger at the girl. The stepmother has thick blond hair that hangs halfway down her back. Sarah imagines her youthful and beautiful, with aquiline features.

"You should certainly be sorry," the stepmother says again. "That was private property. Private. Do you not know anything at all?"

She pauses, waiting. The daughter stares at her, her eyes round and horrified.

"Do you, literally, not know anything at all?" the stepmother asks again. "Did your mother not teach you about courtesy? Privacy? Other people's mail?"

The daughter says nothing. Her eyes shine, brilliant, then tears begin to slide down her cheeks.

"Justine," says the husband. "This is my daughter you're talking to."

The stepmother whirls on him. "Don't you get into this! Don't you defend her!"

After a moment the husband answers, speaking so low they can't hear him.

French Braid appears. "How is everyone doing here? Are you enjoying your meal?"

Warren beams at her as though she is his daughter.

"Delicious!" he says.

When she leaves, he says, "How is your nutty white fish?"

"Good," she says. "Hints of oak and old leather."

"Was it your idea to get divorced?" he asks.

"My idea, yes," she says.

"What was it like?" he asks. "Getting divorced."

"The worst thing I've ever been through. But I'm glad I did it."

He nods. "What was the worst part?"

She looks down at her glass, shifts it. "Really it was the feeling of becoming dishonorable. I had broken a vow. To my husband and the community. I was so ashamed." She looks at him. "I felt as though I shouldn't show my face in public."

He nods. "That would be bad. But probably no one else saw it that way."

"No, but I did," Sarah says. "And so did the kids. They were so angry. My daughter was in college, and she stopped speaking to me. She wouldn't come home for Christmas. I didn't even know where she went. I didn't know if she'd ever speak to me again. What I'd done was permanent, and I didn't know if what she'd done was, too."

It had been terrible. She was afraid she'd lost her daughter. Meg wouldn't answer her phone. Sarah had tried to reach her through her friends, but they wouldn't speak to Sarah. During those awful weeks she had waked each morning in tears, the day already a nightmare. She'd ended her marriage, broken her promise to the world, and now lost her daughter.

"Bad," Warren says.

She nods. The conversation beside them is getting worse.

"How can you not understand, Melanie?" the stepmother asks. "How can you pretend that you don't understand what you've done?"

The daughter stares at her without answering, eyes huge. The waitress—not French Braid but another woman—arrives and sets down their desserts. The stepmother waits until the waitress has gone.

"Don't you think that this will just disappear, because it won't," she says.

"I didn't mean to send it behind your back," says Melanie.

"Oh really?" says the stepmother. "How did you mean to send it? When did you think I'd find out?"

The man says, "Melanie, you should really have talked to her first." He's in his sixties, gray hair and horn-rimmed glasses, pouchy cheeks. He wears a pin-striped suit, an elegant silk tie.

Now Melanie looks down at her plate. Her shoulders shake; she's sobbing. No one speaks. Finally she raises her head. "Look, I don't want to stay here anymore. I'm going home."

"You are not going home!" says Justine.

The father looks at her. "Justine," he says, "why are you being so mean to her?"

The daughter's eyes are on him. Justine whirls to face him.

"Are you taking sides?" she asks. "Are you telling me what to do?"

"This is really awful," Sarah says quietly. She reaches for a piece of bread and tears off a strip.

"Do you think we should say something?" Warren asks. "Offer refuge to the daughter?"

Sarah shakes her head. "It would make it worse." She listens, her eyes on him. "But it's really bad."

"Your mother," Justine says, leaning forward. "Let me tell you something about your psychotic mother."

"Don't you say a word about my mother," Melanie says.

Sarah says, "I can't concentrate on anything while this is going on."

"I know," Warren says, "it's like trying to stand up in a hurricane. Shall we go?"

She had finished her fish.

"Where would we go?"

"We could go have a drink in the bar at my hotel," he says.

"I have my suitcase," she says. "I've been lugging it around all day."

"We'll bring it and check it."

"Let me tell you something," Justine says, leaning forward.

Melanie stares at her, mascara running down her cheeks. She pushes her chair back and turns to her father.

"I'm leaving, Dad."

"No!" Justine says, pushing her own chair back. "No, you are not leaving. I'm leaving. The two of you can have your own talk. Clearly you're not interested in what I have to say."

The father, cowed, says nothing. Melanie stares at Justine as she stands. The stepmother turns to get her bag from the back of the chair and Sarah sees her face for the first time. Justine is not nearly as young or pretty as she'd thought. It was the thick blond hair, halfway down her back, that had suggested youth, beauty. Sarah had created a face to go with it. But here is the real one, close-set eyes, a pointed chin, downturned mouth. Hollows under the eyes, a thin neck.

"I'll see you later," Justine says without looking at her husband. She stalks toward the door, her heels clicking against the bare floor. Melanie's face now crumples and gives way, her eyes tightly squeezed, her mouth distorted.

"We can't leave right now," Sarah murmurs. "It will seem as though we agree with her."

"No," Warren says. "Let's have coffee."

They wait in silence for French Braid to clear. Melanie is still crying; her father is talking too quietly for them to hear.

Sarah's thinking about the choice she had made, when Warren had seemed so confusing. Bucharest had frightened her, and so did his being fired from the camp job. She had wanted someone to rely on.

Rob had seemed so smart and energetic. Rob the planner. Rob the reliable. By the end of the marriage, the sheriff's office was delivering papers to the house. Summonses or subpoenas? By then his office was the little room over the garage. The sheriff would knock at the kitchen door and Sarah would point at the garage. He's up there, she'd say. The sheriff or warden or bailiff or whoever it was would walk across the driveway. When she asked Rob about it he'd wave his hand. It was nothing, he said. Just the way business worked. Everyone does it. She had no idea what he was doing or what he was talking about. It turned out it wasn't fraud, just debt.

She'd known nothing about choosing a husband.

French Braid appears. "How was your dinner?" she asks, solicitous, insincere.

"Delicious," Sarah says, smiling.

"I don't think we'll have dessert," Warren says. "Two coffees?"

Sarah nods. "Decaf cappuccino for me."

French Braid sets their plates neatly on her arm and speeds off. Melanie and her father talk quietly. Sarah hopes he hasn't taken Justine's side. She doesn't want to look closely, doesn't want Melanie to see that she is being observed. Pitied.

"I feel so sorry for her," Sarah says. "And to have it all happen in public. Would you want pity from strangers?"

"No," he says. "I don't know if I'd want pity, really, from anyone."

Melanie is sniffing, wiping her face with a Kleenex.

"We weren't supposed to show our emotions," Sarah says. "Never let anyone see you break down. But why is that admirable?"

"The Puritan model," he says. "Suppress emotion. Self-reliance. Don't ever admit to fear, or uncertainty, or vulnerability. It's a good model if you want to establish a global empire. Maybe not so good if you're part of a family."

"In my family the worst thing you could do was make a scene," Sarah says. "Never raise your voice in public. Or in private. It was really that we weren't supposed to disagree with our parents. Especially my father."

"That's the thing about fathers," he says. "They don't want you to disagree. Because then what? When your children challenge you the world ends."

"But you're not like that with your daughter."

Warren shakes his head. "I hope not. You lay down rules for your kid without meaning to. You say things you expect her to agree with. Suddenly she jumps on you with a totally different opinion. You have a reflex reaction. It's wrong."

"What's your daughter like?" she asks. "Tell me about her."

"Kat's a pistol. Bossy." He grins. "She's a Lakers fan."

"Is that baseball?"

Warren raises his eyebrows.

"Sorry," Sarah says. "I don't watch sports."

"Basketball," he says. "But I cherish the hope that you will now. Now that you're in my life." He looks at her hopefully. "A boyfriend started her off, and now she's a fan. A fanatic."

WHEN KATRINA COMES HOME they always watch the games together. She sits beside him on the sofa. She wears black-rimmed glasses and her long glossy dark hair is loose on her shoulders. Her skin is very pale, poreless, her limbs solid and rounded. She wears stretchy exercise clothes, loose clinging tops, yoga pants, hoodies. She shouts at the players.

"You dirtbag!" She turns to Warren. "Did you see that? Can you believe they didn't call him?"

Warren hadn't cared about basketball before, but now he enjoys it, the pounding turmoil on the court, the big, flexible, swift, loose-limbed bodies, the ferocious concentration. The long silent arc of the ball, curving toward the net as though drawn by magnetic force.

"They should take him off the court," Katrina says. She leans back and tucks up her legs underneath her. She holds the remote, she always does. She's a techie, and likes control. At the intermission she mutes it and turns to him.

"So, how are things, Dad?" She leans back, pulling her knees up to her chest and folding herself into the corner of the sofa. She smiles, her teeth shiny. "What's going on with you?"

When Katrina was little she used to come with him to see the houses as they were under construction, checking on work under way. Once he'd taken her up to Maine to look at an old summer-house the new owner wanted to renovate. It was off-season, in the fall, and cold. They'd stepped inside the front hall, a big square space with a wide staircase on one side. Kat had set off alone through the house, while Warren talked to the contractor.

When he was finished he called for her, and she came back down the stairs.

"What did you think?" he asked.

"There are too many bedrooms," she said. "They're too far away. I wouldn't like to live here."

"You won't have to," he said. His breath unfurled in the air as he talked.

HE TELLS SARAH that Kat lives in Brooklyn. Williamsburg. She works for a tech company. Everything now is tech. It's as though the big solid buildings he has spent his career preserving are meaningless. The material world is over, superseded by the gig economy and databases and revenue streams.

"She's a designer. Corporate web designs. And she likes opera."

"She does!" says Sarah. "Mine don't. Good for you."

"I started when she was little," Warren says. "Every year for her birthday I took her to a different one, just her. Janet doesn't like it, but Kat grew up with it."

"Good job," Sarah says. "I'm impressed. And what about the boyfriend? Do you like him?"

"He's a good guy. Christopher."

French Braid arrives and sets the little cups smoothly before them.

"What if you didn't like him? What if she wanted to marry someone you don't like?"

"I don't know. If it were someone who made her unhappy I'd be very concerned."

Sarah holds the cup in both hands.

"They're sort of at the heart of everything now, aren't they? Twenty years ago, at dinner parties, we talked about our own lives, what we were doing. Our children were little, they were marginal. We tugged them along in our wake. We told funny stories about them, they were for comic effect. Now they're central. At dinner parties we talk about them, what they're doing. We're marginal. At sixty."

"Do you think we're done?" he asks.

"No," she says. "Just that now the big moves will come from them. They're in full spate. We're in the eddies."

"But that's not how I feel," says Warren.

Chapter 2

THEY TAKE A TAXI TO HIS HOTEL. IT'S NOT QUITE RAINING, but misting; the streets are glossy with moisture. The streetlights are haloed, brilliant. People move quickly along the sidewalks.

They don't speak. Sarah looks out the window, already regretting this. She has no intention of having an affair with a married man.

After her divorce, some of her married men friends behaved as though she gave off the pungent odor of sexual availability. At a cocktail party, on her way back from the bathroom, she'd run into Norman Spofford.

"Sarah Watson," he said. He stood in the middle of the hall. She turned sideways to pass, but he set his hands on the wall on either side of her, trapping her. He had heavy jowls and his face was red from drinking. He leaned in. She could smell his breath: smoked salmon, chopped onions, and red wine.

"Norman Spofford," she said. She ducked under his arm and slid past. Did he think she'd be grateful?

The last thing she wanted was some awful liaison, everyone in the community noticing whose car was parked where, his wife getting drunk at a party and making a scene. The last thing Sarah wanted was a public imbroglio. The last thing she wanted was someone else's husband.

She'd seen men since then, had relationships. For a long time she'd seen a man who was not quite single, though he was separated. It had turned out later that his wife thought the separation was temporary, and so had he. That had made her wary of separated men, and she definitely didn't want to see married ones. She didn't want a man who was lying to his wife.

The taxi stops at a light and she watches out the window. On the sidewalk a couple is walking toward them, both in their early thirties. The woman is much shorter than the man. She's holding his arm, looking up at this face, watching him as he talks. She wants him to look at her. She laughs, throwing her head back, opening her mouth wide. But he doesn't look at her, and she turns serious again. She seems desperate. Somehow the power imbalance seems related to size: she is so tiny, hanging on his arm, though that can't be right, Sarah thinks. The woman stares at him, willing him to see her. He won't.

She wonders if she should say something to Warren, to make it clear that she won't have sex with him. The cab is tiny, and her knees are pressed against the back of the front seat. The driver is listening to Middle Eastern music turned very low. She shouldn't assume he wants to go to bed with her. He's married; she'd be insulting him. He's only asked her for a drink. She watches the couple walk past. The man's hands are in his pockets, and he looks straight ahead, as though there is not a woman hanging on his arm.

Getting out of the cab, Warren takes her suitcase. He rolls it across the lobby to the front desk. The man shakes his head.

"I'm sorry, we can't hold anything for you down here," he says. "I can have it sent up to your room. Or you can take it with you into the bar."

Warren turns to Sarah. "Shall I have it sent up? I'll go up and get it afterwards."

She nods.

The bar is dark, with paneled walls and hunting prints. A piano plays quietly for two businessmen in dark suits and a couple over in the corner. Warren orders wine; Sarah, Perrier. When the waiter leaves, they smile at each other. She now feels mute and awkward: the suitcase up in his room seems enormous. She wonders again if she should tell him she won't sleep with him. She once read that men think about sex every forty-five seconds. Was that only for twenty-year-olds? Warren is sixty.

"This is much better," Warren says. "But I feel sorry for Melanie."

"At least she's grown," Sarah says. "She doesn't have to live with Justine."

"No," Warren says. "But I'm sorry she has a spineless dad."

"But he does have to live with Justine," Sarah says. "He has to choose."

"He shouldn't have to choose between his wife and daughter," Warren says.

"He chose to marry a second wife," she says. "That's what started it."

"A bit judgmental?" Warren says. "Maybe his first wife died."

"Maybe," Sarah agrees. "But the second one is awfully vengeful. As though she's protecting her territory."

The drinks arrive. Sarah uses a little plastic sword to stir the piece of lime; bubbles rise in merry drifts.

"Divorce," Warren says. "It messes things up."

"Our generation was bad at staying married," she says.

"You asked for your divorce?" he says.

"I'd had enough."

"Was he having affairs?"

"It was money," she said. "And lying about everything. He never got a real job. He had these wild ideas. He knew nothing about business, but he wouldn't go to business school and get a job at a real company. He expected my parents to support us until he became president of the world. I wouldn't ask them to. I had a little money, but not enough for us to live on. He'd get some semi-professional job through a friend and then lose it. After all that idealism! He was going to change the world!" She shakes her head.

"How did you manage?" he asks.

"Scraped along. At the grocery store sometimes I'd have to wait to see the total at the checkout counter, and if I didn't have enough to pay for it I'd have to take things off the counter." This still makes her angry. "Rob never planned ahead and he never told the truth. At the end I couldn't stand the sight of him. Once I heard him coming into the kitchen when I was coming down the front stairs and I hid in the hall closet."

She'd slid in between the overcoats. He called her from the kitchen, then started walking through the house. In the living room he said her name, then went upstairs. She listened to him get farther and farther away.

"He was crazy to let you go," Warren says.

"I didn't give him a choice," Sarah says.

He nods slowly. "But he protested."

"He decided I had gone mad. Actually crazy. He had lunch with a friend and he drew a picture of my brain on the napkin. He pointed to the part that had been affected."

Warren laughs. "Affected by what?"

Sarah shrugs. "Anti-marriage dementia."

"And where is he now?"

"He died eight years ago. Pancreatic cancer. It was very sudden. He died nine weeks after the diagnosis."

"Did you see him at the end?"

"Yes," she said. There at the end, when he lay dying, yellow and wasted, everything from his life stripped away, she had told him she loved him. Of course she had forgiven him then, all his energy, his intentions, his humor, and intelligence all to be lost. His life about to be lost to the world. Of course she had forgiven him: he was a person.

Warren nods. "So that's the resolution."

"Not exactly a resolution," she says. "But an ending, anyway." She looks up at him. "What about you? How's your marriage?"

He says nothing for a moment. "Marriage is complicated, isn't it?"

So he's not happy. She waits.

"You make it work as best you can," he says.

She nods.

"Janet works hard at it," he says. "So do I. We love our daughter."

She waits, then asks, "Is that why you stay together? Your daughter?"

"Not exactly," he says. Then adds, "No, of course not."

"What does it mean, that you work hard at it?"

He swirls the wine in his glass; it kisses the rim. "It means I try not to think about it. I try to think about what will make Janet happy." He looks at her. "I do things that will make us both happy."

She wonders if he's had affairs. During the seventies and eighties it seemed everyone had. The sexual revolution had made it inevitable.

He changes the subject.

"Tell me what happened to your sister?" Warren asks. "Lynn."

"Lots of things," Sarah says. "She got married and divorced. No children. She lives outside Providence now. She's running an organization that preserves gardens. Not running it, but she's very involved." She pauses. "Did you go out with her after me?"

He shakes his head slowly, holding her gaze. "It was you I wanted."

Hearing this gives her an odd feeling, a kind of dangerous thrill. She mistrusts it, she mistrusts all exciting currents and eddies. Rob had been a romantic. He was always making sentimental comments, trying to excite that nerve, make it twitch.

"She told me you liked her better," Sarah says.

One day that summer, the summer when Sarah and Warren had been a couple, the two sisters had been upstairs in Sarah's room. They were changing into their bathing suits, about to go out to the pool. Lynn's suit was a dark red tank. She was wiggling to get it over her hips, her breasts jiggling. Her nipples were large and flat, different from Sarah's.

"You know Warren would rather go out with me." Lynn got the suit over her torso and put her arms through the straps. "He doesn't dare tell you." She pulled the suit up over her breasts. She raised her hands to lift her hair off her back. They both had long hair; Sarah's hung nearly to her waist, though Lynn's grew only past her shoulders. Lynn resented this. "But he doesn't want to upset you."

"How do you know?" Sarah asked.

"He told me." Lynn slid her fingers into the crotch, tugging the suit into place. "Everyone knows. But you."

Her eyes were darker than Sarah's, with overhanging lids. Sarah said nothing. She was already in her suit.

After a minute Lynn asked, "You coming down?"

Sarah shook her head. "I have to shave my legs."

Lynn shrugged and left. Sarah heard her on the stairs, yelling to someone below: friends had come over to swim. In the bathroom Sarah set her foot on the sink, balancing her heel on the rim. She ran the water to make it warm. Lynn lied, so there was that. She sluiced water over her calf, then furled the shaving cream into her hand. When Warren came to pick Sarah up he talked to Lynn, laughing and teasing. She slid the razor up her calf, slicing through the moist white cloud, opening a smooth stripe of skin. She'd thought Lynn was lying. But she'd never dared ask Warren.

"That was never true," Warren says. "If I'd wanted to go out with her I would have. I never went out with her afterwards. Ask her."

"She wouldn't necessarily tell me," Sarah says.

The white-clothed tables are far apart. The two in the corner are talking quietly, leaning close. The businessmen talk loudly, laughing.

"Why did you marry Janet?" she asks.

"I don't know," he says, his face open. "I'd finished graduate school, I'd come home, and I was starting real life. She was there visiting a friend, she was pretty, and I was ready. How do you know what you'll need to know before you marry someone? Trollope said all you need is a quiet turn in the conservatory at a ball." He turns earnest. "Janet and I have different views of the world, but we respect each other."

She nods. It sounds like baloney. "That's the important thing," Sarah says. "I guess. Is it? I don't really know what the important thing is. Obviously I failed to grasp it."

"Don't blame yourself."

"Who else should I blame? Rob was Rob. He was the person I married," she says. "He didn't change. I didn't realize what he was like. I wanted him to be someone else."

"Were you two friends?" Warren asks.

"I guess," she says. "In the beginning. He was charming. I thought everyone loved him. Later one of his friends told me that none of them trusted him. That he used to snake their dates. And lie, of course."

"Really?" Warren said. "Snake their dates? That's pretty bad."

"I didn't know until later. I believed what he told me. He had great plans. But he didn't think he should have to do anything to carry them out. He thought he should get a wonderful job because he was a wonderful person." She shakes her head. "A friend of ours, Ian, was made director of the Yale Art Center. Rob asked him to lunch and asked him how had gotten the job. Ian had gone to graduate school and taught art history at Amherst, and published a lot. He was highly qualified. But Rob acted as if Ian had just pulled strings. Ian never forgave him." She straightens the coaster. "Were we friends? I guess we weren't. It was all fizz and excitement."

"You weren't friends, and you couldn't trust him. So what kept you together? Great sex?"

"It was never that great, actually."

"Ours was great," Warren says. She thinks he's boasting about his marriage, but he adds, "Yours and mine, I mean."

She laughs: it had been.

The businessmen stand up to leave. The piano music has stopped; the couple has left. A waiter stands in the doorway.

"I have to go," Sarah says. "I'm staying at a friend's, I don't want to show up too late."

Warren raises his hand for the waiter, then turns back to look at her.

"Thanks for coming," Warren says. Now he is serious, sober. "I didn't know if you'd want to."

"I wanted to hear about your life," she says. "You go along from year to year and you think you're part of the lives of everyone you've known. You sort of feel you own them, even if you don't see them, because they live inside your own mind. Then you're sixty, and you realize the people you knew have been leading their lives apart from yours. Remember in *To the Lighthouse*, when someone tells Mrs. Ramsay about friends she hasn't seen in years? They've built a conservatory. Mrs. Ramsay remembers the time they went on the river together, and she was so cold. She can't believe that they're the sort of people who would build a conservatory. She's shocked to realize that they had been carrying on their lives without her." She smiles at him. "I wanted to know what had happened to you. If you'd built a conservatory."

"Because you used to own me," Warren says.

She is stilled.

The waiter returns with the bill in a folder. Warren tucks his credit card inside and hands it back. He looks again at Sarah.

"Why did you ask me to go to Romania?" she says.

"I wanted to be alone with you," he says.

She had never thought of that. "Is that all?" His face is open. It was his openness she had always liked, the sense that he was there, available.

"What did you think I did it for?" he asks.

"I thought you were being rebellious. People were challenging the establishment, calling the government fascist. If you wanted to challenge everything, I didn't want to do it with you. It sounded scary and reckless. That's why I broke it off."

"Is that why." He sets his folded hands on the table.

"I didn't think you knew what you were doing. I thought we'd be arrested. I didn't want to be a waitress in some horrible place. I felt I was incidental, that what you really wanted was the trip."

"We'd never have gone to a Communist country," he says.

"That was just a joke. We'd have gone places you wanted to go. I didn't care where we went. What I wanted was you."

After a moment she says, "I'm sorry. I didn't understand."

"You broke my heart," he says lightly, smiling.

She remembers sitting in the phone booth in the dormitory hall at college, looking down at her scuffed blue slippers, telling him—what had she said? That it was over. Mesmerized by what she was doing.

"I wish you'd told me why," he says.

"There wasn't any point. I thought it was an awful idea and you thought it was great. I thought that was what you were like. Someone I didn't understand. Reckless."

He shakes his head. "I was just trying it out. If you'd told me you didn't want to do that, I'd have come up with something better. I'd have had a million alternatives."

"I didn't know you as well as I'd thought," she says.

"I wasn't reckless," he says.

"Except driving your parents' car without a license. And getting fired from teaching at that tennis camp." she says.

He shakes his head. "I wasn't fired. I quit."

"I thought you were fired. What happened?"

"The guy who ran it, the director, was a sleaze. He was hitting on the girls, flirting and hanging out with them, the students. He was in his thirties and they were teenagers. He hit on the girlfriend of one of the other teachers, who was a friend of mine, and he called the guy out on it. The director fired my friend and I quit in protest."

"Everyone thought you were fired."

"Well, I wasn't."

The waiter reappears and Warren signs the bill. He puts his credit card back into his wallet, and slides this into the inside pocket of his jacket. He is practiced at all this, all these dealings with the world, credit cards and tips and arrangements. This has all happened since she'd known him. She feels a surge of disappointment at herself, at the depth to which she had failed to know him then. It's odd to talk about their earlier selves as though they were other people; they sort of were.

"Let's get your suitcase," he says. "Do you want to come with me or wait here?"

"I'll come up," she hears herself say.

At the elevator he pushes the button and the doors slide open. Inside they are alone as they are lofted upward. She looks at the floor. She is only getting her suitcase. She can feel his body close by. The elevator surges to a stop and the door opens.

"This way," Warren touches her elbow to guide her down the hall. At the door he slides the card across the panel, and the tiny light flicks from red to green. He opens the door and waits for her to go in.

The room is dark. She steps past him and then stands still, sightless in a strange place. She can't sense its size, and for this moment it feels vast and limitless, like an underground cavern, vaulted chambers opening into one another. She feels him moving behind her; she shivers suddenly. In the dark nothing has happened yet. They are suspended in this moment before.

He turns on the light, and the room springs into being. The square bed, pale and blank, takes up most of the space. Against the wall is a dark wood cabinet. Her suitcase stands just inside the door.

Warren puts his arms around her.

She closes her eyes to pay attention. She wants to be aware of everything, every movement, the sense of him folded around her. His smell is intoxicatingly familiar. It's a shock. She yields, breathing it in. Her body yearns for it. She feels the shift of his weight toward her. She wants to know everything. She wants to live this part over again, this time right.

He stands with his arms around her, not moving.

She wonders if she will be enough. The phrase comes into her head, though it's not quite what she means. Person enough? Something like that. Beautiful enough? Young enough? There are lines in her face, her neck is getting cords. The flesh has begun to fall away from the bone. She may be sliding toward gaunt.

What is it that men want? Underneath everything is the familiar beat of fear, galloping, urgent, unstoppable, the fear of having done something wrong, being something wrong. Even now, with nothing to fear (because this is not substantive, she wants only one night, to make up for her mistakes), she is still afraid.

She is his equal. He has no power over her. She is no longer in that vulnerable place in which a woman waits for a man to choose her. She has her own life, she doesn't need to be chosen. Nothing he does can give him power over her. She can spend the night with him and then never answer his emails. If she chooses. She will not be beholden to him in any way. Yet she is afraid, she is always afraid. Of failing. Of rejection. Some whisper of fear is always present.

She puts this from her.

She waits, eyes closed.

Warren draws away from her. He sits down on the bed in front of her and takes hold of both her hands.

"I don't want to do this unless you're certain you want to," he says.

"What would convince me?" she asks.

He shakes his head. "You would be the one to know that." His hands are warm, and he gently squeezes her fingers. "I want to do whatever you want."

To her surprise, her eyes fill. She doesn't want him to know this, and keeps her face still. After a moment a tear spills over and she reaches up to touch her cheek, to make it disappear.

"Ah, don't," he says. He pulls her down beside him and puts his arms around her. He strokes her hair, his hand slow and gentle. "Shh," he says, as though to a child, "shh. Shhh."

"What do we have?" she asks.

"Whatever we want," he says.

Now she remembers how it was to be held in his arms, now she remembers how he handled her, as though she were his. As though she were a treasure.

She undresses with her back to him. The cool air goosefleshes her arms and tightens her nipples. She is afraid again, fear and cold envelop her, tightening her skin, contracting her veins. She folds her skirt and puts it on the chair, sets her shoes beneath it. When she is nude she turns toward him. She's about to slide under the covers, but then she straightens, lifting her head. She won't hide anything. He should know what she is. She stands looking at him, arms at her sides, her chin lifted. He's balanced on one foot, taking off his shorts. He smiles at her. He gives a little nod. He lets the boxers drop to his ankles, steps out with one foot and then kicks up the other ankle, flipping the boxers into the air. He catches them and drops them onto the chair. He stands facing her on the other side of the bed. His body is sixty years old. The thin cluster of hair on his chest is gray, and a narrow track of it leads down across the fleshy swell of belly. She remembers the set of his shoulders, the breadth of his chest. Though there are now hollows below the shoulder bones; gravity tugging at him. His eyes: he's smiling at her. He leans over and pulls the sheets back. She gets in.

The sheets are cold against her legs, her arms, her nipples, and the cold makes her more frightened, but now this is joined by a kind of ecstasy, a fierce rising delight. He slides his arms around her and draws himself close, pressing his chest and thighs against her. Now she feels the heat of his body. He's erect; she feels him against her thigh. He slides his hands slowly down her arms.

"Look at me," he whispers. "Open your eyes."

She does, and there he is, so close. He is overwhelmingly familiar, his lovely, dry, clean, sun-baked smell, his presence, and the way his arms take hold of her. It is Warren. Then she closes her eyes again, because she finds herself sliding into a place she remembers, a familiar darkness, intimate, delicious. His hands are the same, warm and knowing on her skin. He is going so slowly. And she stops being frightened, and lets herself slide further into the place, this secret cocoon, made by the two of them. It's a surprise to her, that she could find it again.

He comes first, but doesn't stop until she comes, too, moving his face down on her body, and then she does, in a kind of explosion of trust.

Chapter 3

SHE DRIVES OUT FROM THE CITY, THROUGH FITFUL RAIN AND the steady slap of the windshield wipers, which say, Warr-en, Warr-en, over and over. She is clasped in a cloud of something more than contentment, closer to elation. Something illuminates the shimmer of drops on the windshield, the smooth rush of cars alongside her.

She turns in to the gate, flanked by the high wire deer fence, and presses the button for it to open. Within, she bumps slowly down the long dirt track and turns the corner. The house looms comfortably through the mist, white stucco with black half-timbering and gabled windows, shadowed by the benign presence of the sugar maples.

The dog stands in the driveway, her black shape silhouetted against the pale gravel. The dog is always there, waiting, when Sarah arrives. She is always free; the property is surrounded by the high deer fence. She goes in and out of the mudroom through a dog door. She's tall and lean, elegant and long-legged. Her dense pelt is clipped close, tight tiny curls like felt, all over her tapering torso. On her legs the hair is long, like thick fur tights. When Sarah gets out of the car the dog is in front of her, yawning with delight. Sarah says her name and the dog twists with pleasure. She raises a forepaw, opening her red mouth wide. Sarah says her name. She carries her things into the kitchen, the dog behind her. Sarah sets them down and then turns to the dog.

She crouches. "There you are," she whispers.

She puts her hand on the dog's hard bony head. The dog shows the flexible tip of her raspberry tongue, then closes her mouth politely. She is not a licker, though sometimes she gives Sarah a long, meditative swipe. She shows her affection in other ways: It's not exactly affection. It's something both more expansive and concentrated. The dog belongs to a small devotional cult that is entirely dedicated to Sarah. The dog is the only member.

Sarah whispers her name twice: Bella. She rubs her ears, where they meet the head. The dog closes her eyes and leans hard against Sarah's hand. They are partners in this, Sarah giving Bella pleasure by caress, Bella giving Sarah pleasure by being alive. Sarah puts her arm around Bella's warm body, though dogs are not huggers. Dogs allow you to embrace them with your arms, but they embrace you only in their minds.

Sarah stands. The kitchen is silent. Everything seems paused: the light is muted, the long stone counters blank, the white cabinets closed, the air stale. Arriving home in the morning is strange. It feels as though she has interrupted the house in something.

"Now," she says to Bella, "what shall we do?"

Bella lifts her head, alert at the question, ready for the answer. She's always in the same room as Sarah. If Sarah leaves, Bella rises smoothly to her feet and follows. Wherever Sarah stops, Bella waits; if Sarah sits down, Bella sinks to the floor, head high until she knows Sarah will stay. Then she sets her head down on her crossed paws, keeping Sarah in full view. Only at night, in the bedroom, will she relax. Then she spreads herself out on the floor like a flag, her long legs crossed like scissors, finally certain that Sarah will not leave.

What Bella would like to do is go for a walk with Sarah, or for a run, or to play a game. She wants Sarah to look at her, speak to her. She wants to be in Sarah's mind, thinking Sarah's thoughts with her. But she will settle for keeping her dark gaze steady on

Sarah's face. She is part of Sarah. Her mission is to be part of each one of Sarah's moments. She waits. When Sarah turns away to fill the kettle, Bella goes to the corner and lies down on her green dog bed. She sets her nose elegantly on her forepaws, but her gaze does not shift. She is still watching Sarah.

Sarah is looking for the exhibitions file when her phone rings: her daughter. Sarah rarely calls Meg because her daughter's days are so crowded. If Meg's at work, she's on her way to a meeting or already in a meeting or trying to find an email or in the midst of a project with a deadline. If she's at home, one of the kids is sick or hungry or she has to run an errand or speak to someone else right then. Meg is always too busy to talk unless she makes the call herself.

When Meg does call, her voice is serene and unhurried. Then she's alone in her tiny cubicle-office, or in a cab, or waiting in line at a store. Then they talk peacefully until suddenly Meg has to hang up, she is about to get into an elevator, or she has reached the checkout clerk, and is talking to the girl as well as Sarah, Oh, thank you so much, no, oh, oops, I'm sorry, here's the card, thank you, her voice still close to Sarah's ear, as though she were still talking to her. Though then she was living her real life, not just talking to her mother.

Listening to her daughter, from this position of intimacy, Sarah hears Meg thank the checkout girl, ask for paper instead of plastic. Meg is friendly and courteous: she moves easily through the world, as though it's her trusted partner. All this fascinates Sarah: Meg's remarks to a stranger, her intonations, her diplomacy. At one time Sarah had known everything about Meg's life; now, somehow, without asking permission, her child lives her life by herself. Meg's thoughts are her own. Sarah has no right to ask to share them.

Though Meg is sometimes shockingly indiscreet. Jeff would kill me if he knew I was talking about this, she would say, then, thrillingly, describe a fight. I ended up standing on the bed, jumping up and down and screaming at him. I was shouting, Okay, then. Is this what you want? How do I look now? Sarah can't remember what the fight was about, only the wonderful image of her daughter in midair, face red, feet bare, hair flying, yelling out loud. He'd kill me, he's so private, Meg says. Luckily for Sarah, Meg is not.

Indiscretion is Sarah's friend; she's avid for information. She wants to be part of Meg's life, the way Meg had once wanted to be part of her life.

Those tiny people, clinging to your leg, your hip, they complain, they whimper, they raise their arms to be picked up, they want to ride your hip, interrupt your conversation, pat your lips as you speak. They come in to your bed when you are deeply asleep, burrowing into your unconsciousness, demanding that you abandon your sleep, deliver your attention, prove your affection. They are burdensome, beloved. They want something all the time, they want your breath, your thoughts, your heart. They depend on you; you must give yourself over. It's you, the mother, who knows about the world, who lives in it, who must explain it to the child. Now it's the reverse. Now Meg doesn't depend on her mother for anything. She knows exactly how to live in the world. It's Sarah who waits for her daughter's words, her gaze, her thoughts, her words and attention.

Sometimes Meg is firmly private, drawing strict boundaries between them. This is familiar to Sarah; maybe she created the pattern. Sarah had never told her mother anything. Her mother had come from another century, she would understand nothing, Sarah was certain of that. Sarah's generation had made up a whole new life, one her mother could never fathom. Jeans, wild hair, drugs, sex. Bare feet: her mother was disgusted by them. And Sarah had dismissed as archaic everything that had come before her own generation. She had never asked her mother for advice; when Carola dispensed it she was brusque and opaque. The only advice about sex came from a comment Carola had made once when they were in the pantry. Sarah reached up to a shelf and was hit by a sudden cramp. She winced, and bent over. "What is it?" her mother asked. "Cramps," Sarah said. "I'm always regular." Carola turned away. "Make sure you keep it that way," she said.

Not that Sarah had wanted to plunge into the hippie world. She knew about it: the whole world knew about Haight-Ashbury and the Summer of Love. Some of her college classmates plunged in. Sarah had gone with her friend Shelagh down to the East Village to stay at Shelagh's boyfriend's pad. They called it a pad in quotation marks, signifying both mockery and thrill. The lock was broken, so the front door had to be left open. The apartment was filthy, and stank of rotten vegetables. There was no furniture, only mattresses on the floor. Shelagh's friend, Fritz, was blissfully happy at their arrival, hugging them each lengthily, though he'd never met Sarah before. People kept coming in and out, long-haired, wearing bell-bottoms that dragged on the floor, the edges ragged. They drawled, and called each other man. Sarah and Shelagh sat on a mattress while Fritz rolled a joint, licking the paper with a long liver-colored tongue. After smoking it Shelagh turned giggly; Sarah went straight to sleep. She had never wanted to repeat the visit, though Shelagh went often. Sarah had grown her hair very long, and began wearing suede and fringe, but she didn't like drugs, and didn't hate everyone in the government. She didn't want to go on marches, either. She was opposed to the war but she hated crowds.

She didn't want to discuss any of this with her parents. She hardly wanted to discuss anything with her parents.

When she told them she wanted to marry Rob, her father said, "That the fellow with the silly belt?"

The belt was rough and handmade, with a big brass buckle. Sarah thought it dashing.

"That's the one. Rob."

"When do you want to get married?" her mother asked. "We'll have to get on the club calendar."

"We thought right after graduation," Sarah said.

"Let me know dates," her mother said.

Her mother was fixed and inaccessible. It was what Sarah expected; all she had known.

After her mother died Sarah had found letters from her in

the attic. Carola had written to her mother, when Sarah was five months old. "How is Sarah?" Carola asked. "Is she better?" There was nothing in the letter about what was wrong, nothing about Carola missing her. The rest was an account of the trip—she and George were in Italy, in the Veneto. Evidently the trip was lengthy. They had seen quite a lot of palazzos. They had visited friends.

Sarah couldn't imagine a young mother leaving her five-month-old baby to go off on a long vacation. The thought chilled her. She had never asked her mother about it; she didn't want to hear the answer. How could Carola have left her? Hadn't it ripped the heart from her chest?

Sarah had been determined to be a different kind of mother, though she wonders how much better she had been. When Meg had asked her about drugs Sarah had been just as rigid and repressive as her parents.

"Never take them," she'd said sternly. As though by forbidding it she would prevent it. Of course Meg had taken drugs. It was a miracle that she hadn't gotten caught up in them. She nearly had, too, she'd told Sarah much later. She told Sarah her advice had been useless.

She was useless at advice, which was strange, because she felt brimming with something—goodwill, energy, love, many thoughts.

So of course Meg now doesn't ask Sarah for advice. Anyway, everything is different. Screens and pornography, pedophiles, lethal allergies. Meg is far better at negotiating these. Sarah is grateful for Meg's confidences, for the portal into her daughter's life. She's grateful that the awful years are over when Meg was angry at her all the time.

With Josh, easygoing and generous, there has always been less friction. He has double-jointed fingers, a high forehead and a wide surprisingly red mouth. He wears those dreadful black-framed glasses, like glasses for bears. He's easygoing, but hardly ever wants to talk about anything. He lives in Seattle, working at something Sarah doesn't understand, for some tech company—systems operations, or software. He lives with two roommates, one male, one female, in a small, undistinguished apartment building. Sarah has visited. The girl, Cara, has neon-blue hair and teaches yoga. At night she chants: Josh hears her through the thin walls. The guy, Arnie, has a long meager ponytail, and works at a nursery. Plants, not kids. They are both affable and mild. Josh loves Seattle.

When Meg calls, Sarah is in the kitchen, looking for the exhibition file. She'd kicked off her boots by the door and now she is walking on the cold stone floor in her stockinged feet.

"Hi, there," Meg says.

"Hi, lovey." At her daughter's voice everything in Sarah begins to lift and soften.

"What's up?" This is a form, not a question, though Sarah feels it as one, a request for information.

"Actually, I have some news. Last night I had dinner with a man I used to go out with. Before your father. I hadn't seen him in years. Decades."

"Cool," says Meg. "I guess. Was it? Was it a date? What was it like?"

"Kind of strange, but fun," says Sarah. "It made me think of what I was like forty years ago. What we were both like."

"What's his name?"

"Warren Jennings."

"I'm assuming he's a nice guy, or you wouldn't have had dinner with him."

"Yes," said Sarah. "He is a nice guy. He's married now."

She doesn't want to say more, certainly nothing about spending the night. When is the right time to make your daughter your sexual confidante? Maybe never. Also she doesn't want to expose him to Meg's caustic tongue. Before Meg's own marriage she'd been casually cruel about Sarah's men. The one with bad breath was "Blowtorch," and the one who kept canceling plans, "I-Prefer-Not." But after Meg married Jeff she has become kinder, less judgmental.

Jeff is tall and solid, with pale blue transparent eyes and quizzical lines across his forehead. He's a math professor at Columbia. He teaches string theory. Or physics: something impenetrable.

"And what else?" Meg asks.

"I have an exhibition meeting at the museum this morning. We're choosing shows," says Sarah. "Which would you rather see, netsuke or nineteenth century English watercolors?"

"Probably not," says Meg.

"Neither?"

"Probably not," says Meg again, "but that's me. I'm in the kid-trough here. I only want to take them to things that are big, bright, and unbreakable." Sarah's not interested in this; she waits to hear why Meg's called.

Meg's voice turns slower, more intimate. "So I have a question for you," she says, but then is silent for a moment.

"Okay," Sarah says.

"What would you think about me having another baby?"

Sarah answers at once, as though speed is important. As though part of her duty as a mother is to answer quickly. Later she'll remember this, how fast she answered.

"I'd think it was great," she says.

It is great: another child will enlarge the family, expand Meg's lovely footprint in the world, add another member to their tribe. Maybe all familial love is really a covert urge for tribal supremacy.

After a moment Sarah adds, "Why would you think not?"

"Jeff doesn't want another," Meg says. "It's expensive, we don't have room. He looks pained when I bring it up."

"Men are always frightened by babies," Sarah says confidently. She is thrilled to be invited into this important meeting. "But there's always room to fit one in. It can sleep in your room for a year."

"And then what?" Meg says. "We're cramped as it is. Jeff's an academic. I'm in publishing. We'll never be rich. We'll never have a big place."

They live in a big gloomy building on the Upper West Side, in a dark apartment with high ceilings and many small rooms. There are three bedrooms, one of which is Jeff's study.

"But it's Columbia housing. Won't they give you a bigger one if you have another child?"

"You can apply. You usually get it, but not always. What if we have the baby and then we don't get a bigger place? Jeff would have to give up his study. He'd never forgive me."

"Why do you want another?" Sarah asks.

There's a pause.

"I just do." Meg's tone is now muted, confessional. "It's like an addiction. When I see a baby I want to grab it and eat it up. I know, hormones. But it's how I feel. I'm dying for one."

Meg's daughter, Eleanor (nicknamed "Busby"), is five; her son, Nate, three. Why not turn Meg's arms into a cradle again? The idea fills Sarah with elation.

"Then do," she says, magnanimous, "have a third. Go for it." As though they're looking at the dessert menu, and Sarah's buying. They both laugh.

Meg's voice turns tentative. "I wondered why you hadn't had any more."

Sarah doesn't answer at once. She doesn't like talking about herself to her children. Her own life seems huge and blurred, too unwieldy to have meaning, the dark stain of her divorce spread across it. She doesn't know what story she should tell, how to tell it.

"Actually," she says, "by the time I had you I knew the marriage wouldn't last."

"You knew then?" Meg asks. "That was a long time before you got divorced."

"Yes." She'd known even before that. "Otherwise I'd have had another. I loved having babies. If you want to, do it. The new one will fit in somehow."

Meg has moved back to her own marriage. "We'll think about it." She says she has to go, and clicks off.

Maybe Sarah's told her too much, offered too much advice.

She thinks of Josh—when should she tell him about Warren? But it seems still too nascent, too unformed, to talk about. She'll wait.

Sarah wants to go over the exhibition proposals. There are five: nineteenth century English watercolors, probably a snooze; African masks; French turn-of-the-century posters, maybe too well known; netsuke; and Bloomsbury. She loves the idea of Bloomsbury, though really because of Virginia Woolf, not the muddy colors and clumsy neoclassicism of Duncan Grant, or really Vanessa Bell, either. She's drawn to them by the famous sister, the luminous presence that rests on the edge of the art. She wonders if Woolf is the reason the paintings receive the attention they do, or if the art is important on its own merits. No one will ever know.

She doesn't much love self-centered Duncan Grant, who took male lovers while he lived with Vanessa, who herself was in love with him, letting her look after him while he painted minor works and carried on with lovers. Wasn't it more insulting to Vanessa for him to have had homosexual affairs than heterosexual ones? An insult to her sex as well as her person? Or was it homophobic to think so? Of course, Picasso was cruel to his lovers and slept with every woman he met. You can't judge art on moral grounds. And you can't blame Grant for being a minor artist. Minor artists are part of the history of art, which is constantly being reassessed. She forgives him, she forgives them all.

The more she thinks of them, the more interesting all the shows seem: Now she is fizzing inside, and the day shimmers before her. Outside, the rain has increased; it grays the windows. The bright drops make halting, irregular paths down the panes. The heavy thunder of the downpour is exciting. She feels as though she's in a secret cave, carrying a bright light inside her, one known only to her.

But where is the file, which she knows she left in the kitchen? She can picture it on her desk under the window, but she finds it upstairs in her bedroom. As she picks it up Warren's face comes into her mind, his serious gaze. This is what I do, she thinks, as though he's asked. She feels his awareness, his curiosity and interest. It unlocks something in her, and she feels a quickening.

She takes the file into her office, which is a card table in Meg's old bedroom. She puts on reading glasses and opens the section on English watercolors. Looking through the images, she's surprised at how strong they are. She'd expected modest domestic scenes, but these are vivid and radiant, great mountain escarpments, wide turbulent rivers, majestic peaks. The green countryside is lush and untrammeled, with a hidden energy in the dense foliage, a limitless fecundity. The tilled fields and smooth hillsides, the moist and fertile earth. She is excited by it, as she always is by art, by someone's passionate interpretation of the world.

Chapter 4

HEADING DOWNTOWN TO MEET A POSSIBLE CLIENT, WARREN leaves the sidewalk and jogs down the long stone steps to New York's underworld. It's Hades: dank, labyrinthine, crowded, infused by an infernal din. Strangers push past him as he makes his way to the turnstile.

Warren slides his Metro card through the slot and pushes the revolving arm, which balks with a thud. The screen flashes: ERROR. People divide smoothly around him. He slides the card through again and it works. He goes through and feels a man shove quickly past. Warren deliberately slows his pace; he's not late. Near the stairs is a group of musicians: two brass horns, a guy on rhythm, playing something Latino, high and jazzy. He likes finding musicians here in the bowels of the earth; they're so brave. Sometimes it's a single violinist, playing an ethereal solo against the thunder of an arriving train. It's a hard way to make a living. Warren drops some change into the red-lined box. The trumpeter blinks, smiling with his eyes as he moves the horn to the beat. Warren smiles back, lifting his chin in salute.

On the subway he stands, holding a strap. People crowd closely. The car jolts around a curve, throwing him against someone's shoulder. Warren thinks of Sarah: her kind eyes, the shape of her mouth. Her hair is short now, like a little boy's. When he'd known her it had been long. It slid down around his shoulders as she leaned over him. Thick and coarse, like an animal's.

The car slows suddenly and forcefully and someone pushes to get off. The doors slide apart, then together. The car moves again into darkness. He thinks of her years with Rob. He thinks of her hiding. What had first drawn him to her was her opinions: He'd heard her at a party, talking about a movie. The critics had gotten it wrong, she said, it meant something completely different. He can't remember the movie, only that she had been so confident and so friendly. She'd been right, too, or anyway she'd convinced him. He tries to remember the movie, but it's gone. He remembers standing outside the circle, watching her face, the way she spoke to the others. Then Janet comes into his mind, in her red wool coat, walking up the stone path to their house. The subway car slows hard, stops.

The street is dwarfed by tall sleek buildings, and the air carries a briny whiff from the harbor. In the lobby he shows his driver's license to security, and is waved to the elevators. On the twenty-eighth floor the receptionist sends him down the hall, where Henry McCain stands waiting in the doorway. He's big and bluff, with rough pitted skin and coarse hair that falls over his forehead like a pony's. He's in his shirtsleeves, a dazzling white shirt, maroon suspenders.

"Welcome," McCain says, smiling.

It's a big office. One whole wall is glass, and Warren goes over to it, to look down on the harbor below. The view itself—the height, the bright boats, the pale green statue, the sizzling blue water—is a wealth signifier, like a sable coat.

"Spectacular," Warren says, turning back.

"Thank you," McCain says cheerfully. "Glad you could come down. Have a seat." He sits at his desk. "Let's talk about my new house. I liked the pictures you sent of the houses you've done on Nantucket. And Bridgehampton."

"Good," Warren says. "Tell me what you liked about them. Anything—windows, staircase, room size—whatever strikes you."

McCain leans back in his chair. "Good question. Let me think. I love that big dining room in Bridgehampton, with the windows looking out on the water."

Warren nods and makes a note. "What we do is deliver a feeling for the client—a feeling of space, or privacy, or shelter. Silence or sociability. So I want to know what houses you like, what details you like. The roofline. The windows. The materials: glass and steel? Or shingle and brick? The way the light falls. I want you to feel this is your house, one you feel is immediately familiar."

McCain smiles. "I like these questions," he says. He leans back in his chair and puts his hands behind his head. "This is a really exciting project. We've always wanted to build a summer place."

Warren shakes his head. "Hear, hear," he says. "And I want to know what your wife wants, too."

Henry McCain leans forward. "Of course. She'll be a big part of it."

They talk about the plot—Henry has already bought a piece of land—and the siting of the house. The number of bedrooms. How they like to entertain. Warm colors or cool colors. Austere or cozy. Warren has brought folders of their projects, so they can look at them together. Henry points at the things he likes: open space, bare floors, wide porches.

"How many summer houses have you done?" he asks.

"Twenty or thirty," Warren says.

McCain shakes his head. "These are great," he says. "I love them." He holds up one of the sheets. "What about this one. Would you build this one for us?" It's glass and steel, at the edge of a beach.

Warren smiles. "I'm glad you like that one. I like it a lot. But we never do the same house twice. You tell me the elements that you like and we'll incorporate them into a design that's yours."

McCain nods. "Got it." He looks across his desk, the houses fanned out on it—blue skies, open spaces. The modern ones with big windows, austere planes. The beaux arts shingle styles, with dark trim, swooping rooflines. "I'd love to spend time going through them. Could you stay for lunch?"

"Not this time," Warren says, "but I'll come back."

The reason he'd come down here was Sarah. Of course he'll come back.

At the airport he boards the shuttle, buckling his seat belt, knees crammed against the seat in front. The plane taxis onto the runway. The engine roar cuts him off from the rest of the world, seals him into a space of private isolation. As they start the race toward takeoff Sarah's physical presence comes to him with force, her skin, the thick animal smell of her hair. This is part of the tumult and confusion of the plane as it lifts suddenly into the air and then tilts shakily, leaning over Long Island, groaning and flapping. He's aware of her as the landing gear shrieks, folding up inside the metal belly. He's aware of her as the engine stalls and he looks down on the miniature grid of roadways. Long Island wheels below them as the plane banks and tilts, sliding sideways. Then it levels, and the ground falls away, the cars and buildings become inconsequential. They begin to rise steadily, and the plane turns north. Warren feels himself lifting off, freed, away. Now Sarah fills his mind completely.

Why had he married Janet? When Sarah asked him that, he'd felt his marriage wrapped around him like skin, close and tight. He's never let himself think of leaving.

He'd slept with a few other women. It was the times, it seemed sex was in the air, easy and natural. It seemed that women were ready and willing, that there was no moral issue around sex anymore. He'd thought Janet might have had a fling or two. He'd had nothing long or serious, or not serious for him. The last one had been with a lawyer called Angela. He'd first met her on the sidewalk near his office: They'd both been trying to buy a newspaper from a broken stand. She'd been laughing as she struggled, and he'd tried to help. The two of them had dropped coins into the slot, banged the plastic hood, rattled the flimsy mechanism. He'd been drawn by her laughter and her energy, her bright shock of red hair, the rat-tat-tat of her heels as she stamped her feet at the machine. He still sees her sometimes on the street, her office is near his. Their relationship had lasted several months, ending painfully. She hadn't wanted it to end. She was divorced, and didn't care that he was married. He'd felt worse and worse about it, and when he had finally told her he wouldn't see her again she had held him tightly and cried, soaking his shirt. Please, she had said, please. He put his arms around her, trying to comfort her, afraid he was making it worse. After that he hadn't wanted to risk creating such unhappiness. And the times had changed. No one thought sex was simple anymore. That had been years ago.

Janet had known about these flings, he was pretty sure, though she'd never said anything. He'd been grateful for her silence in the service of their marriage. But this—with Sarah—was entirely different. He wasn't going to give it up.

That morning, lying beside Sarah in bed, he had run his finger down her neck, from the lobe of her ear down to the point of her shoulder. She had always been slight; now her flesh seemed to be seeping away. The skin was subtly corrugated by age, becoming soft and slack. He was touched by the way her body was moving through its allotted span. He was there with her, stroking this skin. He was touched to be part of her life in this way. He slid his hand behind her head, cupping the bone, lifting it slightly, holding the heft of it.

She had closed her eyes, and he felt as though he were holding her mind in his hand, her thoughts. She had leaned her head hard into his hand.

"Being held," Sarah had said, "is what I miss."

He drew closer, pressing himself against her, so that their bodies shared each other's warmth.

WHY HAD HE married her?

Janet's laugh was raucous and energetic; Warren had always liked it.

"Oh my God," she would say. "I can't believe this." Then she'd give her machine-gun laugh, tilting her head back. She was striking, though not really beautiful, blond hair, big dark eyes, a flat square face, gleaming white teeth. There was something polished about her. She always looked trim, organized.

One night they had come home drunk from a party and lay side by side in bed in his apartment. Janet said she had the whirlies. He didn't answer: he was in some shadowy, ambiguous space where speech was difficult. Janet said she thought they should get married. His eyes were closed; it took him a moment to understand. He hadn't been planning on this, but right then dispute seemed impossible. He made an effort to speak. Okay, he said.

They spent their honeymoon in Barbados. They arrived in the late afternoon, tired from traveling, and when they got off the plane the moist heat closed around them. The hotel was bland and modern, cheaply built, a two-story box with rough stucco walls. Their room was small, with sliding glass doors that stuck, opening onto a tiny balcony. They unpacked into the flimsy bureau and musty closet. Warren thought of the relentless sun waiting outside and wondered what they would do here. The sheets smelled of mildew, and big complicated insects buzzed brainlessly against the screens.

The first night they ordered margaritas and were too drunk to have sex. In the morning they had hangovers. After breakfast—silent and uncomfortable—Janet put on a bikini and coated herself with amber Bain de Soleil. They went out onto the beach. Janet lay on her stomach on a chaise longue, her book propped in front of her. Warren, who didn't like the sun, lay under the palm-thatch hut and tried to read. When he looked over at Janet, her book was facedown, and she was asleep.

Warren read until he was too hot: his fingers were damp on the page. He put down his book and set out to walk down the beach. It unrolled down the island, white, powdery and apparently endless.

Down near the point a big wooden boat lay upside down on the sand. A local man wearing ragged shorts and a straw hat was scraping the bottom. Warren said good morning, and the man looked up and nodded. Warren asked a question about the boat. The man was in his sixties, thin and ropy-muscled, with blunt fingers and white teeth. They talked for a long time, mostly about fishing. Eel, bonefish, snapper. All the time they were talking, Warren was aware of Janet behind him. It was as though an invisible cord connected them. He could feel her lying there. He felt uneasy at spending all this time without her, as though he had deserted her, or at least as though she would think he had. He had spent time on something she would think was worthless. When he finally thanked the fisherman and turned back, he could see her in the distance, stretched out motionless. This time the sand scorched his feet. It had gotten hotter.

When he reached her, Janet was still asleep, her head turned to one side. Her lips were slightly parted; a strand of glossy hair lay across her mouth, shifting with each breath. Beads of transparent sweat were gathered along her hairline. Her book lay in the sand. Warren sat down under the thatch awning and picked up his own book. In the distance he could see the fisherman. His name was Eli. He was sanding the boat with short, purposeful strokes. When she woke up Janet asked him where he'd been. When he told her she said, "Asking about how to catch eels?" Her tone was amused.

At dinner they ordered margaritas again and Janet told him the plot of her novel. A woman makes a fortune in dress designing, then meets the man of her dreams, who saves her from financial disaster when she nearly loses everything.

"After that, you might think she could trust him." Janet held up her index finger. "You'd be wrong." She laughed, that wild, raucous, infectious rattle, which made him laugh, too.

"My god, this fish is so good," she said throatily. "If I lived here I would have it every day for the rest of my life." She took a long sip of margarita. The rim of the glass was coated with salt; she licked her lips extravagantly.

"It's really good fish," he said.

When they got home from the honeymoon, Janet was pregnant. The birth was difficult and she was given a C-section.

Afterward, when Warren saw her, he was shocked. Her skin was lightless and cadaverous. Under her eyes were dark greenish rings: she looked like a creature. When the baby was brought in, Janet took it without speaking. She held her against her chest. Warren looked down at the crumpled red face. The eyes were tightly shut, just dark slits in the soft rosy creases. The clenched pink fists waved jerkily. It didn't seem yet like a person, though it was fierce and gravid with life.

Janet looked up at him and smiled, her eyes shattered, her throat slick with sweat. She was now empty; she'd been gutted.

"So what do you think?" she asked.

He felt guilty: He had brought her to this. He was complicit. He was in it for life.

The plane descends through a white wintry haze, sliding toward the cold gray chop of the harbor. The plane hits the runway smoothly, settling into its race down to the end. He's back.

In the cab to the office, his work world surrounds him again. He thinks about the library in the house they're designing in Finbury, the big main room, its five tall windows that wash the floor with light. For some reason he remembers Kat in the empty summer house in Maine, her frosty breath visible in the cold air. Her confident opinion.

His own office is downtown, near the Prudential. It's mostly one big open room. He wants everyone to feel connected, all of them involved with all the projects. On the outer wall are plate-glass windows, looking out onto the complicated geometry of the city. The interior wall is lined with photographs of houses they've built. The desks are arranged in a rectangle. Beyond this is a conference room, and beyond that a small office that anyone can use. Warren's desk is out with everyone else's.

Laurel, the office manager, greets him, her long dark braid swinging across her back. She's slight and quick, and wears tortoise-shell glasses, a loose stretchy long-sleeved top, and baggy pants. On her wrist is a shiver of silver bangles.

"Hey," she says, "you're back. How'd it go?"

"Pretty well." Sarah's face appears in his mind; he puts it from him. "I think he'll want to build. He's going to look over our houses and make a list of things he wants. Then I'll go down again and we'll start talking about size and cost."

Jack, one of the other architects, comes over. He's a short, stocky, cheerful man, with small deft hands, slanted eyes, and pointed ears. There is a touch of the elf about him. His husband Curt plays the oboe with the Boston Symphony.

"Yo," Jack says. "Can we talk?"

"Let me divest myself," says Warren.

They meet in the small office.

"The frontage on the Finbury house," says Jack: there's a zoning question.

"How is the zoning board?" asks Warren. "Are they pro or con?"

"I'm watching to see," says Jack. "I can't tell yet."

When they've finished, Jack leaves, and Laurel peeks into the doorway, carrying a yellow pad.

"Can I come in?" She sits down.

Sarah's face comes into his mind again; he holds it there as he's thinking about other things.

Laurel is in her late thirties, long straight nose and sculptured features, deep-set eyes and high cheekbones. She's rather beautiful, but casual about her looks. She doesn't present herself as a beauty. She's been here for six years and knows everything. Everyone likes her.

"First of all"—she pushes her glasses up on her nose—"we need to renegotiate the rent."

"What have we got to?" Warren says.

She reads the figure and he whistles.

"At some point he'll price us out of the market. Can we negotiate?"

"I think no." She sets down the pad. "They have no reason to. The market's hot."

"So we have to sign."

She nods.

Warren steeples his hands. He can pay it, but he doesn't like being held hostage. Boston is full of space, and the office suddenly feels small and too public. How can he call Sarah, while he sits shoulder to shoulder with Jack? He can't keep going off to the office. He has no privacy here. He feels a ripple of impatience: the rising rent, the cramped office, the Finbury zoning board.

Laurel watches him. She's almost miraculously diplomatic.

"We might move," he says.

"Why?" she asks.

"I'm tired of wrangling over the rent. And this building isn't really appropriate, we shouldn't identify ourselves as purely modern architects."

"Where would we go?"

"Somerville," he says. "Cambridge, somewhere farther out."

She nods again, studying him.

"You think it's a bad idea?"

"I don't know," she says. "Let me find out about rents elsewhere, the cost of moving."

Now Warren feels uncomfortable, as though he's revealed himself in some way.

"Okay, good." He hasn't committed to leaving.

"You know it will cost us something, not to be in center city," she says. "In the way we're seen. The address says something about who we are."

"You think we should stay."

"We should consider the options."

Their building is part of Boston's urban renewal, and when they'd first moved there it had been exciting, the new city—glass and steel—rising from the old one—brick and slate. But now the building seems like all the others, tall and austere. Conventional.

Laurel pushes her glasses up her nose. "Next topic. Salaries." She smiles.

"Okay." He likes giving raises, rewarding his colleagues. The lift this gives him makes him think of Sarah. Makes him think of calling her.

When he finishes with Laurel he goes back to his desk to answer emails. By the time he's ready to leave, everyone else has gone, the office empty. The outside has gone dark, turning the big windows opaque, shadowy mirrors that conceal the city beyond. He's alone. He could call her, but now it seems furtive; he imagines Laurel coming back for something, her instant understanding that he's being surreptitious. He doesn't want his conversation with Sarah to be covert. He doesn't want to bring her into this room. He begins gathering his things together.

He remembers that evening, asking her to go around the world. To Romania. They were in his car, the top down at first. She hadn't liked it down, and he'd put it up. All he'd meant was adventure. It still seems like a possibility, as though that moment is still available to be lived. As though, if he explained it properly now, everything could proceed as he'd meant it.

He drives home through the winter dusk, the dimming hour *entre chien et loup*. The headlights are on, but the darkening sky is still visible; along the horizon lies a yellow-gray haze. The windshield is crosshatched by bare gray branches; icy slush hisses against the tires. He feels the pull of his house, his wife, his known life. When he turns into the driveway he sees the house through the semidarkness. Downstairs, the kitchen windows are lit; upstairs, the bedroom ones are bright squares in the dimness. Pulling up to the garage, he turns off the ignition and sits in the ticking car. Now he wonders why he hadn't called Sarah from the office. He can't do it now. Janet could look out and see him parked there.

He goes in through the back door, into the kitchen. It's silent and empty. The room is austere, with slate counters and a somber tiled floor, a huge double-doored stainless steel refrigerator and a bleak industrial stove. Janet had it done over several years ago. He'd liked it better before, when it had yellow walls and a bright patterned tile floor. Now it's cold and echoing, black and gray, like an abattoir. It had cost an enormous amount to make it look this way, and Janet has more or less stopped cooking.

He goes through to the front hall and takes off his coat. He thinks of Sarah, hiding, huddled among the overcoats. The sense of her is so strong that when he opens the closet door he expects to see her gazing out at him. But the row of coats is undisturbed; he hangs up his own and shuts the door. The living and dining rooms are dark, but he hears the murmur of voices from above. He goes up the stairs. At the end of the hall the door to their bedroom stands open.

Janet is lying on the bed, wearing a long red velvet robe. She's watching a game show. The audience laughs loudly. She looks up at him. The remote is lying next to her, but she doesn't pick it up.

"Hi," he says.

"Hi," she says. "You're back."

"I am," he says.

"I've already eaten," she says. "I didn't know you'd be home for dinner."

"Ah," he says. He's pretty sure he'd said so.

"You didn't say so." She picks up the remote and aims it at the screen. "I hate that ad." Her hair is pulled back by a hair band, also bright red, but different from her robe. Her face gleams with cream. She clicks the remote, but she's not turning off the show, just changing channels. "How was your trip?"

"Good." He takes off his jacket.

"Want me to make something?" Janet asks.

"No, I'll do it."

He goes downstairs, rolling up his shirtsleeves as he does. As he passes the closet he thinks again of Sarah. Will she now haunt the front hall?

In the kitchen he wonders what odorless, trackless meal Janet had eaten. Yogurt? Some frozen thing. He gets out eggs and the heavy cast-iron skillet. For the renovated kitchen Janet had bought new pots, gleaming stainless, with long pointed handles, but he'd asked to keep this. He likes its serious heft, its blackened patina.

He cracks the shells and the eggs slide into the bowl, smooth and gelatinous. He adds a heavy plume of milk. He wonders if Sarah is making scrambled eggs at this moment. He's never seen her kitchen. He pictures her leaning over a table, reading, the light shining down on her hair.

He feels the day's motion still within him, rattling through the underworld on the subway, roaring through the sky on the plane, the cab through traffic to his office, driving back through the frigid twilight. Now he is home, stilled, with his secret.

His marriage has been formed around Janet, it has knitted itself around both their shapes. He doesn't expect change from her, but he feels himself shifting.

He turns on the burner; the flame flares, blue and avid. He drops a pale chunk of butter into the pan; it skates across the slick black surface, sizzling.

This room is where Kat grew up. She did her homework here, at the wooden table, or curled up in a ratty armchair in the corner. Once, during an argument with Janet, teenage Katrina leaned too far backward and her chair tipped over with a crash. Lying on her back, kicking her pajamaed legs, her bare white feet aloft, she shouted, "You're still wrong." He doesn't remember what the fight was about; he'd felt sorry for her, the noise and fright of falling. Teenagers struggled so hard to make a place for themselves. Kat and Janet had fought over everything. Earrings, clothes, tattoos. He'd gotten along with her better than Janet had. He thinks of her bare white feet kicking in the air. Though she'd stood up unfazed. He pours the egg mixture into the pan.

As a teenager Katrina had been distracted and distant, pulling strands of her long hair across her face, inspecting her fingernails, preoccupied by some drama running continually inside her head. Her parents' question irritated her. Often she was flamboyantly rude. They'd had to choose between ignoring it and making a scene. Often, when Warren chose one, Janet chose the other, some unspoken balancing mechanism at work.

Janet was furious when Katrina admitted to a piercing—a tiny gold ring set in the soft skin above her navel.

"That's your only body," Janet told Katrina. "How dare you mutilate it!" She was so angry she began to cry.

"It's not mutilated," Katrina said.

"This is purely sexual. It's a sexual declaration," Janet said. "Why don't you just wear a sign? 'Rape Me!'"

"It's not that bad, Jan," Warren said.

But Katrina erupted, her voice rising high and thin. "You know nothing! It's my body, not yours. You know nothing at all! How dare you scream at me! You're both assholes!"

She stormed out of the room, bare feet slapping against the floor, tears in her voice. Her door slammed upstairs. The room vibrated.

Janet turned on him. "You encourage her. You think everything she does is fine."

"Everything she does is a shock to us," he said. "But this is her generation. We have to get used to it."

"Get used to our daughter looking like a slut?"

"Don't call her that," he said, angry. "She's trying things out."

"Thank you for your support," Janet said.

That cold day when they had left the house to be renovated, Kat had reached for his hand, slipping her fingers inside his. As they went down the flight of front steps he heard her counting under her breath, soft whispered numbers, keeping track of the world.

This cold gray place holds a history of no one. The old room has vanished, as though family life has been erased. He's here for no reason.

He sits down with his plate. The toast is barely browned, and some of the whites are still glutinous. He's impatient, he wants to get on with things.

Chapter 5

SARAH'S MEETING IS AT THE MUSEUM. IT'S A SMALL MODERN building with white walls and big windows, outside the Village. The Tapp had been started forty years ago by women volunteers, and volunteers run it still. In this affluent community, outside the city, the wives wanted interesting work; they didn't need salaries. They were educated and professional, and they ran the museum well.

Jean Gerson, head of the committee, is small and energetic, with short thick swirly graying hair.

"Shirley, talk to us about English watercolors," she says cheerily. The conference room is upstairs. Outside is a stand of birch trees, leafless now; dappled light falls through the bare branches across the white table, on the women's heads and faces.

Shirley Anderson describes the Golden Age of English Watercolor, the artists, the scholarship.

Jean looks around. "Who likes it?"

Sarah says, "I like it a lot. The images are gorgeous. I was surprised—they're so powerful and so ripe! All that rippling foliage. It's kind of sexual."

Someone laughs, and Jean does, too. "Really!"

Sarah's face turns hot: Is she so obvious? Sex has begun its ticking beat inside her body?

"But do we want to do more dead white males?" Nancy Wilson asks. She's Sarah's friend. "Dead white Anglo-Saxon males?"

"They did do a lot of things well. We can't just exclude them all now that we're feminists," says Shirley.

But the response is mixed, and Jean moves to netsuke. Candace Woods, who has long streaked blond hair and a jutting chin, explains that netsuke are toggles, meant to attach a portable pocket to a kimono sash. They were decorative and political, made in all sorts of forms—people and animals and objects.

"What are they made of? Ivory? Do we have to worry about that?"

"The early ones were," says Candace. "And they're protected. The later ones are made from other stuff. Whales' teeth, palm nuts. The carapace of the hornbill. Mammoths' tusks."

"Mammoths' tusks?" asks Sarah. "Real ones?"

"Apparently. There are mammoths in northern China. Buried in the ice."

"They cut up mammoth tusks to make knickknacks?"

Candace nods. Sarah thinks of the huge bodies, dim and hoary, thousands of years old. Surely they should be protected. Isn't anyone in charge of things?

Someone says that tiny objects don't bring in crowds. Candace says that netsuke has its own audience, and besides, diversity. They table it.

They move on to Bloomsbury, introduced by Nancy Wilson. She has short, prematurely white hair, rising in a crest above her forehead. Bright dark eyes, owlish horn-rimmed glasses and a quick, birdlike manner.

"You all know about Bloomsbury," she says. "Virginia Woolf, suicide, complicated sexual arrangements. But this show would be about something more than that—the currents of a new kind of art, the counterpart to the French Fauves, which were wild and bright-colored. This is an English response to abstraction: somber, intense, some neoclassical, some faux-primitive. It's a really interesting period." She passes around pictures. The paintings are semi-abstract, big solid forms and muted colors. There are photographs of Monk's House, where Virginia and Leonard lived, furniture and panels painted by Vanessa and Duncan. There is a sculpted head of Virginia on a windowsill, a nimbus of light around her long face. There are pictures of Charleston, the decorated chimneypiece. Landscapes by Dora Carrington, the strange exotic birds by Simon Bussy.

"I love this material," Sarah says. "But I'm a Woolf fan."

Candace says, "Isn't the Woolf wave sort of over?"

"It's definitely still a thing," says Nancy. "Woolf is still big."

"I don't know," Candace says. "I think everyone who knows about her knows about her. The paintings are kind of dreary. We need at least one blockbuster next season. I don't think Bloomsbury will be it." She looks around, irritatingly confident.

"Do you think netsuke will be?" asks Nancy. She's unfailingly pleasant. "A blockbuster? Or English watercolors? Bloomsbury will be bigger than either."

They vote against the African masks and the posters. The masks are owned by a demanding collector, who wants a lot of money spent on the show. And everyone has seen Toulouse-Lautrec's high-kicking chorus girls and Mucha's dreamy maidens. They vote yes on Bloomsbury and netsuke; Sarah volunteers for Bloomsbury. At the end of the meeting, they stand, collecting their things. Nancy says to Sarah, "I'm glad you're helping. It's going to be fantastic."

Sarah's glad to be working with her, glad that she has a big project to focus on.

On the way home it starts to rain, and the windshield glitters silver. The wipers switch back and forth, chanting, Warr-en, Warr-en. She can't not hear it.

AS THEY LEFT the hotel that morning they stopped on the sidewalk before they went in different directions. In public Sarah couldn't think of how to say goodbye. Awkwardly, she put out her gloved hand. Warren took it and raised it to his mouth. He turned it over and kissed the palm, pressing it hard against his lips.

"Goodbye," he said.

"Thank you," Sarah said, idiotically.

"You're very welcome," he said.

WHEN SHE GETS HOME the dog is standing in the driveway. She's just come outside, the dog door is still swinging. Bella waits, ears and tail lifted, wagging gently.

Sarah makes a sandwich and sits at the kitchen table. She puts her book beside the plate, laying a knife across the pages to hold it open. One of the luxuries of living alone is reading while eating. In her parents' household it had been forbidden. She's now deep in rereading *The Age of Innocence*, in thrall to the doomed love affair between Ellen Olenska and Newland Archer. She loves this book, though she always hopes for a different ending. By the time Wharton wrote it she'd changed her view of society. In *The House of Mirth*, society was merciless, but later Wharton saw it as benevolent. In *The Age of Innocence* it protected the family, order, duty, honor. The two adulterous lovers, whose passion challenged all those things, sacrificed their own happiness to the greater good. The novel celebrated honor and renunciation—both of which are anachronistic now, Sarah thinks. Renunciation has no value. You're not supposed to sacrifice yourself for the common good or for someone else's happiness. You're supposed to put yourself first: self-actualization, not self-sacrifice. The Puritans had put God first, not the individual. In Europe they put community first; now in America it was the self. Your own happiness should be paramount. Honor was not considered.

She finishes her sandwich and closes the book. Archer has traveled to Newport in the hope of seeing Ellen, but they never quite met. Near the beach they stood at a distance from each other, Ellen facing the sea, Archer behind her. She knew he was there.

Motionless and mute, each waited for the other to act. He waits for her to turn, she waits for him to speak. Wharton makes silence a response.

Sarah's desk is beneath the kitchen window. Outside is the sweep of brown lawn under a sheet of pallid sunlight. The orchard beyond is a soft thicket of browns and blacks, still leafless, though the buds are swelling toward spring.

The desk is empty except for a pewter mug—a polo trophy won by her grandfather—holding pens, and a small Persian box with a design in dull blue and gold. It had been her mother's, and had held her paper clips. The box gives Sarah a sweet tiny rush of feeling. It still holds her mother's paper clips, she has never emptied it. She feels a nearly magical connection to the box, and to the paper clips inside, which her mother had touched. She can't explain why—her mother had touched many things in the house—but the little box is charged. It was part of her mother's daily life, and is still here, whole. She knows this feeling is only hers. Her children may know that the box was her mother's, that the paper clips were hers, but it can't matter to them as it does to Sarah. She never uses the paper clips. She wants to keep the link intact, as though the presence of the paper clips themselves, light and silvery and insubstantial, means that her mother might use them still.

Her mother is now a mystery. Sometimes Sarah feels pity for her long marriage, locked in her husband's shadow. Had her mother been miserable or happy? Had she adjusted, forming herself around his shape and giving up the idea of her own? Surely she'd have said she was happy. If you believed you were happy, did that mean it was so?

Sarah wonders about the trip to the Veneto, leaving the baby behind. What had her mother been thinking?

When she was in her forties, Sarah had gone cruising with her parents in Maine. One afternoon the wind had come up hard and fast, pushing the big mainsail over. George was below, looking at the chart, when the boat started suddenly to heel. He shouted an order up to the two of them. Sarah was at the helm, Carola on the side, by the winches.

"Head off, head off," George yelled, "and let off the jib!"

Carola tried to loosen the jib, but the line had gotten tangled. It was taut as a rod, the heavy wind against it; Carola struggled as the boat leaned farther and farther. George came up the ladder, yelling before he reached the deck, his face red.

"What's the matter with you?" He shoved her aside at the winch, taking the line from her hands. The big sails bucked and snapped overhead, seawater raced down the lee gunwales. The wind roared and the heavy boat tilted dizzyingly. He struggled to free the line. When he did, it ran, sizzling, through the whirling winch. The boat slid grandly upright as the freed jib billowed outward.

He turned to Carola. "Didn't you hear me?" He was still yelling, over the wind.

Carola looked past him, at the horizon. "I wish I were dead," she said distinctly.

Sarah, her hands on the helm, looked up at the sails, holding them full and taut, balanced between wind and water.

It's a mystery, another generation.

Her mother is lost now, dissolved into that dark mist. When she was alive something had kept Sarah from talking to her, some unarticulated family rule, and now it's too late. When Sarah was a teenager she'd felt prohibited from telling her mother anything, as though membership in her generation had entailed a vow of silence. She'd never told her mother about Rob, not when things were happy and certainly not when they were bad. She'd felt her marriage was her responsibility, she had no right to complain. She'd been afraid her mother would say so. Her mother had never offered emotional comfort. Though when Sarah was a child, when she had a fever her mother would rub her back with alcohol. She remembers the long strokes on her hot skin, the sharp medicinal tang, the sense of safety.

The pewter mug and wooden box both carry this charge of

affection, but only to Sarah. To the next generation they'll be detritus, given to Goodwill. The things from the house in Villanova are flotsam from the family crescendo. She hadn't taken much: the big glass lamps from the living room, a small bronze nymph paperweight from her mother's desk. Some favorite pieces of furniture. Her father's cashmere sweaters had all gone to Goodwill. Josh didn't want them. He hadn't gotten along with his grandfather.

She sits down to pay bills. She was never rich the way her parents had been. They hadn't talked about money, and Sarah had had no idea of how much there actually was. It turned out after they died there hadn't been much left. What had seemed like an ocean had become a modest pond.

Her father had died four years after her divorce. It had been sudden: He was walking up to the house from his car. He'd died almost instantly. It was November, a cold rainy day, and for a while no one saw him outside. It was an aneurysm, they couldn't have saved him. But Sarah couldn't rid herself of the image of her father lying on the walk, cheek against the cold stone, the damp seeping into his camel-hair coat. The rain on his face.

For months afterward it seemed that he wasn't really gone. She felt his presence nearby, as though there were some way to reach him. She'd never felt close to him, but after he died she was stunned by his absence, as though something in her had been sheared off. She had never found favor in his eyes, but she'd thought that a time would come when they could open themselves and see into each other's hearts. After he died she'd kept that hope like a held breath. What was she to do with it? The sense that she had failed him was as familiar as grief; it was the way she grieved.

Her father had left everything to their mother, except for the trusts, which he didn't control. Sarah and Lynn each got a modest amount. Lynn didn't need the money; she'd married a rich businessman from Oklahoma whom she'd later divorced, with lashings of acrimony. She'd gotten a lot in the settlement, but she wanted more. She wanted a place in Sardinia: real estate was cheap there. She and Sarah wondered how much was still left, but they didn't dare ask the family lawyers. There might be some clause in the will that disinherited any child who asked. It would be just like him, they thought.

Sarah had never felt rich, growing up, despite the big house, despite the fact they seemed rich. There was some tension around money, something that tightened the air around the word. Sarah was given a small allowance. Her parents disapproved of her spending, though her father owned thirty-four pairs of eyeglasses, laid out in their cases on top of the grand piano. In his closet were stacks of cashmere sweaters in rainbow colors. Many were unworn, still with their price tags. On the floor were rows of bespoke shoes from London, with handmade wooden shoe trees. Her father seemed driven to spend money. He bought paintings and furniture. He was on the boards of the museum, the symphony, and the hospital. Carola was not, but it was her family that had made him prominent, and he never forgave her for that.

Six years after Sarah's father died, her mother had died of cancer.

Sarah spent the last week with her, visiting the hospital every day. Her mother was weaker each time. Her face was stained from within; great bruises bloomed across her cheeks, her hands, her arms. She looked beaten: The blood vessels were giving way. Carola's long body was emaciated, scarcely raising the white sheet. Her big face was mottled, the skin taut over her sharp bones. Oxygen hissed quietly into her nostrils through a transparent tube. She gazed into the middle distance, her mouth slightly open. She didn't look at Sarah, though Sarah spoke to her.

Sarah smoothed the thin hair back from her mother's forehead. They had rarely touched each other. Now her mother slowly blinked, then turned her dark gaze on Sarah. Sarah took her mother's weightless hand. The back was spotted with brown, and the veins were blue runnels under the transparent skin. Her hands had once been beautiful, pale and smooth, with oval nails. Sarah put her mother's hand against her cheek.

Carola died the following morning, before Sarah reached the hospital. The nurse called while she was driving over. It was raining, and when she arrived Sarah ran from the car holding a newspaper over her head, which seemed disrespectful. Water was sluicing down the windows when she came into the room. Her mother lay still; her face looked as though it were made of clay. She was gone.

Sarah took her mother's hand; it was cold, and surprisingly heavy. She began to cry silently: what a waste. The words kept repeating themselves in her mind.

"It was Dad," she said to her mother. "I know he made you take that trip." The tears seeped down her cheeks, down her throat. "It was Dad," she said again. "I know you loved me."

It seemed impossible that she had lost them both. I'm an orphan, she thought. Surely the word referred to a child, not an adult. Yet she was also still the child of her parents. She felt exposed, as though nothing now would protect her from the sweep of the sky.

After her mother's death Sarah had received the rest of her inheritance. It was not a lot, they had been spending capital for years. Lynn was furious, but Sarah didn't care. She had a job, and her children were on their own paths. She didn't want a house in Sardinia.

Sarah pays her bills, credit cards, dry cleaner. The lawn service. Writes checks to charities and nonprofits. She supports social justice and the environment. And the arts. She feels a responsibility. She's not rich, but she's rich compared to most people.

Afterward she goes for a walk with Bella. The dog is energized by the damp scent-bearing air. She trots down the driveway with authority, head and tail up. When they turn off into the woods she stops abruptly, dropping her nose to the leaves, sniffing carefully. Here there is a pile of rocks below the road, an old culvert. There's often a musky scent in the air; Sarah wonders if it's a fox's den. Bella always stops to investigate. Sarah admires her focus. Bella is a Zen master, always present, always in the moment. She lifts her head and looks at Sarah, eyes bright. Sarah smiles at her, and Bella bounds back onto the road and breaks into a canter. She throws her head to one side joyfully.

In the morning Warren sends her an email, with a link to a travel piece. "You might think of Bucharest as a dreary gray Soviet-style city," the article begins, "but you would be wrong."

Warren adds: I am often wrong.

She's at her laptop when it comes in, sliding across her screen. She doesn't answer at once. She means to wait several hours before responding, but it's actually only twenty minutes. Electronic communication is so swift and silent it's like thought. Often she isn't sure if she has only thought about sending a message or actually sent it. Maybe it's especially true of people who live alone?

She writes back, I still don't want to go.

He writes: We could go somewhere else.

She doesn't answer. She doesn't know if this is a joke or for real, and in any case she's not ready to go on a trip with him.

She's researching the Bloomsbury show, looking up Dora Carrington and her paintings. The landscapes are beautiful and evocative: massive mountainsides lowering over small farmsteads, winter-bare trees against bleak fields. Everything has a powerful emotive charge. Why wasn't she more famous?

Warren sends a link to the plans for the library that will be the center of the house in Finbury. It's charming, with big mullioned windows and clusters of chimneys. The wooden columns inside mimic classical marble ones.

She feels a curious excitement: he is including her in his life. She looks closely at the plans. They use architectural terms she doesn't know. He must speak this language: architrave, stile, soffit, all those arcane words. He's gone beyond her. He's acquired a world of knowledge she does not have. This fascinates her. When she'd first known him they'd shared the same landscape of knowledge, but now he's ranged far beyond it. He can report to her from places she has never reached.

She's looked him up online: he's a good citizen. He's on the boards of the Museum of Fine Arts, several architectural organizations, and one for underserved communities. It seems he never sleeps. She wonders what his life at home is like. Is Janet a good cook? What do they talk about? She pictures him in the kitchen as Janet stands at the sink. Does he put his hands on her shoulders from behind? Does she lean back, into him? Does she ignore him? Maybe he never puts his hands on her shoulders. Maybe he merely walks past. They've been married so long, they're accustomed to each other.

But she doesn't want to think about Warren and Janet. She thinks about Warren alone.

He sends her emails that make her laugh. Comments, jokes. Once he sends a link to a conference on residential architecture at which he's speaking. He writes, Strange doings in San Francisco.

She writes back, What will you say?

He answers, I'll let you know after the talk.

She sends him images of Carrington's work.

Isn't she great?

Instead of, Yes, he writes, Tell me why you think so. She can feel his interest. He wants to know what she's thinking. She says she likes the way Carrington infuses the landscape with emotion, how she creates a distorted naturalism. Like the Mannerists, only more beautiful.

He writes, I see what you mean.

She falls into the habit of sending him short, quick notes, like journal entries. I dreamt last night that I was a tornado.

You are a weather event, he replies. You are a hundred-year storm.

She doesn't tell anyone about this. Not Meg, not Josh.

Sarah has friends, but few close ones. She's shy, and uncomfortable with intimacy. She listens to others talk about problems, fears, secrets; she sympathizes, but doesn't offer up her own. It feels safer to keep her secrets to herself. While her marriage was failing she told no one. She was ashamed; it seemed like her fault.

Sarah doesn't want to talk about what's happening; she doesn't know quite what it is. She hadn't wanted to see a married man. Is she betraying the sisterhood? But it's not her responsibility to protect Warren's marriage. It's Warren who's responsible, not her. And the more she hears about Janet, the less she thinks Warren should be with her. At first, learning about her, she thought of them as a pair. But now she feels more and more connected to Warren, as though they are the pair. Now she can't imagine Warren with Janet. Her moral landscape has shifted. What she is doing now seems right.

She wonders if Bella will accept Warren; her breed are one-man dogs. She tells Meg and Josh. I'm seeing someone. Someone nice. They tell her they're glad. Meg asks what Warren reads; Josh asks what he does. She doesn't tell them he's married.

She and Warren send texts and emails. She tells him about the exhibition. He tells her about the latest project. One day he calls to tell her about a funny conversation he overheard in a coffee shop. When she sees his name on her phone she feels a bright flutter in her chest. After that they talk often; he calls whenever he can. She calls him rarely; he's explained about his office, the lack of privacy. She asks for a video. That day, after everyone leaves, he walks around the office, scanning the rooms with his cell phone. "In here is the conference room," he says. The room is hung with photographs of their buildings. He moves closer, focuses on one. "Here's one of our summer houses. See the granite facing on the ground floor? It's from a quarry in Stonington, Maine. It supplied granite to half the post office buildings in the East."

Everything he tells her is new, it's like discovering a whole new cuisine. She savors the information, the points of view. He tells her that every week they have a life drawing class. A model comes to pose, and they all draw her. This informs the hand, the eye, he tells her. Keeps them quick and responsive. She has never imagined architects doing this.

He calls to say that the zoning problem has been resolved about the house in Finbury. Excitement is in his voice. It's novel, this combination of art and commerce. She's dealt with people in the arts world, impecunious and passionate, or in the financial world, comfortably aware of their philanthropic power. She hasn't known someone who's passionate about the arts who's also practical, determined to integrate them into the utilitarian world.

"That's so great," she says, "that's great, Warren."

She has said his name as though she owns it.

She stops thinking about the fact that he's married. She thinks of two parallel worlds, two lived lives. She thinks of the universe in which they'd gone to Bucharest. That summer when they traveled through Eastern Europe. When they arrived in a somber Hanseatic city, a plaza ringed by massive gray stone buildings, turreted and slate-roofed. They walk across the cobblestone square to the fountain in the center. They're both hot, carrying heavy backpacks. The straps have carved runnels in her shoulders, and she has a blister on her heel. They set the backpacks by the edge of the fountain. It's dark stone, a square tall pillar with a spigot on each side, spurting a thin stream. They lean in, raising their faces toward the cool spray. She cups her hands, filling them with water. She dips her face into it, feeling it against her hot skin, her closed eyes. She remembers all this: the blister on her heel, the slate roofs, the water on her face: the summer they went to Eastern Europe. They had never gone to a Communist country.

It was her fault that this had not happened.

On his next trip to New York Warren comes for the day, but he gets a hotel room. I'll be there at two o'clock. I hope to see you.

That morning she gets dressed for the city. Bella understands at once. Black pants, black turtleneck, a blazer. Earrings. Sarah doesn't look at Bella. The dog watches every movement. Sarah has breakfast and sits at her desk; Bella lies on her bed, not relaxed, her eyes on Sarah. At the end of the morning Sarah stands and picks up her bag. Bella stands, but her tail is down. She doesn't follow her to the door. Sarah carries the dog bed to the mudroom, then calls Bella. The property is fenced, and the swinging dog door lets Bella go in and out of the mudroom, which holds her food and water, her bed. She is completely safe. She hates Sarah leaving.

Bella walks past Sarah without looking at her. In the mudroom, Sarah locks the back door, then crouches down. I'll be back, she says, good dog. Bella listens, her eyes mournful. Sarah goes outside and after a moment Bella pushes through the swinging dog door and follows her. She stands motionless, ears down, watching Sarah walk to the car. Sarah can't look at her.

The drive in is nearly traffic-free. She surges down the highway as the roads swoop and cross, join and diverge, closer and closer to Manhattan. She reaches the hotel sooner than she expects. He has texted her the room number; he's already there.

When Sarah knocks, Warren opens the door almost at once. She wonders if he's been standing by it, waiting. Her pulse is thrumming. She feels herself begin to expand into excitement, heat, and energy. She wants something from him.

"Hi," she says, now shy.

"You're here," he says.

She steps past him. The room is dark; the lowered shades create an erotic twilight. Her body has become soft inside; it has been waiting for his.

They undress without speaking. He sets his watch on the bedside table; it makes a small metallic clink. She sits on the bed to take off her shoes. Her bare skin tightens in the cool air. Her heart is loud and insistent. She lifts the bedclothes to get in. He is already there, his dark eyes fixed on her. She slides across the sheets to meet him.

"I've been waiting for you," he whispers. His whisper is arousing. He seizes her by the upper arms, draws her close.

Now when he comes to New York they meet in the middle of the day. Sometimes he has meetings before, sometimes he just comes to see her. Sometimes they order sandwiches after they have sex, and watch the news, as though they share a life. One afternoon they watch the president at a press conference, with his beaky nose and little eyes and down-turned mouth. He talks about Iraq, and says America is winning.

"We shouldn't be over there in the first place," Sarah says. She is lying in bed, propped up against the pillows, the sheet pulled over her breasts. Warren is already dressed, sitting on the end of the bed.

"No," he agrees.

"Plus he doesn't believe in global warming."

Warren doesn't answer, and she looks at him.

"You believe in it, right?"

"Our whole economy is based on oil. There are practical problems about giving it up."

"But we can solve them if we support alternative energy." Sarah feels panicked at this conversation: It is dangerous to talk to men about this. The subject itself is a trigger: if men disagree they are scornful and derisive, peremptory. Sarah's throat narrows; she can't bear it if Warren is one of those. She feels the planet at risk. She can't talk about this easily. She feels it as something huge and threatening, she has to beat it back. "Americans are inventive, they'll figure it out."

"True," he says. "But it doesn't seem as urgent to me as it does to you."

"It does feel urgent to me," she says stiffly.

Warren turns and leans over her, sinking his elbows into the pillow on either side of her. He takes her face in his hands.

"I can see how you feel it," he says. "I don't disagree. I just don't feel it as strongly."

She is always prepared for a man's dismissal of her ideas. Rob had mocked and ridiculed her. She is unprepared for this, for Warren to disagree and be gentle. The touch of his hands, and his sympathy, surprise her. Her eyes fill, and she closes them for a moment.

"Thank you." She smiles at him.

They start watching again, the pundits disagreeing.

"Do you and Janet agree about politics?"

"Yes," he says. Then he corrects himself. "I shouldn't say that. Sometimes. I don't know that we do."

"Is she liberal?"

For a moment he doesn't answer. Then he speaks, his eyes still on the screen. "Not exactly," he says. He turns to her. "I don't know what Janet is."

He lowers his head into his hands and runs his fingers through his hair. "I don't want to hear what she thinks."

Sarah puts her hand on his shoulder. He runs his hands through his hair again.

"When I go home everything turns gray," he says. "I'm just waiting to see you again."

WARREN STOPS telling Janet when he comes down to New York. Once, his flight home is held up, delayed for two hours by the weather. He has to call Janet to tell her. New York? she says. I didn't know you were going. No, he says, I didn't bother to tell you. I had a meeting. I thought I'd be back early. Well, she says after a moment, I hope the weather lets up.

Chapter 6

AT THE BEGINNING OF APRIL SARAH GOES TO LONDON WITH A group from the museum. They take the day flight, arriving in the evening. The hotel is in Chelsea, handsome warm red brick, with white fluted columns. The bellboy takes Sarah to her room, which is small but pleasant. Discreet patterned wallpaper and mahogany furniture, worn fitted carpet, faded curtains at the tall windows. A big mirror over the bureau. Below it, doubled by its reflection, stands a huge bouquet of flowers, furled in silver paper.

"Welcome!" says the bellboy, an elderly South Asian. He glances at the flowers, smiling. "Someone is very pleased to see you."

Sarah doesn't respond. She's chasing through her purse for a pound coin. Does she have one? She knows who the flowers are from, she can't look at them now. She finds the coin and holds it out.

When the door closes behind him she doesn't move for a moment. The air is still, and the flowers give off a sweet, light fragrance, filling the room. She moves to the bureau. Within the silver paper is a layer of fine white tissue, then a cornucopia of deep magenta roses, crumpled pink taffeta carnations, arching bugles of white lilies. Around them is a pale green fizz of foliage. Taped onto the glass vase is an envelope. On the card is handwritten: *XXX*.

She knows he hasn't touched this himself, knows it was written by someone at the florist's shop, but she puts it in her wallet.

She texts him. *They're beautiful.*

They're in different time zones now, it's late in Boston. But a few minutes later she hears the little silvery chime on her phone as the text comes through. *Carnation, lily, lily, rose.*

Thank you, she writes. She's puzzled by the answer, but she puts away her phone, the others are waiting downstairs. In the elevator, as it shudders downward she feels herself rising: she's brimming with something, the ripple of promise, expectation.

The others are in the hotel dining room, down in the basement. She makes her way to the table. The others are tired, but Sarah is ebullient. She can feel the flowers waiting for her.

When the drinks arrive, she takes a sip of wine and starts talking. "I love London," she says. "I remember the first time I came here, I was sixteen, and I came with my parents. We went to Madame Tussauds. All those murderers!" She is full of energy.

Nancy nods. "I remember Madame Tussauds."

Sarah goes on. "We saw them changing the guard at Buckingham Palace. Christopher Robin went down with Alice!" She laughs. "And we went to *The Mousetrap.*"

Candace says, "We took the kids."

"And Gilbert and Sullivan. *The Mikado.*" Sarah sings in falsetto. "Three little maids from school are we!" She's laughing, she can't contain herself.

Jean Gerson says, "Sarah, what are you on? I'm ready to die. What is up with you?"

Sarah smiles, holding her secret.

That night she has trouble sleeping, though she's tired. She feels full of expectation, buoyed by it. Warren seems so close. They have been seeing each other nearly every week for nearly three months. His mind seems so close.

The next day is the National Gallery, where a curator will show them Early Netherlandish paintings. He's in his forties, tall and narrow, in a crisp dark suit. He seems more like a PR person than a scholar—Sarah thinks of scholars as young and tousled and impecunious. But maybe this is what museums want.

He is deferential to the point of irony. He stops before a diptych. "In this image," he says, keeping his head low politely—he's taller than they; Sarah wonders why Englishmen are so tall—"you see the extraordinary attention to detail that was a hallmark of these northern painters. Look at the careful folds on the white headdress, the expression on the terrier's face, the exactitude of the pattern on the carpet." They all stare at the heavy napkin folded around the woman's head, the bright-eyed dog at her feet, the geometric design on the Oriental rug. "The Netherlandish painters produced religious works, but the material world," he says, speaking slowly, as though to children, "was of crucial importance to them."

Does he speak with such insulting courtesy to all groups, or does he think Americans are idiots? He's like a salesman in a very expensive shop, hands clasped behind his back as he leads them to the next painting. His condescension interferes with her attention. Later Sarah will remember the pricked ears and bright eyes of the terrier, the heavy linen folds of the headdress, the complicated carpet, without remembering why.

After lunch they visit the Tate. They have no guide here, and Sarah sets out on her own, drifting through the vast high-ceilinged rooms hung with gilt-framed canvases. She prefers to look at paintings alone; if she's with someone else she feels scrutinized, or as though she must share her thoughts. Alone, she feels her consciousness expand, untrammeled, like Mrs. Ramsay's self.

The Impressionist rooms are filled with peaceful scenes, luscious colors, those celebrations of the middle class. People at leisure, boating, picnicking, having tea. One wall is dominated by a painting of two little girls in long white dresses, standing in a garden at twilight. They're lighting Chinese lanterns; the fading daylight is eclipsed by the warm glow of the lanterns. It's a strange, beautiful painting, unconventional in its execution, despite the conventional subject—little girls and flowers. The subject is sentimental, but the picture is not at all sentimental. The composition is oddly cropped, the space ambiguous. And there is the curious mingling of natural and artificial light. All those whites—the dresses, the lanterns, the radiance of the tall trumpeting lilies. Sarah leans in to read the title: John Singer Sargent, *Carnation, Lily, Lily, Rose.*

She takes a picture with her phone and sends it to him.

He's at the office, and writes back at once. I hoped you'd find it.

She's struck by his modesty, by the fact that he doesn't say, I knew you'd find it. He's hopeful, not certain. He's aware that she is leading her own life. His awareness opens something up inside her. She was not expecting this, someone so alive to what's between them.

The trip is five days long, all museums and galleries, but Sarah has become distracted. Listening to an authoritative young woman explaining Rachel Whiteread's inside-out house, Sarah's thinking about Warren. She has lost the sense of absorption she usually finds in museums; afterward she has little memory of what she's seen. Warren is as much a part of the trip as the art; when she sees something she thinks of telling him about it. She's just waiting to get back to him.

One evening before dinner Nancy Wilson knocks on her door. Her room is down the hall from Sarah's.

"It's me," Nancy says. She has very white teeth; Sarah wonders if she has had them bleached. "I just wanted to see your room."

"Come in." Sarah's glad to see Nancy, who's unfailingly cheerful. She's married to a friendly, balding lawyer called Gerald, who can never remember Sarah's name.

Nancy's dressed for dinner, dark blue suit, gold earrings, heels, a quilted leather evening bag with a gold chain. Her brilliant eyes are set off by makeup. Her thin, fine hair is like a silky pelt. She looks around and says, "Oh, they gave you one of the small ones."

"Really?" Sarah asks, gullible. "Is yours much bigger?"

"Vast," Nancy says. "It echoes when you walk in."

She grins and Sarah starts to laugh.

Nancy shakes her head. "No. Just the same." Then she sees the flowers. "Whoa!" she says. "Who are these from?"

Sarah doesn't answer.

Nancy looks at her with interest. "You have a boyfriend?"

After a moment Sarah says, "I guess I do."

"You go, girl," Nancy says. "Who is it?"

"A guy I used to know in college," she says. "He's married." Now she's said it out loud.

Nancy nods. "Okay."

"I'm not married," Sarah says. "I'm not cheating on anyone."

Nancy holds up her hands. "I'm not judging." She moves over to the flowers. "They're gorgeous. I wish I had a lover."

"They're to match the Sargent at the Tate," Sarah said. "*Carnation, Lily, Lily, Rose*." At once she wishes she hadn't told this detail, it's too intimate. But she's proud.

"That painting of the two little girls?" Nancy asks. "Wow. That's amazing. Gerald would never think of that."

"He is amazing," says Sarah.

"I always thought it would be cool to have an affair," Nancy says. "So romantic." She touches the ruffled petals. "I never did, though. I'm pretty sure Gerald did, years ago. One affair is enough for a marriage."

"What happened?" Sarah asks. "Why did you think he was having one?"

"We have a little sort of cabin in our backyard," says Nancy. "Gerald used to use it as a study. He'd go out there and work on weekends. One day I went out to tell him something. Our sons were playing on the trampoline, jumping up and down, waving as I walked across the lawn. I opened the door and he was on the phone. He turned and looked at me, and I knew from his face. For a moment neither of us moved. Then he said, 'I have to take this call!' It made no sense, he was already taking it. It was clear he wanted me to leave. I turned and left. I didn't want to hear whatever he was going to say."

"What did you do?"

Nancy sighs and sits down on the bed. "Nothing. I was a complete coward. I kept thinking I would say something. During the day I'd get pumped up and angry and I'd walk around the house saying tonight's the night, and rehearsing what I was going to say."

Her gaze is interior, remembering. "But I couldn't. I was so afraid of what would happen." She looks up at Sarah. "My cousin Becky is fifteen years older than me. This happened years ago, her husband was having an affair with his secretary. When there were secretaries. It went on and on, everyone knew about it. Sometimes he'd be with the secretary at holidays, Thanksgiving and Christmas."

Sarah sits down on the desk chair to listen.

"The other woman would call him at home, pretending to be someone else—Becky knew her voice. Finally Becky couldn't stand it. She had it out with her husband—he was called Tick—and she said, This can't go on. You're disgracing me and your children. You have to choose." Nancy looks up at Sarah. "So he chose. He left Becky and married the secretary. Becky never married again. She never really recovered. She was broken."

They sit in silence.

"But that was a long time ago," Sarah says. "Women recover from divorce now. They learn to code or something. Look at me!"

"Well, my whatever it was, was years ago, too," says Nancy. "Crisis. I didn't want to be single. I kept thinking about Becky. I didn't want him to walk out, and I knew he could. It's such a fragile thread, either one of you can break it. It felt like my choice was to keep the marriage going, keep our life whole, the kids happy, the house the way it all was—and hope it was good enough. Try to last her out." Her eyes are serious. "I think that's what happened. I don't know. I never want to hear. I never want to know." There's another silence. "That was years ago. I don't feel anything now where I used to feel all that confusion and deceit. I know he's back. I don't know if he's happy about it. I don't want to know."

Sarah thinks of jovial Gerald, pushing his glasses up on his nose. "Hello!" he'd call, as Sarah arrived. He'd be extra-friendly because at first he couldn't retrieve her name. She would give him a peck on each cheek.

"Sarah!" he'd say, delighted. "Welcome!"

He would seem so open and candid.

"But you're sure it all happened?" she asks Nancy.

"I know it. I don't know why he stayed. But he did." Her face is filled with the memory. "As soon as I realized, it made sense of all sorts of confusion—trips he'd taken, times he was late. It's like this awful place where we struggled in the dark. I never want to know about it. I never want to know her name, or what happened."

Sarah nods.

They are both still. Below in the courtyard a suitcase is noisily trundled across the cobbles. The flowers on the bureau declare their soft, erotic presence.

"I'm the other woman," Sarah says.

"I know," says Nancy.

"I don't know which side to take," Sarah says.

Nancy smooths the skirt over her lap and stands up. "You don't have to take sides. My story is over. Maybe your friend's marriage is different."

"It sounds it," Sarah says.

"Everyone's marriage is different," Nancy says. "I'm not judging. Ready to go down?"

Sarah nods.

Nancy goes to the door and puts her hand on the knob. She turns back to look at Sarah. "Is he kind?"

Sarah nods, grateful. He is kind.

WHEN SHE GETS BACK she drives in to New York to spend the whole night with him.

Driving into the city, folding her car into the long rush of traffic along the darkening highway, she feels light and powerful, encased in her small lighted space. The wide stretch of windshield offers the darkening world. She stays in the fast lane, where there are fewer cars and she is in control. She doesn't like the middle, where she's boxed in on either side, or the slow lane, where she's stalled by huge thundering trucks.

She has driven these highways for years: big open 684, flanked by farms and woodlands, curving down through the county to the Hutchinson, enclosed by concrete walls, leading to the Cross-County; making the diagonal trek across lanes toward the Major Deegan, the racing urban highway. She's used to this high-speed maneuvering, watching behind, ahead, both sides, cars surging past or falling away, keeping pace with the long continual scroll of the divider, the lanes yielding, narrowing, widening.

She must change lanes to get off at the Willis Avenue Bridge. The highway dips beneath an underpass. She glances in the rearview mirror, turns on her blinker, and slides sideways toward an empty space. She turns to look as she moves and finds another car beside her at seventy miles an hour. She's sliding toward it. Her scalp goes icy. She turns the wheel, trying not to swerve, heart thudding. The driver looks over, furious. She shakes her head in apology, but he still glares. She's missed him by inches; her body fills with cold.

She's missed the Willis Avenue exit and will have to take the Triborough. Cars sizzle past. It's dark now; the highway lit by the sodium glare of the streetlamps. She's cold, but she doesn't dare look down to turn on the heat; she doesn't dare take her eyes from the road. She feels the cold touch of that near-miss.

THIS RESTAURANT IS SMALL, French, not grand. A long narrow room, a mirror along one side. A sense of Gallic festiveness. He's in a booth at the back, watching for her. When she comes in he raises his hand and smiles; she feels a lift, a warming.

She sits down across from him and he puts his hand out on the table, palm up. She gives him hers awkwardly, her fingers closed, like a paw. He takes her hand carefully and raises it; he kisses the back of it. She suddenly shivers, a chill running through her like an electric shock.

"Welcome back," he says.

"Thank you," she says.

"I missed you," he says.

She says nothing for a moment. Now that he's in front of her he seems too large to contemplate.

"Tell me about your trip," he says, and she describes it, the wonderful art, the snooty curator, the fatigue at being part of a group. He watches her, as though everything she says is interesting.

"It was fun, being with the others," she says. "Kind of tiring to be on a schedule, but I did things I wouldn't have done otherwise. And I really like Nancy."

"Because?"

She shakes her head, not ready to tell him Nancy's story. "I just got to know her a bit."

He nods.

After a pause she says, "Tell me what we're doing. You and I."

"Trying again." He puts his other hand over hers.

"What if it's too late?" she says.

He raises her hand again. He's watching her face. He turns her hand over. Gently he opens it and kisses the palm.

"I feel it's not too late."

"You're married," she says.

"I'm going to get divorced."

She looks at him, uncertain. Has he just decided this because of what she said? Is this like Bucharest?

The waitress appears, to recite the specials. When she's gone, Sarah waits for him to speak. He looks at her gravely, still holding her hand.

"I don't mean to frighten you," he says. "This isn't about you." He looks down, then back at her. "Or it is about you. Having you in my life again has made me realize I can't spend the rest of it like this."

"What is it you want?"

"You," he says. "I've never stopped."

"You don't know me now," she says.

"I do," he says. "Ever since the opera I've been thinking about you."

"Not really me," she says. "You've been thinking of someone I was when I was twenty."

"No," he says. "I've been thinking of you."

She watches him.

"We'll go as slowly as you want," he says.

"What about Janet?"

He looks down. "This isn't . . ." He pauses. "It was never great, being with her." He looks up. "Now it's a prison."

He is tethered to Janet. She is like a stone, barnacled, mossy, sunk deep in cold black waters, linked to him by a long, heavy seaweed-hung rope. The thought of her is unbearable. He had promised her his whole life until death, but his heart is failing. His body refuses hers.

"I'm sorry," Sarah says.

"This isn't sudden, for me," he says. "It must seem it to you, but it's not."

"What will happen next?" Sarah says.

"We'll go as slowly as you like," he says. "I need to get things in order before I tell Janet. I have to talk to a lawyer."

She waits.

"I think you and I should get married," he says.

"I have to think about it," she says.

"Okay," he says. "But that's my hope."

"Where would we live?" she says.

"I have to live near Boston for a while still," he says. "Could you imagine it?"

She thinks of her house, the soft fields, the reservoir glimmering beyond the woods. "I have a dog."

"Whatever you want," he says. "I'm yours."

She can't really absorb this.

"When will you tell her?"

"I have to talk to a lawyer. I want to make her comfortable. I need to see how to go about it."

"What about your daughter?"

"I'll tell her after."

"What will she think?" she asks.

"She's grown up," he says. "She must know the marriage isn't great."

"Mine were angry. Meg was angry for a long time," she says. "But they were much younger."

"I hope Kat will forgive me."

"She will," Sarah says. "You're her father. She loves you. She'll have to."

"I'm hoping." He doesn't think Kat will take sides. It's his marriage, not hers. She's left home, she's gone. He thinks of the gray kitchen. He now wants only to leave, he wants never again to enter the closed chamber of his marriage, facing Janet, her chapped lips, the way she swallows. Having to talk to her.

IT'S THE SAME HOTEL. This time he turns to her as soon as he shuts the door, before he turns on the light. He holds her, saying something she can't hear, a sigh, or a single syllable.

"What?" she whispers.

"I'm glad to have you back," he says. "My god."

The way he says it shakes her.

He pulls back, holding her shoulders, to look at her. His face is shadowed, and she can only see the outline of his head, but she feels the force of his gaze, sees the bright gleam of his eyes. He says her name.

This time she undresses in full view, standing beside the bed. She still feels awkward. The culture has made this moment into a spectacle, the revelation of the woman's flesh, as though she is climbing out of a cake. But Sarah has never felt her body was something to celebrate. She has always felt ungainly, too lean. Her shoulder-points are too bony, her elbows too sharp. She slides off her underpants and looks up. He's watching her. He's on the other side of the bed, taking off his socks, ripping them off his feet and flinging them away. The bedside lamp illuminates him from below. His neck and throat are bright and his face is in shadow, but his eyes are brilliant. They are focused on her. His body is lit by the lamp, illuminating the curve of his belly, the dark tangle of soft hair, the long pale penis, now upright, swaying as he moves. He slides down onto the bed and holds his arms out.

"Come to me," he says.

They trust each other now, and she gives herself up to his hand, his mouth, his skin against hers. The deep comfort of touch. She closes her eyes, yields. Afterward they lie flank to flank, and he puts his hand over hers.

He says, "I figure we have forty more years. We missed forty years, but we still have forty more."

"You're going to live to be a hundred?" she says.

"Easily. Now that I have an incentive," he says.

She turns toward him. "They won't be the best years of our lives," she says. "Getting old."

"They will be the best," he says. "For us."

"Your chest hair is turning white," she says.

"I'm old." He turns toward her, rising up on one elbow. "Your roots are turning white."

"I'm old, too," she says. "But I don't feel it yet. How will we know when we are?"

"It'll be something we don't expect," he says. "Like not knowing how to do something. The internet, like that."

"That's already happened," she says. "But really. I feel the same as I always have. I wear the same clothes, eat the same way, exercise the same as I did when I was fifty. Or forty. How will I know?"

"Something will happen," he says. "Something will change."

"Remember, we kept count, once, having sex?" she says. "Thirteen times in one weekend? Or twenty-two? Something like that. What was it?"

"Exactly," he says. "I don't remember. But it's not happening again."

"What's better about getting old?" she asks.

"We know more now," he says. "We don't see things as catastrophic. We can take the longer view. And we're not old, by the way."

But she had never not taken the longer view. She had always looked ahead, as though she did not exist in the present, as though her real self were somewhere in the future.

THE NEXT MORNING she seems asleep when he wakes up. He gets out of bed quietly and goes into the bathroom; he has to catch an early shuttle. He has a zoning commission meeting. Zoning commissions always want to discover something. He has to remind them that he's on their side. Sometimes it's a matter of class. The head of the commission, Eric Clayton, comes from South Boston; Warren's accent is against him. Each time he opens his mouth he antagonizes Clayton.

He cups his hands beneath the faucet, dousing his face. Janet will be sitting at the kitchen table, in her flowered bathrobe, watching the news. She'll be eating toast, sliced into halves. She'll hold each buttered slice with the tips of her fingers, then wipe them carefully with a napkin.

He covers his cheeks in shaving cream. He can feel Sarah in the next room. Her presence is like a light. He feels buoyed up, exuberant. She is his secret.

When he comes out of the bathroom she's dressed and standing by the bed. She holds herself very straight, her head held high like a deer. She's in a red sweater and black pants. It's amazing that she's here in the room with him.

Her face is open and naked, still slack from sleep.

"I'm sorry I can't have breakfast," he says. "I have a nine o'clock shuttle."

She shakes her head.

She thinks he's already left, entered the rest of his day, the airport, the shuttle, the meeting. He's ready to walk into his office.

She's already gone, too. She's thinking about getting her car, the drive home. She'll be home by midmorning.

He puts his arms around her and pulls her close. "I'll be thinking of you all day."

So he's not gone yet.

"During your meeting with the Southie?" she says.

"Even then." He likes the fact that she has memorized his day, entered into it.

"Why doesn't he like you?" she asks.

He sits on the bed to put on his socks. "He doesn't dislike me. He'd just rather I'd come from his background. I have to work for his trust."

He stands and puts on his shirt. His chest is still damp from shaving, and when he buttons it up a small dark patch appears.

"I don't mind working for it," he says. "People are tribal. But I'd like it if I didn't have to work for it over and over."

"Do you trust people?" asks Sarah. "Generally?"

"Generally, yes," he says. "I do."

She feels that there is a list somewhere, she must ask him all the right questions. What has she not asked him? What do you need to know about someone?

He looks up, the shirt now fastened up to his chin. "What else would you like to know? Do you have a list?"

She laughs. "I don't have a list." It's too silly to admit. She likes that he has picked up on her thought. Still she thinks there's something more she needs to know, she just doesn't know what.

When she comes out of the bathroom he's dressed, a stranger. He comes over and kisses her carefully. She closes her eyes: his smell is intoxicating, his breath, his skin clean and warm. Her body opens to him.

He gazes at her intently, as if he is memorizing her.

"I'll call you later." He picks up his briefcase.

"Yes," she says.

They don't have a way to say goodbye. They haven't used the word love.

He sets down his briefcase and puts his arms around her again. "I love you."

She's startled again. She feels pleased and panicked. She nods, smiling. She doesn't say it back.

AT THE END of the driveway the dog is standing by the house. Sarah wonders what Bella does when she's alone. She doesn't like thinking of the dog without her.

Bella is always waiting when she arrives. Today she wags her tail quietly, pleased but restrained. Sarah understands that the restraint is reproof.

Sarah crouches and whispers her name. Bella tilts her head toward Sarah. Sarah rubs at her ears; Bella closes her eyes. How would it be to live with someone else? She's used to being alone. In the hotel that morning, as she brushed her teeth, she was aware of Warren on the other side of the door. She's used to the luxury of privacy. How would it be to be not alone? Sometimes she listens to a meditation tape before she goes to sleep, slipping in earbuds, lying on her back. Would it be too strange to do it with someone next to her? Would it be rude?

She goes upstairs. Bella follows, nodding on each step, making a soft four-beat rhythm with her padding footsteps. Sarah unpacks; Bella lies down, head raised, watching her. Sarah sits down on the floor beside her. She rubs Bella's throat. Bella closes her eyes, leaning into Sarah's hand.

"Beautiful girl," Sarah whispers. "Beautiful girl."

Bella has a large vocabulary. She knows all the obvious words—walk, dinner, vet, no, good dog. Bad dog, though Bella is almost never bad, and when she is it's deliberate. If Sarah is gone for too long—a week or more—Bella destroys something. It's always something of her own. When Sarah came home from England the zipper on Bella's dog bed had been chewed through. Once Sarah had been staying with friends in Maine. They'd gone to the grocery store, where Bella wasn't allowed. Sarah tied Bella's leash to the fence beside the store. When Sarah came out Bella was sitting by the fence, very erect, her eyes on Sarah. A piece of the leash hung down straight from her collar. The other end was still tied around the fence. She had chewed it through, though she hadn't moved. It was a rebuke.

Bella's mission is to align herself with Sarah, to become neurally connected. She studies Sarah, watching for signs of intention. She knows all the commands, sit, lie down, shake hands, roll over. She despises them: They are beneath her. If commanded to sit, Bella will lower her haunches to where they graze the ground, then lift them immediately and stand, as though she had never sat down in her life. If asked to shake hands, she'll raise her paw impatiently, bat twice at the air, then set it down. At the command to roll over she will throw herself to the ground and roll over in one swift motion, like a dolphin, then leap to her feet, eyes flashing, insane with contempt and impatience. She does all these things quickly, her manner perfunctory and condescending, like a math genius asked to do short division at a party. She finds tricks pointless, embarrassing to all concerned.

Bella is more interested in words that deliver information. When Sarah leaves, she says, "I'll be back." Sarah thinks Bella understands this, though Bella may think it means, "I'm never coming back." Her ears droop, her tail stills. When Sarah talks on the phone to Meg, the last thing she says before she hangs up is, "I love you." When she hears those words Bella leaps to her feet, knowing that now Sarah will do something new. Living with Bella is like having a familiar, a small unpredictable spirit who knows you intimately, who is deeply involved in your life in ways you don't quite understand, who feels she shares your soul, and who is always, always present.

PART II

Chapter 7

SARAH CAN'T OPEN THE CABINETS IN MEG'S KITCHEN.

She's in charge of making dinner: Meg's at a conference in Cincinnati and Jeff's working late. Meg has asked Sarah to come down and help out for the evening, to feed the kids and put them to bed. Of course, Sarah said. She wants to make it clear that she's part of their family, because she's not sure she is.

Sarah crouches to get out a pasta pot, but the cupboard door has a special childproof device. They all do, tricky plastic contraptions that Meg unlocks with one deft gesture. Sarah can't open them at all. She tugs at it, feeling idiotic. Maybe this is what getting old is: you simply can't make things work. She's always nervous in Meg's house, afraid of doing the wrong thing.

Sarah is still crouching when Jeff comes in. He's a big man, not fat but solid. A shock of caramel-colored hair curves onto his forehead. His face is wide, with high cheekbones, and his eyes are long and narrow, Slavic.

She looks up. "Hi," she says, "I didn't know you were going to be here."

"I thought I'd bring my work home," he says. "In case you needed backup."

"Great," she says, "thanks. Actually, I can't get this cabinet open," she confesses.

Jeff crouches easily beside her. He has a pleasant smell, dry and clean, like the pages of a new book. She leans away from him, avoiding touch. She has a horror of appearing to flirt.

Jeff snaps it open easily. "There you go."

Jeff's field is string theory. Sarah has asked him about it, but the very idea empties her mind. She can't manage to hold his answers in her head. On other subjects he's courteous but abstracted. He's not much interested in art or books. She doesn't know what to talk to him about, and they have a courteous, distant relationship. She doesn't know what he and Meg talk about, though they have long ago moved from the time in which they were exploring each others' ideas. Now they are facing each day together, dealing with the practicalities of child care, schedules, doctors' appointments, their jobs, all that.

Sarah is trying to get dinner on the table. It's not a big task—two kids, one meal—except for those impenetrable cupboards. Also, the stove is not a real one but an electric cooktop, burners sealed under glass, like some high-tech simulation. Some of them work and some don't, and it's not clear which is which. The oven is set into the wall, with nothing so simple as on or off, but a host of cryptic buttons and dials, like the dashboard of a jet plane. There is also a grim microwave, which will destroy metal, plastic, and certain kinds of china. The kitchen is an obstacle course. Sarah is happy never to use either of the ovens, but she must use the cooktop, and there's no way around the cabinets. She's glad Jeff appeared.

And she's glad to be called on for help. Before Meg was married Sarah had felt as though she and her daughter were part of each other. Hadn't they once shared the same body? She'd felt that whatever Meg was doing, Sarah was vicariously part of it. But now she's been taught that this is not the case: Both Meg and Jeff keep her at a distance. Jeff had been friendly at first, but now he is not friendly, though he's not unfriendly. He's pleasant but distant. As though she is an alien mathematical theory, something proposed by a competitor, something he's holding under observation.

She doesn't know how to act toward him. They are not quite friends. Their shared interests are Meg, Busby, and Nate. Not much else.

She wants to bathe both children before dinner, but this project is like dragging heavy sacks through a swamp. She tells them both to get undressed, then goes to the kitchen to put on the pasta water. When Sarah comes back to her room, Busby has not moved. She is still kneeling on the floor, intent on a game that involves playing cards, toy animals, and tattered ribbons.

"Come on, Bus." Sarah doesn't want a late bedtime, she thinks the children don't get enough sleep.

Busby doesn't reply. When Sarah opens her mouth to speak a third time, Busby says, irritation in her voice, "In a minute."

"Now, lovey," Sarah says.

Busby stands reluctantly and pulls her tights down over her plump legs. She doesn't look at Sarah. She pulls her shirt off, then crouches again to the game. "Come on, Bus," says Sarah. Busby doesn't look at her but doesn't touch the animals. It's a standoff.

Sarah goes back to Nate's room. He's lying on his bed, surrounded by dinosaurs. He doesn't look up.

"Come on, Natey." She kneels beside him and puts her hand on his head. He shakes it off, staring fixedly at *T. rex*. "It's time for a bath."

"No," he says, frowning.

He is determined to stay here, dry, which is so known and so comforting, and resisting wetness, which is so strange and alien. Children's plans are continually interrupted and destroyed.

"One minute," she says.

She goes in to turn on the bath. Ancient white tiles cover the walls, the grout darkened with age. She twirls the heavy spigots of the tub, and water thunders down from them. Steam rises in plumes. She goes back to the kitchen, where she turns down the heat under the boiling water and puts in the pasta. She goes back to capture the children. Herding Busby, she carries Nate, naked and protesting, into the bathroom, and lowers him into the tub.

"Noooo," Nate whispers, shivering. Busby stands on the bath mat and shakes her hands, whimpering fretfully.

"In," says Sarah. Busby steps in, shivering, reluctant, as though into freezing acid. She crouches, then, and splashes at the rising water. As they settle in, the warmth begins to seep into them, and they relax. Their limbs stretch out, their skin turns moist and pink. They stop complaining and start playing. Bus kneels in front of the faucets, polishing them with her fingers. Nate, behind her, lies on his belly and puts his arms around her waist. His mouth hits her spine and he quickly kisses the bony nub, just above the buttocks, then blows against her vertebra like a conch shell. She ignores him, singing under her breath. They slip and slide against each other, they are like two parts of the same animal. Sarah soaps a washcloth and moves it over them, from one body to the next, sleek rosy skin.

When she has finished, she's drenched by a big wave sloshed by uproarious Nate. She gets them finally to the table in their footed pajamas. Their faces are damp and pink, their hair in dark ringlets. They smell clean and fresh, like plants.

But when she puts the plates before them Busby's face crumples with distaste. She hates carrots, she says, and lies back against her chair, kicking her feet.

"You can put the carrots to one side," Sarah says.

"I miss Mama," Busby says. Self-pity begins to overcome her. Her face crumples and she makes little percussive grunts, prelude to tears.

"I do, too," Sarah says.

"I miss her, too," Nate says anxiously.

"We all do," Sarah says. "Take a bite."

Jeff comes in and sits down, putting his cell phone on the table.

"Thank you for making dinner," he says to Sarah. "Hello, munchkins." His attention is like a spotlight. The children turn toward him, craving his gaze. Busby says fiercely that she hates carrots, and Jeff leans toward her. Nate bangs his spoon on the table.

"Da-da!" he shouts.

"In a minute," Jeff says, "I'm talking to Busby."

Nate collapses against the table with a wailing cry. He wants air, sustenance, survival. Sarah puts her arm around him. Busby raises her voice, wanting to keep primary status.

"I'll throw up," Busby says. She is near-teary at the thought of her own distress.

When the children are quieted, Sarah asks Jeff about Meg's conference.

"It's an annual publishing thing. It's the first time she's been invited, so she's pleased."

Sarah nods. "What will she be doing, exactly?"

"I think representing her boss's imprint."

His answers are polite dead ends. She wonders what this actually means. Will Meg sit in a booth in a conference center? Give a speech in an auditorium? She doesn't quite have the nerve to ask him for more information; Jeff acts satisfied, as though the world is complete as it is.

They finish the meal talking to the children. Afterward Jeff thanks her and goes back to his office, and Sarah puts the children to bed. Busby reads to herself while Sarah reads to Nate. Then she turns out his light and sings him a folk song. She tries to remember "The House Carpenter," which has a beautiful melody, and is about a bad wife who leaves her husband and baby, and who asks her lover where they are going. "What hills, what hills are those, my love? That lie so dark and low? Those are the hills of hell, my love, where you and I must go." Kind of horribly judgmental for a bedtime song. They are all like that, these folk songs, about the grim fates that befall the people who break the moral codes. She can't really remember most of the verses but fudges it, hoping Nate is asleep. His face is set against the pillow, the rounded nose, the impossibly long curved lashes, the faint greenish rings below his eyes, which are open. He's not asleep. She sings one verse over and over, softly, barely audible, until she sees his eyes slowly blink, blink again, close. She tiptoes out, shutting the door soundlessly, and goes into Busby's room. Busby does not look up from her book, frowning and pretending not to see her. Sarah sits down beside her.

"Would you like me to read?" she asks.

Busby nods without looking at her, and gives her the book. While Sarah reads, Busby watches her. The story is about a group of humans and non-humans making a dangerous trek through a nocturnal landscape. Busby officiously corrects Sarah's pronunciation of the made-up names: her mother's versions are the only true ones, apparently. At the end of the chapter Sarah says, "That's all for tonight."

At once Busby says, "More. Mama always reads two."

Sarah hesitates, torn between being responsible and being loved. She reads three more pages. When she turns out the light, Busby asks her to sing the song about the shepherdess. Busby listens, her cheek on the pillow, her index finger, with its tiny fingernail, slowly stroking the sheet. Sarah sings the verses over and over, nearly hypnotizing herself, until the finger stops moving. Sarah leans over and kisses her, setting her lips on the satiny hair, feeling the warm head below. She closes the door quietly and goes into the kitchen to do the dishes. At once she feels their loss, and she regrets her hurry. Why does she do this? She feels driven by the clock, hurrying them to the bath, the table, to bed. Snapping at their heels like a sheepdog. What is wrong with her? Why can't she just enjoy her time with them? They'll remember her as crabby. But sleep, sleep is the elixir of happiness for children.

When she's finished the dishes she knocks on the door of Jeff's study.

"Yes," he says, and she pushes it open. The room is dim. Jeff is sitting at his desk, facing the door. His computer sends a glow onto his face and the packed bookshelves behind him. He looks up; the glow makes his glasses opaque.

"All through," Sarah says. "I think I'll head home."

"Thank you for coming in," Jeff says, but he doesn't stand up, or even move. "It was really a help to have you."

"Happy to do it," Sarah says. She means it, because doesn't this earn her something, in the family exchange of gratitude, acknowledgment, respect? Love. This means she will be less likely to be set down on an ice floe and sent out to sea. Or it will not happen so soon. She's happy to donate her energies to this family, though she'd much rather come when Meg's there. Her daughter's presence is the whole point. For all of them.

Jeff is still looking at her politely, but he's waiting to go back to work on his mystifying subject. He's impenetrable. She tries to think of something to say about string theory, something not foolish or derisive, but fails. She would like to meet Jeff somehow, enter easily into his thoughts, become friends. He waits, saying nothing. Sarah nods and closes the door.

Driving home, she watches the highway signs as they loom up and fall away into the darkness. She should become a better friend to Jeff. She feels walled outside him and the family he and Meg have made; their family excludes her. But this can't be true, can it? Isn't she a part of Meg's life? That can't change, can it?

She calls Josh. Amazingly, he answers.

"Hi," he says. "What's up?"

"Not much. I'm on my way home from Meg's. I spent the evening there. She's away."

"And how was that?" he asks. Josh is always like this, responsive, reflective, comforting, asking questions. A bit like a therapist.

"It was fine," Sarah says. "I can't open their kitchen cupboards."

"Because?" Josh asks.

"They have these childproof gadgets on them," Sarah says. "It makes me so incompetent. I can't get anything out or put anything away."

"Mmm," says Josh. "That sounds frustrating."

Sarah laughs. "Yes. It was. How are you?" Her evening is now put into a different perspective.

But Josh never divulges much. Everything is fine, he says. He's going hiking this weekend with some friends. She asks him where, but it doesn't matter, she's never heard of the mountain. She asks about his girlfriend. She's traveling a lot on business, he says. She works for a start-up. He hasn't seen her much, but she's fine. They text all the time.

"How about the guy you're seeing?" he asks. "How's that going?"

"Fine," she says. "He's fine."

"What do you talk about?" he asks.

"Um. Books. Politics. His work. Mine at the gallery. Everything. You'll like him."

"That's good, Mom. I'm glad you've got someone."

She's touched by this, the idea that Josh has been watching, the thought of her happiness in his mind.

"Thanks," she says. "Me, too."

"Has Bella met him?"

She laughs. "Not yet." Now the highway is getting complicated. "I've got to go, Josho. I love you."

All evening Warren has been present in her mind, a running backdrop. She'd wanted to tell him about the locked cupboards, the hated carrots. String theory. What is he doing?

She calls Meg, but it goes to voice mail. Meg must already have heard from Jeff. Sarah should have called as soon as she'd left, Meg would have taken the call then. Now Meg knows everything's fine; she doesn't have to hear Sarah's version. Sarah has missed her chance. She's disappointed. Isn't she sort of owed a conversation? Though maybe not. She's owed nothing.

Being a mother is paying it forward, sending that energy and feeling to someone who needed it at first to survive, but who, the older she becomes, needs you less. The older you become, the more irrelevant you are.

Chapter 8

JANET PULLS OPEN THE BOTTOM DRAWER OF THE FRIDGE AND takes out two frozen chicken potpies. She's wearing a long red velour robe, slit up the sides, with a plunging V-neck that exposes a horizontal strip of lace from her nightgown. She shoves the freezer drawer shut with her knee. The gesture widens the slit in her robe, revealing her white calf, a little starburst of blue veins. She sets the pies inside the metal cave of the microwave. She pushes a button and the oven begins its secret whirring. She drops the empty boxes on the floor and steps on them, crushing them with her soft Belgian shoes. She drops the flattened boxes in the trash.

Warren is setting the table, taking down the blue water glasses from the cupboard. He's aware of each one of Janet's gestures: the dismissive knee-shove, the swift ripping open of the boxes, the trampling of the cardboard. He closes the cupboard door. Each moment takes him closer to the end of this life. It's as though he's watching from behind a screen as Janet moves, unaware, toward an ambush. He can't warn her. He opens the freezer drawer and scoops out ice cubes with a loud metallic rattle. He puts the cubes in the glasses and holds them under the tap. The water shatters the ice with a harsh crackling noise.

Janet pads briskly back and forth in her soft-soled shoes. The robe flows against her bare legs.

"How was your day?" he asks. He won't tell her until they've finished dinner. He feels it approaching him like a waterfall on a river.

"Fine," she says. "I had lunch with Caroline, about the gala."

For thirteen years Janet has been the gala chair of the Boston Adult Literacy Program. She is good at running it, at choosing venues and caterers, organizing the committee. She has made the whole thing glamorous and successful, she and her friends in their long dresses and glittery earrings, their high heels and glossy hair. It raises huge sums each year.

"How's it going?"

"Oh, fine. Now everyone's saying they'll take tables, but in a couple of months they won't be answering their emails," Janet says cheerfully. "The weasels."

Warren puts wine goblets at each place, setting them onto the table with a sense of finality. He feels the tiny click of the glass meeting wood. Each movement seems freighted, terminal. He wonders if this is the last evening he'll spend in this kitchen. He wonders what Janet will do for dinner when she's alone.

Janet takes a box of salad greens from the fridge. She shuts the double doors, checks the jointure, opens them again, and closes them more carefully.

"It looks shut but it's really not," she says. "Unless you close it in the right sequence it stays open a crack. I guess there's nothing we can do. Poor design."

"Mm," Warren says.

"It's leaking cold," Janet says; then she adds, "Can you leak cold?"

Warren says nothing, and she turns to look at him. "Can you?"

"I think so," he says. "Air-conditioning. Leaving the front door open in July." He wishes not to be drawn into this discussion.

She waggles her head, not agreeing. "It's a funny idea," she declares. "I know you can leak heat. Or water." It's her habit to state the obvious with energy and affirmation. "I don't think you can leak cold."

When they were first married Janet had deferred to Warren's opinions. But that deference had drained away during feminism. He'd liked all that, liked the idea of women coming into their own. He likes women. But now Janet disagrees casually with anything he might say, things about which she knows nothing and about which he knows a good deal. He doesn't know how to respond. He doesn't like arguing.

She accepts his views on money and taxes, but she has her own ideas on everything else, much of it cockeyed. She thinks that France started World War II. Under stress she mixes up right and left. She has never read serious fiction. She thinks Machiavelli is a kind of pasta. She's unabashed by all this. Warren had once found it endearing—her sunny self-confidence, her firm conviction that intelligence and education were overrated.

She takes out an empty mustard jar to make the salad dressing in. Salad dressing is about all she makes now. Years ago she cooked all the time. Once, for his birthday, she'd made a cassoulet, which took three days. In those days the kitchen was aromatic, messy, full of spots and stains and cooking smells.

The microwave gives its annunciatory ping and Janet takes out the potpies. They sit down across from each other. Janet pokes her fork into the browned crust, releasing a steamy burst of heat. She takes a tiny bite and gives a little gasp, fanning her mouth.

"So hot." She takes a swallow of wine. When she sets down the goblet the wine leaves a faint translucent shadow on the glass.

Warren has turned his potpie out onto the plate, where it collapses, steaming.

"Elena brought a new woman onto the board, Alicia Landen, from Los Angeles." Janet talks about her, how she doesn't understand Boston. "She doesn't get it. Alicia has only been here fifteen minutes. It took me years to be accepted." She points her fork at Warren. "I know what you're thinking: What makes you think you've been accepted?" She gives her rattling machine-gun laugh.

"Right," he says, laughing with her.

"We'll never be from Boston," says Janet. "And you know

what? I don't care." She blows on the chicken and takes another cautious bite. "Did Katrina call you?"

He shakes his head.

"I have this feeling," she says. "I think they're going to get married."

"Did she say something?" he asks.

She shakes her head. "I just have this feeling." Faint firm horizontal lines cross her forehead; around her mouth is a spray of wrinkles: her life is making itself known in her face. "I suspect it won't be that way, anyway, him asking her."

"You think she'll ask him?"

Janet nods, gingerly chewing the hot pie. "I mean, Kat's quite—"

"Bossy," Warren says. Kat is definitely bossier than Chris, who is mild and good-natured. He's from the Midwest, and doesn't seem to have opinions. He's in tech, too: analytics.

Janet nods. "Men have trouble actually asking the question." She says this as though it's common knowledge.

Warren says nothing. He won't disagree with her now. She seems to be at a great distance from him.

"Wouldn't that be great?" she asks. "If they do decide? I don't think it's a good idea to live together for years. Indefinitely. Then there's never any reason to commit. She'll just be doing his laundry."

He is hardly listening. Every moment he delays is one more in which this world will exist.

She looks at him. "What is it?"

He will begin by saying her name.

"Janet," he says.

Janet's fork is poised, a pale chunk balanced on the prongs. "What is it?"

"I want to talk about our marriage." He speaks slowly and carefully.

" 'Our marriage'?" she repeats.

She is still calm, still friendly.

"I know there are things about it that make you unhappy." He pauses. "And me as well."

She sets down her fork, the little pale cube of chicken still on it. "What do you mean?"

The look on her face—stunned, fearful—reminds him of the awful time they'd gone to Jamaica. They'd stayed in a big hotel, and had seen an ad for river rafting. They'd gone out on the river with Katrina. Their rafts were flimsy plastic ones from the pool—it was dangerous, though they hadn't known it. They hadn't brought life jackets. The current was smooth and swift and they called back and forth, laughing, and then around a bend they had suddenly hit white water. Janet's raft raced into a rock; she was tipped off into the rapids. As she slid into the foam she looked at him, frightened, and called his name. He was too far away to reach her.

Now her face is set in that same look.

"I'm unhappy, too," he says carefully.

"What do you mean?" she asks again. "What do you mean, 'too'? I'm not unhappy."

"We're both unhappy," he says. "We've been struggling for years." She must know about the affairs. This can't be news. But it saddens him to realize that she thinks the marriage has been happy. How can she not have seen it was not?

"I am not unhappy," she says stiffly. "I don't know what you're talking about."

Warren says, "But I am unhappy."

She stares at him. "What are you saying?"

"I want to separate," he says.

She shakes her head slightly, as if clearing it. "Separate? You and me?"

He nods.

"No," she says, as if to herself, "no."

He feels a knock against his chest, heavy and brutal. He feels as though he is leading a charge, this is something he is committed to doing. He must obliterate the resistance, stamp it out.

"Warren," she says, tilting her head strangely, as though she's lost her balance. "What is this?"

"I want to separate," he says again. "We can start off as a trial."

"We are not separating," she says, her voice rising. "We can go to a counselor. If that's what you want."

It's not what he wants. "All right," he says. He's determined to make this go smoothly. He'll do anything to make it easier for her, anything but cede.

"We're not going to just end things," Janet says.

He doesn't answer. He takes a bite of the chicken.

"I don't know what you mean," she says. "What do you mean, you're unhappy? What's wrong?"

"In many ways I have been happy," he says. "We've had a good long run together. We've raised a great kid."

She waits, her head tilted. "And?"

"And you've been a great wife."

She shakes her head slightly, staring at him. "And?"

"But I want something else." He sounds utterly banal.

"Like what?" she asks. "What else do you want?"

He shakes his head. "I want to separate."

After a moment she says, "I can't believe this. You really mean this?"

He wants to explain, make her understand, so she'll take his side, so she'll nod and agree. But he can't tell her the truth, that this was a mistake from the start. That he'd loved her in a way, and he still loves her in that way, but it's not one that makes it possible to spend the rest of his life with her. He can't tell her any of this. Irrationally, he feels bereft. He is losing her.

And he can't tell her about his feeling for Sarah, that it had been part of his life all along, that it merely had gone underground, like a river, and now it has surfaced, swift and powerful, and now everything from before is over. His marriage is now an obstacle to his life.

He won't go on facing her each night in this gray kitchen. The idea of this going on forever is like the glimpse down a dark shaft, a lightless place where his soul will turn to mineral. Now that Sarah is in his life, staying here would be the end of him. His life is no longer part of Janet's. He doesn't know how to tell her without delivering a mortal wound. He wants to execute his marriage without causing pain.

"I do mean it," he says. "I don't want to hurt you, but I mean it."

"You don't want to hurt me," she repeats. "But you want to leave me."

"I really don't want to hurt you," he says.

She waits, but he says nothing else.

"You have to say something more," she says. "You can't just make an announcement like that after thirty-four years."

"I'll say anything you like," he says, "but this is what I've decided. I'm sorry. I'm not happy in this life."

She shakes her head as though he's an idiot. "Then we'll do something else, Warren. We'll lead a different life. What do you want to do? Learn Mandarin? Sail around the world? Leave Brookline?"

He's impressed by the Mandarin.

But he says, "No. I mean this married life."

She stands, her mouth tightening. "You can't just decide this on your own. This is my marriage, too."

She grabs her plate and carries it to the trash drawer. She slides the uneaten pie into it and shoves the lid shut. She takes her plate to the sink and slams it down on the stainless steel. There is a loud crack, and she yanks open the trash drawer again. She throws the shards of the plate into it, slams it shut.

She turns and faces him. "I won't let you divorce me."

"I'm sorry," he says again.

"I mean it," she says. "You can't just decide."

"I can decide I'm not happy," he says.

"And how did that happen?" She folds her arms hard across her chest. "Suddenly? After thirty-four years? Suddenly you're not happy? You flipped a switch?"

"No," he says. "It's not like that. It wasn't sudden."

She looks down at her folded arms. She is silent for a moment, then looks up. When she starts to speak something happens to her voice, and she has to clear her throat and start again. "It's me? You're not happy with me?"

"Janet." He rises and goes to her. "Not happy enough," he says gently, and puts his arms around her.

She pulls sharply away.

"Don't touch me," she says. "Do you think I'm a fool?"

She turns around, her back to him. He thinks she will cry, but she doesn't make a sound. He wants to comfort her, and also to convince her that there is no chance.

She puts her face in her hands but still makes no sound. He doesn't touch her. He thinks of her face in Jamaica.

"I'm so sorry," he says. "This is my life. I have to save it."

She raises her head and turns to face him with contempt. "Don't you dare say that," she says. She goes to the table and sits down again. "Don't you dare say something so stupid and banal. And selfish. What about my life?"

He says nothing.

"I do not want to get a divorce," Janet says, slowly and with emphasis.

"I'm sorry," he said. "It's what I want." He sits down.

Janet stares at him. "But why?"

"Janet," he says.

"What have I done?" She closes her hands into loose fists, as though she holds something in each one. "What?"

"It's too late," he says.

She looks at him. "I can't believe this."

"I'm sorry."

They sit down again and he pours them each another glass of wine. He tells her he'll take care of her. He says he'll make sure she has everything she needs. He tells her that Kat will understand.

"Why will she understand?"

"Because she's a grown-up," he says.

"Have you taken up with someone else?"

"I'm not going to talk about anything but you and me," he says.

"So you have." Janet pours herself more wine. She takes a swallow and leans back. "You shit," she says. "You sanctimonious shit."

Now he's angry. She doesn't even know what it means.

"Sanctimonious? I'm saying I want to end our marriage. Maybe there is someone else involved. That doesn't make me sanctimonious, it makes me candid. I'm being honest. Don't use a word if you don't know what it means."

She has no respect for words, he thinks.

"You don't get to decide this, Warren," she says. "This is my marriage, too. It's not just your decision."

"My presence in the marriage is my decision," he says. "Whether or not I stay."

She takes a long swallow, her eyelids lowered. She sets the glass down and looks up at him.

The kitchen goes quiet; the refrigerator loudly and suddenly stops humming. Now every movement is audible in the silence and it feels as though their marriage, their whole life together, is present. The light falls from overhead, illuminating the top of Janet's head, the slope of her nose, the soft pouches along her jawline. Her somber gaze is focused on him.

"You promised," she says.

This is a stiletto blade into his heart: he did promise.

"I'm sorry," he says.

She shifts the wineglass, holding it by the base, sliding it very slightly back and forth on the table. The glass makes a faint susurration against the wood.

"I never thought you'd do this," she says. "I've seen it happen to my friends. Every time it happened I'd feel sorry for them, but proud of you, and grateful for my marriage. It's like driving past an accident, you think, How awful, and then you think, Glad it's not me. I thought we were past all that. I never thought you'd do it to me."

"I'm sorry," he says.

By the time they finally stand to go upstairs they've nearly finished the second bottle. The city outside is still. Janet pushes her chair in against the table. She hasn't quite stood up straight, and she rocks slightly, unsteady.

"My god," she says under her breath. She closes her eyes for a moment, then picks up both glasses and carries them to the sink.

She sets them down but doesn't move. She puts her hands on the edge of the sink, leaning forward. She drops her head, and he sees that she's weeping. He goes over to her, but when he touches her arm she flinches.

"Don't," she says.

She covers her face in her hands and then begins to sob noisily, loud raw gasping cries, as though she's being strangled. He stands behind her, arms at his sides.

When they go upstairs he stops in the doorway of the bedroom.

"I'm going to sleep in Kat's room," he says.

He gets clothes for the next day. Janet watches, her arms folded. At the door he pauses.

"Good night," he says. She doesn't answer.

Kat's is now a guest room. The walls are no longer black, but papered with a flowery print. Paintings have replaced the posters. Warren gets into bed, turns out the light, and waits for the relief of sleep. Despite the wine he lies awake, as though a spotlight has turned on inside his brain. He shifts uneasily under the covers, aware of Janet lying alone down the hall. She's adrift in a sea of pain, which he has created. He can't seem to reconcile what he's done with who he is. He depends upon a certain knowledge: He's not someone who breaks promises, or knowingly causes pain. But this is what he's done.

He won't undo it. He won't give up Sarah.

This is like having double vision: there is who he believes himself to be, and who he has become.

The room is dark, but light drifts in from the edges of the shades, a pale dusting of the city's ambient glow. He can see the dim outlines of the furniture, the high bureau, Kat's small desk from middle school, the square-backed chair pushed neatly in. The room still holds Kat's presence. Lying in bed, waiting for sleep, he thinks of her.

When she was fifteen she'd sat in sulky silence through *Die Meistersinger*, and the next year she said she didn't want to go to the opera anymore. She listened to her own music on her earbuds, retreating into a world Warren didn't understand. Being a teenager meant living in a wilderness. She was using pot, probably, Warren hoped nothing worse. He hadn't been great about all that. Kat's affect had been so confusing and volatile, she so easily erupted into tears and shouts, slamming doors. She was so furiously private about her life, alternately sullen and hostile or cozy and giggly, he hadn't been able to have the conversations he should have had with her. He hadn't really asked her about drugs or sex. The sex was arguably Janet's territory, but he should have talked about drugs. How was that electrical line created, so dangerous, so highly charged, that prevented a conversation about the most crucial things?

Once she had come home late, late, he'd heard her downstairs. He'd gotten up and was standing in the upstairs hall when she came up. She was wearing all black, jacket and leggings and those heavy boots that seemed to be fashionable for women, though why? Her hair slid loose around her shoulders, and her eyes were rimmed with black. As she came up the stairs he watched her face, rising higher with each step. She seemed a bit off, unbalanced in some way, but she was smiling.

"Hey, Dad." She seemed delighted to see him. "How's it going?" She spoke slowly, almost crooning.

"Fine," he said. "How's it going with you?"

She nodded loosely. "All good." She had reached the top of the stairs and headed for her room. She put her hand on the doorknob and turned to him.

"Night." She gave him a dreamy smile, then turned. She had trouble getting through the doorway, then shut the door very quietly behind her.

When he went back to bed he said to Janet, "I think she's been smoking pot."

"How do you know? You can't be sure," Janet said.

"She had certainly taken something. She acted as though all her limbs had become unstrung."

"You can't know it's pot," Janet said. She turned over. After a minute she said, "They all do it. What can we say to her? Tell her never to smoke it?"

What to say was the question, and for a long time he lay in the darkness thinking about Kat, what to say. In the morning he waited at the kitchen table. When she finally came down she was brusque and wary, avoiding his eye. She sat down silently with her granola.

"Sweetie," he began, and she looked up at him without raising her head.

"I had the feeling you'd taken something last night," he said.

" 'Taken something'?" she repeated. She raised her head.

"Some kind of drug," he said. "I'm not going to let you challenge everything I say." They looked at each other. "Do you want to talk about it?"

She shifted her head, not quite shaking it. Her expression suggested that she did not.

"I'm on your side, Kat," he said.

She took a spoonful of granola and began to chew.

"I'm aware of what you're doing. I can't stop you, but I want you to know that it can be dangerous. Among other things, it's criminal. So it's more dangerous than alcohol just because of that."

Kat looked at her bowl and said nothing.

"Please tell me you're being careful." He had planned what he would say, he'd assumed she wouldn't answer. How could she implicate her friends?

"I'm being careful, Dad," she said, still looking down, but her tone had changed. She looked up at him. "What do you expect me to do?" She was serious. "Everyone my age smokes pot."

"All I'm asking is for you to be careful," he said. "Don't deal. Don't take hard stuff. Don't use it a lot. You know the risks."

She held her eyes on him. After a pause she said, "Yeah."

"I'm on your side," he said again. He had no idea if this would have any effect. Kids kept their behavior veiled, nothing was overt. Once he'd called her and she said she couldn't talk, that she and her friends were about to start something. Years later she'd told him they were taking mushrooms. She'd come through the drug wars unscathed, as far as he knew.

And at the end of her teens, halfway through college, Kat had turned friendly again. The pyrotechnics of sex and drugs were apparently behind her. One weekend she had called to ask him about a paper she was writing on Scandinavian philosophy. It wasn't a subject Warren knew much about, but they talked about structure.

"Do you think I should put despair first?" she asked. "Should I start out with Nordic despair? Or should that come at the end, part of the conclusion?"

He was so flattered to be asked, so relieved to be back inside the small inner circle of Kat's intimates, he could hardly focus on the paper.

"Let's see," he said. "What's your conclusion going to be? Have you come to some decision about them as a group? Or are you just describing them and their work? You can put your thoughts at the beginning and then explore them one by one, or explore them and then state your opinion about them."

Kat was silent. "I do have opinions about them. Very strong ones. Kierkegaard kind of drives me crazy—he's like just a contrarian. Whatever someone else says, he disagrees with. He wants to be a Christian, so, good, but he actually makes it impossible. He just makes everything more difficult."

"Interesting," Warren said. He knew nothing about Kierkegaard, actually. He was inordinately proud that Kat should know more about this than he did.

It was the first time Kat has done this, involved him with her intellectual life. "So, give us your opinion," he said. "That's the most important thing. But be clear, and show examples. You can make any argument if you back it up with good examples."

She was silent again. "Okay," she said. "Even though he's a contrarian he's kind of my favorite. They're all gloomy, though. I think it's the weather."

Warren laughed. "That sounds like a different paper, the effects of climate on philosophers. Though I'm sure it's real."

"Yeah," she said, meditative. "Anyway, thanks."

"Anytime," he said, delighted.

That winter she'd asked to go to the opera again; he'd taken her to *Norma*. After that it had been sporadic, they hadn't gone every year. But he was certain that it had survived the adolescent turbulence, that she loved the opera, loved its richness and mystery.

The night unspools past him, minute by minute, the darkness stretching across the country, down to where Kat lives now, in lighted rooms, where she is safe.

His eyes are open when the door cracks, and light from the hall slices through the shadow.

"Are you awake?" Janet whispers.

"Yes," he says.

"Can I get in with you?" She opens the door wider. She's still whispering, as though not to wake the terrible creature he has created.

He raises the bedclothes as he used to do for the children when they had nightmares. The bed is only a double, and a bit narrow. In order to fit she turns her back, pressing her whole length against him. There is no room for them to lie separately. He puts his arm around her. He breathes in her smell, musky and intimate. He can feel her sobbing, though she tries to make no sound. He tightens his arms around her, comforting her for what he's done.

"Shh," he says, pressing himself against her, "shh. Shh."

Chapter 9

IN THE MORNING HE CALLS SARAH FROM THE CAR, ON HIS WAY to work.

"I've told her," he says.

Sarah's at her kitchen table, barefoot, in plaid pajamas. She's holding a mug of tea and watching the bird feeder, which is crowded with bright-eyed chickadees and titmice.

"What did you say to her?" she asks.

"That our marriage had come to an end."

"What did she say?"

"She disagreed."

"Where are you?"

"In my car."

"Was it bad?"

"Very."

"I'm sorry," she says. A junco arrives, scaring two chickadees, who explode into the air. "Did you tell her about me?"

"She guessed," he says.

"Now what?" she asks.

"She wants to go to counseling. I said I would," he says. "I told her I have a lawyer, and that she should have one."

She hadn't known he'd gotten a lawyer. "Do you want to talk about it more?"

"Not much more to say."

He stops at a light. He's surrounded by the morning tide of commuters, heading into the day. He feels caught up in the surge, but not part of it. Behind him he feels the presence of the house, which still holds his marriage, which holds most of his adult life. He feels it like a cloud, huge and dark, a shadowy mass, still connected to him.

The street ahead is damp and glistening. It's not quite raining, but condensation mists the windshield, turning it silver. He turns on the wipers for a few brisk swipes. As soon as they stop it fogs up again: the air is trapped. He turns on the air-conditioning with a roar, and a cold blast hits his legs. He thinks of Sarah's pale face, dark smudges beneath her eyes. He feels Janet behind him, sad and furious.

"Are you all right?" Sarah asks.

"Yes," he says. "I'll talk to you later."

As soon as he clicks off, his phone buzzes. He glances down at the screen: Katrina.

"Hi, sweetie." He wonders if Janet was right, if she's calling about Chris.

"Mom just told me." Her voice is gravelly and uneven.

"What did she tell you?"

"You want to leave her."

He is silent for a moment. "I'm sorry."

"Is it true?" Her voice rises. "It's true?"

"The last thing I want is to hurt you," he says.

She begins to cry. "So it's true. But why are you doing it? Why?"

"Kattie," he says.

"She's the same person, Dad. She's the same person. Why are you leaving her?"

He can't talk to his daughter about his marriage. And certainly not like this, on the phone, awash in the sea of commuters.

"Kattie, I can't explain it all. But we're not happy together."

"THAT'S NOT TRUE," she says loudly. "She's happy. Why are you not? She hasn't changed."

He's silent for a moment: Kat is right.

"No, she hasn't," he says. "It's me. I've changed." It has collapsed, the lovely edifice of his family. "I can't go on."

She's sobbing, ugly ragged breaths. "Yes, you can," she says wildly. "You can, Dad."

He says nothing. He can't.

There is a silence. The windshield is opaque again, he turns on the wipers for a brief furious spate, then turns them off. The blades subside through the glittering drops.

"So are you saying you haven't been happy? With us?" Her voice rises, then breaks. "Dad?"

"I've always been happy with you, Kattie. I love you." He remembers her hand slipping into his. She is crying. He hears the harsh breaths.

Finally she says, "How could you do this to us?"

"I'm not doing it to you, Kattie." His own voice is now rough. "Please believe me. I'm so sorry to hurt you."

She's crying hard. He doesn't know how to do this. He's unprepared for her grief, which is like an avalanche, huge and uncontrollable. "Your mother and I were never a perfect match."

"I don't care!" Katrina says. "You married each other! You've been married for over thirty years! You don't get to break up the family! Are you going to divorce me, because I'm not a perfect match for you?"

"I'm not breaking up the family," Warren says. He's now begging her. "I love you. I'm never leaving you. The family was broken when you left. Not broken, but . . ." He gropes for the word. "Dispersed."

"Please don't do it, Dad," she says, still crying, her voice low and raw. "You haven't done it yet. Just don't do it. Don't."

"Kattie," he says, trying to calm her.

"Just don't," she wails. She won't be calmed. "Don't. You'll kill us. You'll kill our family."

The word is shocking. This is beyond him.

"Kat," he says, trying to recover, "I'm not going to kill anyone."

But she has hung up.

The traffic is drawing to a halt, coalescing at a light. They're drawn up in pairs, the drivers looking ahead, ignoring each other, listening to news or music, bobbing heads to private rhythms. He is isolate, trapped in this daytime nightmare, his beloved daughter weeping in pain.

When he calls her back he gets voice mail.

As he drives he turns the windshield wipers on and off, the windshield clouding and clearing. The traffic moves like lava, stopping, starting again, he hears her voice, full of pain, echoing in his mind. All that grief, anguish, accusation. It fills his head. She's right, of course. Though he can't allow his daughter to decide for him.

He calls Janet.

She answers at once. "Hi."

"I heard from Kat," he says.

"She said she was going to call you."

"I felt kind of ambushed."

"Why?" she asks.

"Because she'd only heard one side," he says. "It's hard on kids if they have to take sides."

"I'm going to talk to my daughter whenever I want," she says. "She's my child."

"I hope you won't turn her against me."

"I'll tell her what you've done," she says.

He hangs up. He has no stomach for this fight. His marriage has failed, the life has ebbed from it. He feels a wash of shame at his broken promise. He can't reconcile his two selves. He can't go on living in the house.

When he reaches the office he goes online to look for an apartment. He finds one downtown—furnished, one bedroom, view—and takes it. The rental starts on the first of May; he has a week to get through. He makes a reservation at the DoubleTree. He'll go home tonight after work, pack up, and then leave.

That evening, when Warren arrives, the house is full of cooking smells. Rich, sweet, savory, onions, wine, oil, and meat, complex and sumptuous. Janet turns to look at him from the stove. She's wearing black pants and a turquoise turtleneck sweater. Her hair is pulled into an untidy ponytail.

"Hi, there," she says cheerfully.

"Hi."

She smiles as though they are friends. She raises her wineglass. "Yours is over there."

"Janet," he says. "I'm going to move out tonight. I'm going to a hotel, then to an apartment. I can't stay here."

She stares at him for a moment, but she has some plan, and won't be deterred. "Okay," she says, shaking her head to show cooperation. "That's fine. Whatever you want."

He says, "I'll go up and pack."

"You're staying for dinner?"

He nods. It's the least he can do.

When he comes back down he sets his suitcase by the front door. He comes in to the kitchen, rolling up his sleeves. Janet smiles again and waves at the wine on the counter. He pours himself a glass.

"Boeuf bourguignon," she says.

His favorite, which she hasn't made in years. He takes a sip of wine. She lifts the top and stirs, releasing a cloud of savory steam. She's wearing an apron, the strings are tied behind her back. They're loosening, coming undone.

"How are things at work?" she asks. "What happened with that place in Dedham?"

She never asks about his work.

"Okay," he says, nodding. "We're working with an inspector. I think it will be okay."

The table is set with bright mats, linen napkins, a vase of orange flowers. A green glass jug is filled with ice water, drops glistening on its sides.

Dinner is an advertisement for her cooking: pasta, a salad of crisp white endives and dark watercress, walnuts. French bread, warmed in the oven. Janet serves the boeuf bourguignon carefully, and when some of it drips onto the edge of the plate she wipes it off with a cloth. When they sit down she smiles again.

"This looks delicious," he is obliged to say.

"Good!" she says. "I hope you like it." She is like a bride, shyly brimming with pride and hope.

The stew is rich, the sauce too oily. He eats a few bites, then sips his wine.

"The garage door wouldn't open this morning with the clicker," she says. "I had to do it manually. I don't know who to call."

"Who installed it?" he asks.

"Some service," she says. "Do you have the name?"

"I'll look it up at the office." He wonders how long he will feel responsible for the house, how long he'll be asked to take care of it. Forever; she'll never forgive him.

Janet looks at his plate. "I thought you loved this."

"I do. I'm not hungry."

She takes the salad bowl and tosses the salad with swift, efficient gestures. The pale endives turn dark and coated. She hands him the bowl. Her face is open, guileless, as though they've never discussed parting. They eat in silence.

Janet drains her glass. She leans toward him.

"Warren," she says, "I have something to say." She speaks carefully, as though she's rehearsed. "I want to ask you not to do this quickly, leave the marriage. Because everyone feels like this, like they want to leave, at times."

She has readied herself for this, like a horse gathering himself for a jump. She looks directly into his eyes, not quite pleading.

"You can't just give up on a marriage," she says. "It's too big. It's our whole lives. We have to get through this. Beyond it."

He says nothing. Beyond it is where he wants to be.

"Being in a marriage is like walking a tightrope," she says. "You can't lose confidence. You have to keep going. You can't look down." She smiles anxiously.

He wonders who has provided these earnest platitudes. A friend, or a self-help book?

"Janet," he says, but doesn't go on. She watches him, tentative, pleading, and he feels the surge of her hope. She has given herself completely to their marriage. She'd thought her belief was enough. What else could she offer?

"I love you," she says. "I loved you before you ever noticed me, when I saw you at that party. Everyone was playing Monopoly on the floor and you were lying on your side, leaning your head on your hand, and you started to laugh, and then you rolled over onto your back, laughing. Just the way you did it, so . . . loose." She shakes her head. "I don't mean loose, I mean, easy, you seemed so easy."

She squeezes her eyes shut, remembering. She seems panicked, as though she's lost not just the thread of her thought, but also her understanding of the world, as though she has no idea of where she is. "This is killing me, Warren. Please just stop. Don't do it." Her eyes are filling, glittering, huge. She is frightened.

He shouldn't have come.

"I'm sorry," he says. "I won't change my mind."

She puts her hand over the whole lower part of her face, covering her open mouth, her eyes spilling over. She begins to sob. "Please don't. I don't want you to do this. I don't want you to leave. Please don't leave. Please. You can do whatever you want. Just don't leave me. You can have whatever kind of marriage you want." She puts the other hand over the first, as though she needs both hands to contain her grief.

"I can't stay," he says. "I can't do it. I'm sorry. I'm sorry."

He stands and pushes the chair in. He doesn't know what to do but flee. It feels shameful, but he can't stay. He can't offer her comfort for what he's doing. She is weeping, big wracking sobs that shake her body. She puts both elbows on the table and lowers her face into her hands.

Chapter 10

THE DOOR OPENS ONTO BLACKNESS.

When he flicks the switch the place springs into being, like a stage set. The main room has big windows and bare white walls. The furniture is tan and white. It's anonymous, like a hotel room. His presence is irrelevant here; this is a great relief. Solitude is a refuge. He sets down his computer bag on the table, then stands still, listening. In the room is only the faint electrical sound of some appliance; outside, the city thrums distantly, far below. He puts his hands in his pockets and raises his chin, stretching his neck, closing his eyes. In the stillness he feels himself loosen and expand. He moves outward, like mist, unopposed. He stands like that for a moment, his eyes closed. He feels the silence around him. This shift, this loosening, informs him how tightly the coil of self has been wound.

He's becoming aware now of what it has cost, every conversation with Janet. How carefully he'd had to steer each one, holding part of himself silent and separate. He thinks of the honeymoon, that morning talking to the fisherman on the beach, all the time aware of Janet behind him, lying in the sun with her drink. He'd felt guilty, as though he were somehow cheating on her. As though, by spending time on something she'd disapprove of, he was taking something that was hers. That first morning, feeling her behind him, he'd understood what lay between them: a dead zone.

Janet wouldn't ask a fisherman how to catch eels; she'd think it a waste of time. She spent her energy on people whose language and currency she understood.

Each year at the gala she took the podium and spoke for the literacy program. In her silk dress, with her glossy hair, she gave a smooth and practiced speech, then introduced the director. Trina Rivaux was a beautiful wide-faced Haitian woman, majestic in loose flowing robes, her hair a mass of narrow twisting braids. Janet asked the audience to applaud, smiling and clapping as she gave way to Trina. But she did not look directly into Trina's eyes. She did not meet the other woman's spirit. She withheld herself, as though she couldn't quite see the other woman.

Janet was afraid of people unlike herself. They frightened her, with their mysterious lives, their strange accents and foreign intonations, their unknown needs. She was afraid she'd be asked for something she couldn't understand or provide. She was afraid she'd be somehow embarrassed. Afraid she'd be asked a question in a language she did not speak, challenged in some incomprehensible way. She held herself apart from Trina, from the people who worked in the program, from the students. They frightened her.

Warren enjoyed conversations with people unlike himself. He liked learning what they found interesting or admirable or funny. Other peoples' ideas fueled his own. He couldn't do what he did without listening to different points of view. That was one of the pleasures of designing peoples' houses. He listened to clients talk about their families and their lives. He listened to zoning boards, structural engineers, building inspectors. Each one was a piece of the mosaic, it was his job to make them all fit together.

He couldn't talk to Janet about these things. He could, but she hardly listened. There was a vast shoal of things he'd never been able to talk to her about. He talked to her about the mechanics of their lives, their friends, about Kat. Not ideas. Not art or music or books. Not what the old man in Dedham had told him about how the local library had been used as a soup kitchen during the Depression. Janet would have shaken her head. "A soup kitchen! Really! Food all over the books!"

Now that he's alone, it's a relief.

Here in this place he can let his mind loose, he can expand and drift. He can abandon vigilance. He is alone. He walks through the rooms abstractedly, pulling off his tie and dropping it on the chair in the living room. He likes the privacy, the smallness, the containedness of this place. He is alone; he wants Sarah. She is in his mind constantly; when he turns on music he wonders what she'd think of it, and what she's listening to right then. When he thinks of a project, he wants to tell her his ideas. He wonders what she's doing at that instant. At work he thinks of her. Sometimes he is surprised to remember that no one in his office knows her, none of them realize this new thing about him. He wants to share it.

Kat is not taking his calls. He sends her emails every day or so. I love you, he writes. Hope you're okay. I know this is a rough time. Call if you need anything. I love you. His messages seem hopelessly banal. She doesn't answer. Warren's messages may be echoing in outer space, among the cold and distant galaxies.

He sits down on the sofa and takes out his cell phone. He sends her another message, clicks off.

Janet has found a lawyer, and hers and his have begun to talk. They have made little progress. Warren believes he is being generous; her lawyer disagrees.

WARREN AND JANET start seeing a therapist together.

At the first session they arrive within moments of each other, and file awkwardly into the office together. They sit in two armchairs facing Dr. Klein.

Dr. Klein is in her fifties, with short gray hair, a small mouth, and a look of perpetual concern. She wears long scarves, black pants, and soft-soled shoes. She has a dry gravelly voice.

"I know this can be difficult," she says. "You're both to be commended for being ready to discuss something so important. You're both courageous."

Warren doesn't feel courageous, he feels miserable. He thinks this will be torture.

She asks each of them to talk about their life together, then about their child. Later she asks Warren why he married Janet; he says it was because she was warm and friendly and good-natured. And beautiful.

"Were you disappointed in some way by her, as time went on?" Dr. Klein asks. He says no, that Janet was all those things.

"How do you think things went wrong?" she asks.

After a pause Warren says he believes they are deeply incompatible.

When Dr. Klein asks Janet why she married Warren, she leans forward earnestly. "Because I knew he'd support me and our children," she says. "When we had them. And he always has. Always." As if by reciting the history of Warren's good behavior she could make it continue.

Dr. Klein sits in a trim beige chair, legs crossed at the knee. She nods thoughtfully.

"What do you mean, 'incompatible'?" she asks Warren.

"Our ideas are very different."

"Could you give me an example?"

"About books, about politics, about everything," Warren says. It pains him to say these things.

"That's not true," Janet says. "We have almost the exact same ideas. Opinions about things."

"Could you give me an example of how your ideas differ?" Dr. Klein asks Warren.

It's hard to answer, because for so long he's avoided dangerous areas. He doesn't want to hear Janet's views. Once she had declared that France started World War II. This had been years ago, she won't even remember it. Raising it now will seem pedantic and unkind. But he can't forget it. He's disheartened by her ignorance. He faults her for thinking these things don't matter. He faults himself for thinking they do: He shouldn't put knowledge over character. But he does mind. He can't talk to her about the things that interest him.

It's no one's fault, certainly not hers. But it's his life. He can't go on keeping his mind separate from his wife's. He remembers that first day of the honeymoon, when he felt an invisible cord, binding him to her, while he talked to a fisherman and she lay reading a romance. He'd felt a kind of guilt, for spending all that time away from her, as though he'd been betraying her with that fisherman. He had been taking something that belonged to her. He'd been doing something she considered futile. He's been betraying her all along, leading his real life separate from hers.

"She thinks France started World War II," he says.

Janet stares at him. "What are you talking about?"

They all wait; he says nothing.

"That was years ago," Janet says to Dr. Klein. "I said that once, years ago. He's kept this in his mind all this time. Holding it against me."

He has, he has kept it in his mind. The other things are idiotic, too—the little bow-tie pasta called Machiavelli. How she never reads a serious book. "You read it," she says, "and tell me what happens." He should love her for her character. He knew who she was when he married her, didn't he?

But he had not: she had been beautiful, funny, good-natured, charming. He hadn't noticed the rest. It had become like living in a thicket of barbed wire: he can't move without a tiny piercing of his skin, without doing damage to the living organism of his marriage.

Janet says, "Warren brings these things up to make me uncomfortable. Miserable."

Warren waits for the session to be over. He can't answer truthfully. He'd like to say that being with her makes him feel like a tethered goat. He'd like to ask if he is expected to stop talking about these things forever. If he was supposed to cut out all those parts of himself. "How much of myself am I allowed to keep?"

He can't tell Dr. Klein about the way Janet chews, the way she moves her jaw. That he now winces at her laugh.

He doesn't dare look at his watch.

At the end of that session they leave Dr. Klein's office and stand together in the narrow hall. Warren reaches out to push the button for the elevator, and as though that were a signal, Janet drops her head and begins to cry. She lifts her hands and presses her fists together, beneath her chin. She's wearing her red coat and a black scarf, and the scarf is caught up by one hand. It looks as though she's crying into a shroud. She sobs until the elevator arrives. They move inside and stand side by side as they descend, while she weeps. At the bottom, as the elevator slows, he says, "Janet, I'm sorry."

She puts her palms on her cheeks and sweeps the tears sideways off her face.

"Sorry for what?" she asks. "Which thing, exactly?"

He thinks he will never do this again. When they leave the office, next time he will go down the fire stairs, seven flights, rather than this.

He feels as though his life is being disassembled, piece by piece. He has to focus hard on his own belief. It seems that everyone else—Dr. Klein, with her gravelly voice, Janet, holding back her tears, silent and sorrowful Kat, the world at large—is pressing him to abandon his belief in what he's doing. He can't go back to the gray kitchen, the knobs of bone at Janet's wrists. The evenings together. He can't lie next to her in bed again.

They have been seeing the therapist for several weeks when Janet calls at work and asks him to come to the house that evening. She wants to talk, she says. Warren asks if they can talk by phone, but she says no.

"Face-to-face," she says.

He has refused her so much that he agrees to this.

Driving out after work, he wonders what she has planned.

When he began this process he'd felt in control. He had told Janet, he had talked to Kat, he had called the lawyer. He was in the process of changing the insurance, the accounting, the mortgage, the bank accounts, all of it. It was his project. Like the ones at work, it was full of complications and personalities, but it was something he knew how to move forward. There was satisfaction to be found in marshaling large and complex forces, and though this project depressed him he felt the same energy and determination he felt for his projects at work.

But now he's no longer in control. He's done the things he can do, but nothing has moved. He's not in control at the lawyer's—there has been little progress there. He's certainly not in control at Dr. Klein's, and he may not be in control tonight. It's strange that this is so: What he's doing is simple. He's stated his intentions. People can state their responses, but they can't alter his position. Yet nothing is moving. The opposition is immense, a mountain of stone. He has to get through it to reach the other side, the rest of his life.

At the house all the downstairs lights are on. He uses the front door, like a guest. He comes inside and heads down the hall toward the kitchen, but hears Janet call, "We're in here." He follows her voice to the dining room.

Janet is sitting at the mahogany table, Kat beside her. They're waiting for him.

"Hi, Dad," Kat says, unsmiling.

Kat is at the head, in his chair. Janet sits next to her, as though Kat's her lawyer. Kat sets her elbows on the table and clasps her hands.

"Kat," Warren says. It's a tribunal.

"Please sit down," Kat says. She's wearing a black short-sleeved shirt, and her hair is loose around her shoulders.

He pulls out a chair and sits at her side, across from Janet. Dread begins to pool inside him.

"Mom asked me to talk to you," Kat says. "About what you're trying to do."

"Okay," he says. He wants to sound reasonable.

"Look," she says. She folds her hands on the table. She's nervous. "You can't just do something like this on your own," she says. "This affects all of us. It's not just you. You can't just choose to destroy the family."

She is tense, her eyes bright, charged. She's prepared her speech. He admires her courage.

"I understand why you're upset—" he begins.

She interrupts him. "Don't talk like a therapist," she says. At once she's furious. "And don't patronize me. I'm not 'upset.' I'm telling you what the situation is. What you're doing is morally unacceptable."

"Kat, you're not the moral arbiter here." He's determined to stay calm. "I respect your opinion, but you're not in charge of deciding what's acceptable."

"You know it's not acceptable," Kat says, abandoning her speech. "You know it's unconscionable. It's unspeakably cruel to Mom."

He hesitates: it is.

"You shouldn't be asked to speak for your mother," he says. He doesn't like being ambushed. "If she has something to say, she can say it to me."

"I want to speak for her," Kat says. "She needs someone to defend her."

He won't let this turn into a fight. "Kat," he says, "I admire you for supporting your mother. But this is not your matter. This is between your mother and myself."

"Not true, Dad," Kat says bravely. "It's also between you and me."

"You and I can deal with our own issues on our own. But this is not one of them. This is my marriage, not yours."

"Don't keep saying that!" she says, her voice rising.

"You have to understand it," he says, but she glares at him, her eyes black with fury. "I love you. We both love you. You don't have to choose between us."

"You are choosing," Kat says flatly. She folds her arms. Strands of her black hair lie on her bare arm, sticking to the skin.

"I'm not choosing not to have you in my life." He resents her tone. "How can you say that? I'm choosing between being married and being single. That has nothing to do with you. You don't live at home. I'm not leaving you."

"You're leaving your life with us," Kat says. "You're destroying it. And you're trying to destroy Mom."

"Can you understand that marriage is something that both people must be part of?" he says. "Both partners must want it. Both must be happy."

That makes her angrier.

"Don't tell me you're unhappy," she says, contemptuous. Her voice has turned uneven, as though something is struggling inside her chest. "You can't have been unhappy for thirty-four years." She says the number as though it proves something.

"What if I have?" Warren says.

"You haven't, Dad. We'd have known it," Kat says. Now her uneven voice rises; tears threaten. "Trips, birthdays, Christmas, graduations, everything. All the presents you gave Mom. You can't pretend you were unhappy all this time. With us."

"Kat—" he says, but she interrupts him.

"Say it," she says, her voice now shaking, "admit it. You were happy with us, you were happy. Say it!" She's full of rage and grief. She begins to cry. Furious, she swipes at her cheeks.

Undone by her tears, he can't answer. She's right that he was happy, but a strand of unhappiness was always part of that thick family braid. The whole of his married life contained that running thread of emptiness.

"The thing is," Kat says, setting her forefinger onto the table, "this isn't just your marriage. It belongs to all of us. It's our whole family, our whole life, not just yours. You're divorcing yourself from your family." Her voice is lower now, under control.

"I'm not," Warren says. "Kat, what you can't see is that this is separate from you. When you get married you'll be doing something separate from your family. You'll still be a part of us, but you'll be leading a separate life. We won't get to say whether you should get married or not. Or get divorced."

"You want to sound like you're innocent," Katrina says. "You want to control the narrative. You're like the overclass, defining history."

"I'm not the overclass," Warren says, exasperated. "This isn't politics. This is my life, lovey."

"Don't call me 'lovey,'" Katrina says, her voice trembling with rage. "Tell me something: Who is this woman you want to run off with?"

Warren hesitates. "I'm not going to tell you her name. But yes, there's another woman."

"Where did you meet her?" Kat asks, now quiet.

He shakes his head. "Not your business, Kat. I'm not required to give you my private information."

"You are required," Kat says. "You are my father. I have a right to ask. Your private information is part of my life. I have a right to know everything about you."

"Well, no, you don't," Warren says. "Nor do I have the right to know everything about you, and I wouldn't claim it."

"If you're betraying your promise to Mom, your promise to us, we have the right to know everything," Kat says.

"I made a contract with your mother, thirty-four years ago, and now I'm ending it," Warren says. "I'm doing so openly and trying to be as fair as I can."

"Stop it," Kat says with disgust. "Don't get legal. You're betraying us all. A parent teaches by example. What example have you shown me?"

"For thirty-four years I hope it's been good, my example." He shakes his head. "I take this very seriously, what I'm doing."

"Then don't do it," Kat says, her voice rising again. "You promised. You made a promise."

"I'm sorry. I understand this is a disappointment."

"It's not 'a disappointment.' It's a betrayal." Her voice is shaking.

"How I lead my life is my own decision," he says. "You have to understand that."

"And you have to understand this," says Kat, leaning forward, her voice loud and unsteady. "If you divorce Mom, I'll divorce you." Her rage and grief have taken over the room. "I'll divorce you utterly," she says. Her eyes are dark and hostile.

"I hope that's not true." He has no idea what she means, but he won't go on with this. He stands up and pushes the chair in to the table. Kat leans forward and grabs his forearm.

"You can't just walk out, Dad," she says. "We're not finished." Her fingers close on his flesh, tight and powerful, like a monkey's.

"This is not a conversation," he says. "I won't sit here and be shouted at." He pulls his arm away, yanking free from her grasp, and walks out of the room.

Kat shoves her chair back and shouts after him, "Dad! Don't do this!"

Janet calls his name, and then Kat begins to cry, but he won't turn back. It's like pulling himself from a whirlpool.

He goes out the front door, half-afraid Kat will come bounding after him. Once in the car, he starts it at once, backing fast out into the street. He can't bear to fight with his daughter.

Driving back into the city, he can still feel her fingers clenched on his forearm. Later, when he takes off his shirt, he sees the marks on his skin: three small ovals, dark purple. Contusions.

He'd taught her to ride a bike, running beside her and holding the seat as she wobbled across the lawn. Several times she fell, and once she hit her cheek on the handlebars. She hadn't cried. Later, her small fresh face bloomed with a plum-colored bruise. He'd used the word then.

Chapter 11

SARAH STANDS OUTSIDE HIS APARTMENT AND RINGS THE doorbell. It has an odd two-note rising tone.

He opens the door. She's wearing sunglasses and a bold red patterned scarf, and—though he's expecting her, she has come for the weekend—for a moment he doesn't recognize her. After that moment of confusion, in which a stranger becomes the beloved, delight wells up in him.

"It's you," he says.

"It is," she says.

"I'm glad," he says, and opens the door wider.

He takes her in his arms, folding her against himself. She is now deeply familiar, her shape, her smell.

He releases her. "Let me show you around. In six steps."

In the living room she looks out the huge window.

"Wonderful," she says. "You're so high."

She is right. He is so high here; he is perpetually confronted by the weather of Boston, by drifting fog obscuring the view, rain slashing against the pane, sun irradiating the shallow room. He shows her the bank tower, and the band of lights that notify the public about emergencies.

"Yellow for a blizzard, though you wouldn't be able to see it through the snow."

"In an emergency you don't know what you're looking for," she says. "What would you do if it turned red?"

"She knows it's you," he says.

Sarah turns. "Did you tell her?"

"A friend of hers saw us," he says. "At a restaurant in New York."

She sits down on the sofa, still in her coat. "Now what?"

"Everything gets more complicated," he says. "Her lawyer will ratchet things up. She's really angry. She knew I was seeing someone. But this makes it worse. For some reason."

"Anyone would make it worse," Sarah says. "I mean any specific person."

"They're angry at me."

" 'They'?"

"Janet and Kat."

He stands in the middle of the room, hands in his pockets. Outside, the weather is somber, the sky a high felted gray, the light cool and thin.

"I'm so sorry," Sarah says again.

"Which I hear about from the lawyer." He doesn't want to talk about the settlement. He feels he's being generous; he's being treated as cruel.

"How bad can it get?" Sarah asks.

"She can't stop the divorce," he says. "But she's making it unpleasant."

He'd imagined they could stay friends.

"Kat's the one who's really angry," he says.

"I'm so sorry."

His marriage has a presence, it seems. It takes up space. Sometimes they ignore it, and talk about other things. But it's there.

Sarah's there for the weekend, and in the morning he shows her around his city. He drives her on a tour of his favorite buildings: the architecture school at MIT, the State House, Trinity Church. They end by double-parking, beside a battered red Volvo, next to the church. The stone building towers above them, massive, ponderous, rearing its slate-brown bulk against the sky.

"Henry Hobson Richardson's masterpiece," he says. "Maybe the greatest example of Gothic Revival in America."

She peers up at it, leaning her head against the car window to see it. "Why is it Gothic?" she asks. "Why not Moorish? The bulbous tower, the round checkerboard arches? It makes me think of that mosque in Spain, not Notre Dame."

He picks up her hand and kisses it. "I love you," he says. "You're right. Definitely Córdoba." He feels a deep plunging sense of relief, gratitude, as though the horizon has been opened up.

A man with thick curly hair and glasses knocks on the window. He points to the Volvo; Warren nods and turns around to back up. The man gives him a thumbs-up and opens the door to his car.

The social contract, thinks Sarah. She feels comforted by Warren's commitment to it. Rob had felt challenged by everything, certain that he was being taken advantage of. He argued on the phone with Accounting, he argued at a tollbooth with the collector. Warren goes around obstacles and takes nothing personally. He's like water, shifting smoothly to another channel, finding the way through. He lifts his hand to the Volvo driver, who pulls into the stream of traffic.

On Beacon Street the line of tall nineteenth century brownstones meets the sky. They're set back from the street, and trees line the broad sidewalk. The houses are imposing, but the shops in them, tucked up on the first floor, or down a half flight of stairs, are small and amateurish: haircuts, ethnic clothes, cupcakes. This doesn't have New York's impersonal grandiosity, its soaring skyscraper culture. Boston offers a pleasant nineteenth century presence.

"I like Boston," she says.

"I was hoping you'd say that. I'm wooing you on its behalf," he says. "I can't move my office. I have to live here." He looks at her. "What would you think of living with me?"

They're stopped at a light. People cross the street before them in a purposeful stream. A young woman in a bright pink jacket and long frizzy dark hair stops and looks over her shoulder, tipping her foot up to see the sole.

"Do you mean would I move here?"

"Would you?" he asks.

"It's different now," she says. "At this time in our lives. If we were both thirty, one of us would move. We'd choose one place or the other."

"I'm choosing you," he says. "What shall we do? I'll come down on weekends. Or we could get a place here. In the city. Outside it if you'd rather."

The light changes. The woman in the pink jacket puts down her foot and keeps going. Sarah can't imagine moving to Boston.

"I have a dog," she says.

"I know that," he says.

"What about your daughter?" she asks, changing the subject. "How's it going?"

"Still a work in progress," he says. "I hope she'll change her mind. But she isn't answering my emails."

"I'm sorry," Sarah says.

"What happened with your daughter about your divorce?"

Sarah looks out the side window.

It had been awful. Meg had been in college, and she had stopped speaking to Sarah. She hadn't come home for Christmas, and hadn't called to tell Sarah. It had been humiliating. Meg had gone with Rob to his parents'. On Christmas Day Sarah called Rob's parents, hoping she was there. Rob's mother had answered. Sarah wished her a merry Christmas and asked to speak to Meg, hoping she was there. Rob's mother was very polite, but Meg had shouted at her. "You're so selfish!" Then Meg had wept, and then she'd hung up. Sarah didn't have the nerve to call back, braving Rob and his parents again.

Much later Meg began talking to her again, but she'd held this against Sarah, her betrayal of the family. She still holds it against Sarah, somewhere. Sarah had lost her right to moral authority.

All that's in the past. Sarah's moral authority is no longer an issue, it is irrelevant. Meg has her own family, her own sources of moral authority.

Sarah says, "Now Meg says she can't imagine how we were ever happy together, Rob and I."

"So you think there's hope for me," Warren says.

"Yes," Sarah says.

Though she thinks Kat is fierce and determined, and that your children can spiral out of any orbit you've made for them.

Chapter 12

NANCY AND SARAH SIT AT HER KITCHEN TABLE. THEY'RE meeting about the Bloomsbury show, which is scheduled for February, three years from now. They've made lists of first, second, and third choices. They've sent the first round of requests and are getting responses. They've spread out folders and papers.

"They've said no to these two by Carrington," Nancy says, pushing two images forward.

"Those are really good. Are they promised somewhere else? Or aren't we important enough? It's too late to move the dates." Sarah's big green looseleaf notebook says BLOOMSBURY in block letters on the cover.

Nancy's notebook is a small Moleskine, with a white stick-on label. She's written *Bloomsbury* in a careful hand.

"It's definitely too late to move the dates," Nancy says. "We've already made them public. Some of the paintings have prior commitments."

Sarah thinks of the paintings traveling around the world, being gathered with others to create cultural communities, each one illustrating a new premise: Introduction to the Modern, or The Farm in English Landscape Painting, or From Blaue Reiter to Bloomsbury.

"Do you know anyone at the Baltimore Museum?" Nancy asks. "They have a beautiful Vanessa Bell but they've never lent it."

"I'll look it up," Sarah says. "I've worked with them before."

"They might respond to a gentle nudge." Nancy moves her pencil down the list. Without looking up, she says, "How's the boyfriend? The flower man."

"Good," Sarah says. "He's left his wife."

Nancy looks up. "Is that good?"

"I guess," Sarah says. "But it's no longer just this private thing, us seeing each other when we could. Without the world knowing."

Nancy looks at her. In a moment she asks, "Did you think that would last?"

"I don't know what I thought," Sarah says. "I think I didn't think." She had not thought. She had allowed herself to be carried along in the current made by Warren. She had thought that somehow this was all happening in some alternate world.

"And now how is it?" says Nancy.

"Now it's like the opera," Sarah says. "Fricka and the Valkyries. Each time I hear from him, things are worse."

"What are his kids doing?"

Sarah shakes her head. "He just has one. He doesn't talk about it. I think it's killing him."

Nancy slides an image across the counter to Sarah. "Should we go for this one? It's on our second list but maybe it's time to move it to first?"

It's by Duncan Grant, a naked godlike figure, cavorting clumsily on the grass.

Sarah looks at it. "Yes, okay."

Nancy nods and they both write it down.

"His daughter sort of terrifies me," says Sarah.

Nancy looks up at her. "Because?"

"She doesn't seem to have any limits. I don't know. She won't speak to him. She's cut him off.."

"But she'll come around," Nancy says. "Won't she?"

Sarah looks up at Nancy. "I don't know what she'll do."

WARREN TAKES an early flight to LaGuardia, then a cab from the airport. He hasn't told Katrina he's coming: she still isn't answering his calls. She lives on the edge of Williamsburg, in a block of low nineteenth century houses. Her apartment is on the top floor of a shabby three-story house. It's early June, and two struggling city trees have put out foliage, making a thin green canopy over the sidewalk.

He goes down the two steps to the front door and rings the bell. It's just past eight, he's pretty sure she'll still be there. You can never tell if doorbells are working or not; he leans close to the metal panel to listen.

Her voice is scratchy and distant.

"Who is it?"

"It's me," he says, "Dad."

There is a long silence. Then she says, "What are you doing here?"

"I want to talk to you," he says.

"I don't want to talk to you," she says.

"Please let me in, Kat," he says, raising his voice. "I've come down to talk to you."

"Did you spend the night with her?" Kat asks loudly. "Here?"

"I flew down this morning to see you," he says. "Please let me in. I'm here because I love you."

There is a long silence. Behind him a line of cars moves past. He's not sure the intercom is still on.

"Kat," he says, "I'd like to talk to you."

The buzzer sounds, loud and staccato. Before it stops or she can change her mind, he pushes open the door.

The hall is small and low-ceilinged, with a damp industrial smell. The dull white walls are scuffed by years of impacts: strollers, furniture, packages, umbrellas. A tall battered silver radiator is littered with restaurant flyers. At the end of the hall is a doorway, with a doormat and a pair of sneakers. Before him is the narrow staircase, the stained steps and wrought-iron railings.

As he mounts the second flight he sees Kat standing in her

doorway, her face closed. When he arrives, she opens the door wider to let him in, but she turns and walks away as he enters. He shuts the door behind him.

The pale gray walls are hung with museum posters: Anselm Kiefer, Vija Celmins. A dark sofa stands against the wall, a metal lamp beside it. The furniture is austere and modernist, but the building is old. The plaster walls are cracked, the floors are slanted, the corners askew. Everything is muffled by a century of paint.

Kat faces him. She's barefoot, in yoga pants and a T-shirt.

"Where's Chris?" he asks, wondering if they'll be interrupted.

"Not here," she says. "What is it?"

"I want to talk to you," he says. "You won't take my calls."

"I don't have anything more to say to you."

"Kat, we haven't said all we have to say to each other for the rest of our lives," Warren says gently.

"Maybe we have, Dad." She folds her arms on her chest.

"Well, I think we haven't," Warren says. He moves to one of the stiff armchairs. "May I sit down?"

Kat shrugs. "I can't talk long. I have to go to work."

"Yes," he says. "I'd have come at a more convenient time but I wasn't sure you'd see me."

"I wouldn't," she says.

Warren sighs. "Kat, we have to get past this." She's still standing, arms crossed. He looks up at her. "I love you. You're very important to me. I'm not going to let this wreck our relationship."

"It has," Kat says.

Warren looks down at his hands. "It can't," he says, after a moment. "I won't let it. You are part of my heart. I won't allow you to cut yourself off from me."

Kat flicks her gaze to the window, at the houses across the street. Outside, the city carries on: traffic, the chug of engines, the thudding of music. He waits.

"Dad, you don't know what you've done," she says.

"I understand what you're saying," he says. "But I don't think you understand what I'm saying."

"You just want me to take your point of view," Kat says. "But I won't. Why shouldn't you take my view?"

"Supposing I do. What would you like me to do to fix this?"

"Stay with Mom," Kat says. "Drop all this."

Warren shakes his head. "You don't know what you're asking. This is my life. I can't go on living with your mother." But grief begins rising inside his chest. He feels the sudden dark expanding sense of loss, the loss of all this: the family of his marriage. He remembers Kat, one Christmas morning, lying down on the rug after opening her presents. She was nine or ten. She lay on her back and spread out her arms and closed her eyes. I am so happy, she announced. I am so happy.

"Then you'll lose me," she says. "You will never see your grandchildren."

She stares at him, resolute. Her fixed jaw reminds him of Janet.

"Don't do this," he says. "No matter what you do, I can't go on living with your mother. I can't. If you stick to this, you'll be losing your father, by your own hand."

"It's not my hand, Dad," Kat says. Her voice rises, and color appears at her cheekbones. "Don't keep shifting the blame. It's you! You're doing all of this. Every bit of it is yours! You're a shit!"

The slur pierces him; it's surprisingly painful. But he shakes his head. "You can't see this now, Kat." He feels he's pleading with her for his life, though he won't beg. He's not asking for her pity. How could he ask her to pity him for living with her mother? But it's a life sentence in solitary confinement. "You don't see it now, but you'll see it differently later. I'm not going to let this come between us."

"It has come between us," she says, furious. "How can you not see this? The only way I can prove it is by refusing to talk to you. That's what you've done. Why do you not understand? You have ruined our life. I will never forgive you."

He stands up; he can feel the rage coming from her in waves. She is creating an ocean between them. She is distant, she is nearly out of sight.

"Kat—" he says, but she interrupts.

"It's not just this time. You've done this before. How many women have you done this with?" She says "women" contemptuously. He is now lost.

"What do you mean?"

"I know you've done this before. I saw you on the street with some woman. You kissed her. You stepped into a doorway with her and kissed her. She had red hair."

And there it is.

He's speechless. He can't summon any defense.

Kat is like a tropical storm of rage. She is quivering, her face filled with it, unshed tears of it brimming in her eyes.

"Okay," he says. "I did see another woman."

"It's not 'okay,' Dad!" Kat is nearly screaming.

"No, I know," he says. "It's just—it's not something I did often. It was brief."

Kat stares at him, shaking her head.

"How many?" she asks.

"A few," he says. "All short, never important. All years ago."

Kat makes an exasperated sound, clicking her tongue.

"I don't even know what to say to you. You have ruined my life."

"I'm sorry," Warren says, "sorry it seems that way, but I haven't. I'm sorry I did that—"

"You're just sorry I saw you," Kat says, bitter.

He has lost the high focused energy that had brought him here. He had meant to conquer her with an indefatigable love, but instead she has evoked shame. He can't summon up a defense, or an argument.

"Yes, I'm sorry you saw me, because it was years ago and it was unimportant. I haven't been a serial adulterer. It's not what happened to my marriage. This woman I'm seeing now is someone I knew years ago. I was in love with her then. This isn't a fling. It's a continuation."

Kat stares at him. "Have you been seeing her all along?"

"No. Never. Until this."

"It doesn't make it any better," she says.

"I can't help it. My marriage is over, I need to make you see that."

"I see it," Kat says. "I hate it. I don't want to see you anymore."

There is a pause. He feels helpless: he's done what he could. "Don't break my heart, Kattie," he says. He reaches out, but she steps back.

"Why can't you stay with Mom?" she asks.

He says nothing, and she asks again. Something is churning inside her, boiling up: grief, now, and hurt.

"Tell me why you can't stay with Mom."

He can't tell her why.

"You don't think she's smart."

He steps forward to touch her again, but she draws back. "I do think she's smart," he says.

"You do not," Kat says. "You do not." She puts her cupped hands over her eyes. "You think you're too smart for her." She takes her hands down. "What is she supposed to do, Dad? What am I supposed to do?"

"Kat," he says.

"Mom is a really good person," Kat cries. "She's really nice."

"I know that," Warren says, ashamed. "Of course. I know she is."

Kat shakes her head. "You have to go. I have to go to work."

"Kat," he says, "please let me put my arms around you."

Her face changes suddenly, crumpling. Sorrow fills it. Her eyes turn brilliant with tears, her mouth opens in pain. She turns her face away, and he steps forward and holds her. She stands in his arms, shaking with sobs, and he strokes her hair. She is warm and trembling in his embrace.

"Shh, shh, shh," he murmurs against her head. He feels a deep closeness; a warm current of peace and rightness floods through him. This is how it should be, he thinks. His chest aches, and he hears himself: a sob. For a long moment they stand together, then Kat draws away.

"You have to go," she says. "Nothing has changed. You have

lost me." She takes a long shuddering breath. Her face is bright pink now, and wet with tears, but she is composing herself. She wipes the tears from her cheeks with her fingers and wipes her hands on her thighs. "I mean it. I'm sorry, but you've done this to us. You've judged Mom for something she can't help. It is unbearably cruel. You have hurt her in ways you will never understand. I don't want to see you again." She opens the door for him.

"I hope you'll change your mind," he says, but he sees nothing for it but to leave. He goes down the stairs, into the gloom of the ground floor. He hears the iron clang of his footsteps echoing around him. He wonders if her door is open, if she's standing in it, watching him, but he won't turn to see. He doesn't want to see the closed door. He remembers the time he'd gone to see *Norma* with her, how happy he'd been.

At the airport, in the departure lounge, he thinks of calling Sarah, but his chest feels small and heavy, and he doesn't want to summon up the words to tell her what has happened. He thinks it can't be true. Her face was closed and sullen.

He watches the ground crew outside, striding about in bright vests and big earmuffs. They send semaphore signals, drive back and forth in heavy vehicles. A plane rolls back from a gate, slow and ponderous. Beyond is the runway, with its line of motionless planes, waiting for takeoff.

Chapter 13

SARAH TURNS OFF THE PAVED ROAD ONTO THE LONG DIRT driveway. She bumps slowly past a ragged field of high grass, then turns right, toward her house. She pulls into the gravel courtyard. Warren gets out of the car. He sets his hands on his hips and looks slowly around, turning to see it all, taking in the house, the lawn, the hedge and orchard: it's his first visit. It's warmer here than in Boston. It's July, and the trees are heavy with green, the sky a deep summer blue. The air is soft and warm, the landscape fecund. He looks at the house: white stucco, half-timbered, with a steep roof and gabled dormers. The stucco is brilliant against the black wood.

He nods. "I like it. When was it built?"

"The sixties," Sarah says. "By a Francophile, obviously. We're in Normandy now."

The courtyard is a square of smooth blond gravel. To the right, toward the road, stands a high hedge. To the left, toward the reservoir, the lawn stretches to a meadow. At its edge is a split-rail fence, and beyond that, an orchard. A faint wind shuffles through the trees, drowning any sound of cars on the road.

Warren nods again. "Very nice. It's so quiet. It feels as though we're miles deep in the country."

She feels something inside begin to loosen: He sees the place.

He's looking at everything, the house, the meadow, the orchard, all of it. She feels a rush of gratitude. She can trust him, then.

"And this is my dog," Sarah says.

Bella stands beside her, wagging her tail discreetly. She's restrained by Warren's presence. Sarah crouches down to say hello.

"Beauty," she murmurs, rubbing behind Bella's ears. Bella submits for a moment, pressing her head into Sarah's hand, then draws away, again on duty. She approaches the newcomer, head raised, tail lowered, courteous but alert.

"Hi, Bella." Warren leans down and puts out his hand for her to sniff.

"Now they say you're not meant to do that," Sarah says. "Put your hand out. Now they say it's aggressive, you're asking the dog to bite you. Though Bella wouldn't dream of biting you."

Warren straightens and pats Bella's head awkwardly, bumping against her skull.

She doesn't like it, and blinks, wincing slightly.

"What are you meant to do instead?" he asks.

"I don't know." Sarah's relieved when he stops patting.

They both look again at the house. Sarah tries to see it through his eyes: the high roofline, small-paned windows, faded black shutters. She can't see it as a building; it's the locus of her family's life. There is Josh's bedroom window, where he climbed out onto the roof, there is Meg's, where he climbed in. Her bedroom is on the other side, facing the meadow, a view she'd seen in every season, every hour. The house is her family's history: these rooms hold their days and nights. This place holds her life. Nearly forty years.

She and Rob had planted the orchard, just little bare whips stuck in the ground. They'd watered them, then fenced each one to keep out the rabbits. Rob had cut himself with the tin snips. He'd come through the tall grass limping, as though he'd hurt his leg. But it wasn't his leg: he was holding his arm out, stained bright scarlet. He had looked stunned.

Now the trees are soft wide domes, spreading over the grass.

Sarah says, "Come inside."

She takes him through the front hall, past the gilt-framed mirror darkened with age, a honey-colored table with curved legs. The red-tiled floor is waxed and glowing. She goes through to the living room, where French doors give onto the lawn. Before the fireplace two sofas face each other, the low table between them piled with books. "This is where I read in the afternoon," she tells him. She shows him the dining room, with the long polished table, the wrought-iron chandelier, tall pale curtains framing the windows.

Upstairs, at this hour her bedroom is full of light. It slants across the cream-colored walls, falling on the high four-poster bed, the maple bureau. On the walls are watercolors, landscapes. She wonders how it looks to him. The surfaces are nearly bare. Her bureau holds two framed photographs and her mother's silver-backed brush set. Maybe it looks austere to him.

But he nods, and says, "It's very peaceful."

Meg's bedroom serves as Sarah's study. The battered old brass bed is still there, and Meg's tall mahogany bureau, with her teenage photographs and the small china animals. But Sarah has put a card table in front of the window, and a wire file cabinet on the floor. The arrangement is provisional: to Sarah, it's still Meg's room. She likes it sitting in here, among Meg's things: it's like visiting her daughter. Josh's room has been done over. It's now a proper guest room with twin beds and white curtains. His tattered posters are gone, though his lacrosse stick is still in the closet. She nearly shows Warren this: She feels an obligation to show him every part of her life. She wants to conceal nothing.

Downstairs they settle in the kitchen, by the window. Sarah makes tea, pouring boiling water from her red enamel kettle into soft blue pottery mugs. Warren sets his elbows on the table and looks at her.

"I like your house," he says.

"I hoped you would," she says.

"So how will this work?" he says. "Us, together. Where will we live? How will we do it?"

"I'm assuming you can't leave Boston," Sarah says. "I thought maybe you'd be a weekend commuter, and come down here on Fridays?"

"You can't imagine moving to Boston," he says. It's not quite a question.

"What would I do there?"

"There are things to do." He smiles, and she can feel his energy, his wish to envelop her. "There are people who live quite happily in Boston. And the environs."

"I know. But everything I do now is here."

He nods. "But you could come up part of the time? We could both move back and forth."

She says, "I could. But this would be the center, for me."

"I see that it is." After a moment he says, "The problem is my daughter. I want to have a place for her, wherever I am."

"There's room here." Sarah would be glad to share the place with his daughter, opening it to her. "She'd always be welcome."

He nods carefully, pauses. "But this place isn't mine."

"It could come to be," Sarah says. "It could come to feel like yours."

"But my daughter would never feel it was hers. I want her to feel she has a place with me."

"So you'll get a bigger apartment in Boston?"

"Probably. If you're spending time there, we'll need a bigger place. But if you and I are spending time down here, if you don't want to leave Westchester, I thought we might buy a place together down here."

She looks at him. "Another place? Here?" She can't believe what he's saying. "You mean I'd move to another place, down here?"

"So my daughter would feel it was hers."

She waits for a moment. "You'd want me to sell this house?"

"I think it would make things better," Warren says.

She takes a sip of tea, then speaks carefully. "I've been here for a long time."

"I know," he says. "It's a lot to ask."

"What does your daughter say? Is this something she wants?"

"She doesn't know about it. But she's really upset about the divorce. I've told you. This would be something I could offer her. Something tangible, to show that I want her in my life."

He doesn't know how to deal with this. Kat's response is always with him, always beyond his grasp, huge and formless and violent, like a hurricane. There must be some way he can show her that he is still her father and that he loves her. That they're still part of the same family, which can never be altered. But it's too much for him, Kat's rage and her accusations. He doesn't know how to address the accusations. Nothing he says appears to make any difference. He can't seem to wrestle this into any manageable shape, can't find a way to resolve it. Ordinarily he enjoys figuring out the solution to a complicated problem, what the parts are and how to address them. But this will not reveal its parts, it will not be resolved. Kat is still not speaking to him. Warren has left many messages. He feels her fixed against him.

Sarah nods, watching him.

"I can't lose my daughter," he says.

"No," she says.

"If she were small, I'd have some kind of control. I could have her every weekend. But now I have no way of reaching her. She can just vanish from my life. She can do whatever she wants."

The fear that he will lose her seeps into his thoughts like dark water. What if she simply stops responding? Never answers his calls or messages? It feels like falling into air. Who would he be without his daughter?

"I can't lose her," he says again.

Sarah nods. "No," she says carefully. "But maybe this isn't the way to keep her? To buy a whole house that she can use . . ." She pauses. "Warren, she isn't ever going to live at home again."

"I can't tell you how bad this is," he says. "She's furious. She says I'm destroying the family."

Sarah says nothing for a moment. "She's kind of right. You are kind of destroying it. But you can't put it back together by buying a new house."

"But that's something I can do."

Sarah feels his energy, his determination. She's felt it before, directed at her, his determination to win her. But this seems irrational. She looks down at her cup, then back at him.

"When do you think Kat would come to this new place? How often does she come home now?"

He shakes his head. "I can't look at it like that. I have to do what I can to make this better. This is my daughter. I have to make a place for her."

"You'd ask me to give up this place, forever, on the chance that your daughter might come, once or twice a year, to stay with us?" She pauses. "I don't think she'd come here. I think she'll see you in Boston. I think you should get a bigger place there, that you can share with her." Though she doesn't think Kat will ever stay with Warren in Boston. She'll stay with her mother, in the house where she grew up.

Warren pushes back his chair and stands up.

On one wall are rows of family photographs, trips, graduations, the soccer field, the wading pool. Over the back of the chair is Sarah's sweater. Her dog lies on the bed in the corner. Her cookbooks are on the shelf beside the stove. As Warren stands, Bella raises her head, alert. He looks out the window.

"This is your view," he says. "This place is all yours, and your kids'. Their clothes are in the closets. Their photographs are everywhere. This is your life. How will my daughter feel when she comes?"

"She'll feel it's the house where a family lives. We can't make a stage set. We'll welcome her. I'll welcome her. Why would she feel welcome in a brand-new house? What would we put in it? Could I not put my photographs on the wall?"

Warren shakes his head. He can't rid himself of the memory of Kat's stubborn, stony silence. He can't imagine her coming here.

She has closed herself off from him. This sense of closure is a constant presence, a sheer rock face he cannot climb.

"We won't talk about it now," he says. "Show me around the outside."

They walk across the lawn to the edge of the meadow. A mown path leads through it, and the tall grass leaves pale dry seeds on their legs. At the far edge is a narrow wooden gate, the wood dark with damp. They pass through it and walk through the orchard, the trees still holding apple blossoms, though they're mostly spent now, and petals litter the grass. On the far side another gate opens onto a path through the little wood. As they walk through it they can see the water glinting beyond the trees. Beyond it the view opens thrillingly onto the reservoir.

They stand on a bluff overlooking the water. The reservoir is long and narrow, and they are standing at the center. From here they look across to the other shoreline, where the trees come down to the edge. To each side, in both directions, the water stretches out of sight. Below them the surface is made of tiny waves, flickering with light. The air is fresh and mild against their faces.

"Spectacular," Warren says.

Sarah nods. She knows this view intimately. She has seen it at dawn, before the wind comes up, when the water is dark silk. At sunset the surface is flooded with red, the trees on the far side black, the moving air a vast invisible presence. She likes to breathe in this ocean of air, feel the sweep of it. Now that he's seen this view, stood here, he'll understand that she can't give it up. As though he's thinking exactly that, he puts his arm around her, presses her against his side.

He's thinking he'd like to show this to Kat, stand here with her. He wonders what she's doing right now. He wonders if she has answered his last text, but he resists the urge to check.

"These reservoirs were created in the twenties, to supply water to New York. They were built by stonemasons brought over from Italy. The dams are phenomenal, stone walls hundreds of feet high. The masons brought their families, so we have a big Italian population. We have great food—homemade sausages and pasta. Fresh buffalo mozzarella—though I can never figure out where the buffalo are. Where do they live? Where are the buffalo herds for that mozzarella? Somewhere in New Jersey?"

"One of the great mysteries." He still has his arm around her, and they stand together. The air moves lightly against them. He pulls her close, but he's thinking of Kat, Kat putting her hand into his. Sarah puts her arm around him.

"This is fantastic," he says. He turns his head, looking up and down the shimmering length of light.

They walk back through the orchard, past the apple trees spreading their wide leafy umbrellas. Bella goes ahead at an elegant trot, lifting her paws high over the stubbled grass, or suddenly stopping, nose to the ground, alert to some invisible presence.

They have lunch in the kitchen. Sarah fixes soup, and Warren picks up a book she's reading and asks her about it.

"It's by an Englishman who takes ancient walkways. It's strange."

"Why strange?" asks Warren.

"The writing is beautiful and the walks are kind of madness. One is on a beach on the coast of East Anglia, from the land to an island only accessible at low tide. The path goes across quicksands, and lots of people have died there. Stakes in the sands marked the safe routes, so for four hundred years people used them," she says. "Now the government has taken the island for some kind of testing ground. They don't want people out there, so they took away the stakes. The writer walks the path without a guide. He walks past the quicksand pools, and writes about how beautiful it is, light and mist shimmering on the sand."

"The government took away the stakes." Warren shakes his head. "Wow."

"It's shocking to me," she says. "The idea of eliminating this kind of deep knowledge. Are we going backward instead of forward?"

But he won't allow her pessimism. "We're not going backward," he says. "We're just not. Look at medicine. Antibiotics:

people used to die of infection in three days. Look at artificial knees and hips. All sorts of advances."

"The environment," she says. "Extinction of species. Climate change."

"I know," he says, "it's bad, but we don't really know how bad. I'm hoping science is on it. I have to believe that. 'Adapt or die': that's the rule."

"Okay." She likes hearing a contrary view, it's reassuring.

She's come to trust him. She's no longer worried that he's reckless. She's touched by his feelings for his daughter. She admires the fact that he's never unkind about Janet.

Later he tells her that Janet has refused all his offers.

"So what will you do?" asks Sarah.

"Keep negotiating," Warren says. "Keep the lawyers talking. Finally she'll believe me."

"Believe you that . . . ?" Sarah asks.

"The marriage is ended," Warren says.

"What does she say?"

"That it's not." He looks up at her. "I never thought I'd be doing this."

She shakes her head. She can't help him here. Divorce has become such a commonplace, it has almost lost its moral gravitas. But still it carries a weight of grief. Each family had its own life before it was destroyed by this.

At the end of the afternoon, as it begins to get dark, they go out for another walk to the reservoir. Bella trots ahead, light and elegant, like a dancer. She seems to float over the grass. He puts his arm around Sarah as they walk, holding her close. She's touched by this. She has been on her own for so long, she doesn't expect support. They walk in step, their strides are the same length. This makes her ridiculously pleased.

For dinner she makes roasted chicken with a mustardy sauce, new potatoes with parsley and butter, carrots with ginger, endive salad. He sits in the kitchen while she works.

"Will I disturb you? I know some people don't want anyone in the kitchen while they cook."

"I don't mind," she says.

"I like being here." He's brought the paper in, and reads while she works. She snips the parsley into moist green shards. She likes the sense of order that cooking brings, the way she can make things happen as she wants. The chicken browned on the outside, steaming inside, the potatoes firm and moist.

"It's nicer to cook for two," she says.

"What do you make when you're alone?"

"It's hardly cooking. Scrambled eggs and toast. Melted cheese sandwich."

He folds the paper and sets it down. "Can we talk about getting a house together?"

She turns to look at him. "Getting a house together?"

"What I said earlier."

She's silent for a moment. "Warren, you've seen this place. My whole life is here."

"I can't move into a place that rejects my daughter."

"This place doesn't reject her. I don't reject her."

"But she would never come here. To your house." Kat would be disgusted and furious.

"That's her decision," Sarah says. "If she won't come to see you here, it's up to her."

Warren looks down at his hands. "Please don't do this to me."

"To you? To you?" Sarah says. "How can you say I'm doing it to you? You're asking me to give up my house!"

"She is my child."

He feels grief welling up in his chest, spreading within him, at his daughter's rage. He'll do anything.

"I can't lose her," he says.

Sarah comes over and sits down across from him. "I'm not asking you to give up your child. It won't be this house that makes the difference to her. Don't ask me to give up my house."

At the sound of her voice Bella raises her head, ears pricked.

"Okay," Warren says. His voice has taken on an edge. "Then let's decide what we're doing. Are we planning to live together? I've already made a commitment," Warren adds. "I've left my wife."

"We are, we are," Sarah says. "But this is different. Suppose I asked you to give up your job for me."

"That's completely different," he says. "There's no comparison."

"No, there is," Sarah says. "Your job is unrelated to our relationship. I'd be asking you to give up something that I don't have any rights to. You'd be right to tell me no."

"You don't understand what's happening," Warren says. "Don't tell me I have to stand up to her. If I stand up to her I'm afraid I'll never see her again."

She sees he means it. After a pause she says, "But that can't be true. She wouldn't give up on you."

He shakes his head slightly. "And you know that how?"

"Just . . ." she says, then doesn't go on. How can she be sure of what his daughter will do? Something on the stove is more than sizzling, maybe burning, and she turns away. It's the carrots, steam is roiling up from the pot, though they're not quite burning. She carries the pot to the sink and adds more water. "I'm sure she wouldn't."

He shakes his head again. "You don't know her."

They don't go on talking about it. The meal is ready and she takes out the plates from the oven, where they were warming. They're now too hot to hold, and she gets out her faded, scorched pot holders to pick them up. She's thinking about his daughter and this house. She's not going to sell it. He gets up and begins walking around, opening cupboards until he finds the glasses. He takes down two and fills them at the tap.

"What else shall I do? I don't know where the silverware is," he says.

This confuses her, his asking how he can help. She's been thinking of him as her antagonist.

"Point me at the silverware, napkins, anything else you'd like on the table," he says.

"I'm not leaving this house," she says. She's holding the big spoon in the air like a baton.

He looks at her, his eyes troubled. At this age everything is marked on their faces. Every thought is apparent. She can see his distress.

"Don't do this to me," he says.

"Look at this," she says, waving the spoon at the room. "Look at the reservoir in the evening. You stood there and watched the sunset and felt the wind on your face. How can you ask me to leave this house? I left my marriage. I'm not leaving this." Her voice has risen.

Bella stands up from her bed. She lifts her head and wags her tail diffidently.

"Don't do this to me," he says again.

"I'm not doing it," she says. "Your daughter is doing it to you. Don't blame it on me."

He steps back as though she has struck him. After a moment he says, "We can't let this happen. We can't let ourselves be set against each other this way."

"Please don't set up a false equivalence," she says. "It's not a choice between me and your daughter. Or do you think it is?"

He looks down and shakes his head. "No." He looks up again. "I don't know what the choice is."

"Well, you have to make it. Don't ask me to sell this house."

"I have to keep my daughter," he says.

Chapter 14

"HI, THERE," SARAH SAYS. "IS THIS A GOOD TIME?"

"Not really," Meg sounds distracted. "But I have a minute or two. What's up?"

"I wondered if we could plan a visit," she says. "I could pick up one of the kids for a playdate, or I could bring you all dinner one night."

Sarah has friends who take a grandchild for one day a week, or do school pickups. One flies to L.A. every month for a week. Sarah's distance from the city makes a short visit awkward. Both children are in preschool, Nate for the morning, Busby the whole day. The housekeeper, Adeel, comes in for the afternoons and picks up Nate. If Sarah picks him up she has nowhere to take him: Adeel is always in the apartment, and usually Jeff is as well. It's not large, and Sarah feels like an intruder. She hasn't made a routine; she thinks they are growing up without her. With the new baby she wants a plan: once a week, half a day. She'll give her a bath, feed her, take her to the park. (She's sure it will be a girl.) She wants to connect. Now, September, she thinks she'll make a fresh start.

Because running a museum is like writing in air. Planning exhibitions, wooing donors, running board meetings—anyone could do those things. But her job with her grandchildren is something only she can do. She wants to pass things on to them, something of her family, which is their family. She wants to teach them the rules: How you must never lay a book facedown, because it will crack the spine. You must never let bed linen touch the floor. The correct pronunciation of "tomato." Who their great-grandparents were. The nursery rhyme about toes. She feels a responsibility to pass on the sacred knowledge of the past. Her grandchildren should be her mission. With each year her obligation seems more urgent. In elephant herds, the grandmothers are essential—instructors, guardians, keepers of the peace.

Part of her urgency comes from the baffling fact that this family seems to do fine without her. They have their own patterns, their own games and jokes and stories, their own fights and reconciliations. They have created all these without her. It's a source of sorry amazement. Isn't she a part of their lives, as they are a part of hers?

For a moment Meg doesn't answer, and Sarah's heart sinks. She is a nuisance.

"Actually," Meg says, "could you help me out today? Busby has an ear infection, and she stayed home from school. Could you pick her up at the apartment and bring her to the pediatrician, and I'll meet you there? And could you take her back after? Adeel came in early to look after her, but if she brings Busby to the doctor she has to bring Natey as well. He'll miss his nap, and I don't want him in the doctor's office with all those germs."

"Of course," Sarah says. "When's the appointment? If I leave now I can be there anytime after eleven."

"It's at twelve-fifteen. I'll see you there. Thanks."

Sarah can walk right out the door, she has no plans today. All summer she and Warren have had a sort of schedule, meeting at his apartment during the week, her house on weekends. Today she is free. She reaches the apartment just in time to leave for the doctor's, but it turns out Busby doesn't want to go. When Sarah holds out her hand, Busby begins to whimper.

"Come on, Bus. We're going to meet your mumma," she says.

Busby ducks away, whimpering louder. Sarah and Adeel crouch, trying to persuade her, but she throws herself onto the floor and begins to scream, a high-pitched iron-filing whine like a dentist's drill.

"Come on, Bus," Sarah says.

"No, no, no!" shrieks Busby. "I don't want to go!" She's frantic. Sarah, leaning over the contorted face, the whine drilling into her brain, thinks it's a miracle that more children are not abused.

Adeel, crouching, in her tight jeans and orange sweater, puts her hand on Busby's shoulder. She speaks in a low patient voice, ignoring the screams. She is firm but kind, and has more authority than Sarah. Now, Busby, she says, sit up, don't cry. No, no, no, be a big girl. Finally worn out by the pain in her ear, and her own screams, Busby subsides. She opens her eyes and sits up, face pink, cheeks glistening, shuddering with leftover sobs. Sarah wipes off the tears: her cheeks are hot as a furnace. Now that she is quiet it's easy to see that she's not a demon but a small child, exhausted and in pain, infection throbbing inside her head. She tilts her head toward the infected ear.

"Let's go," Sarah says. "You'll feel better soon. We'll see your mumma." Busby sniffs, still aggrieved. In the elevator she ignores Sarah, staring up at the needle as the floors drop away, but out on the street she relents. When Sarah steps to the curb for a cab, Busby clasps her hand.

The pediatrician's office is in a grimy old high-ceilinged building on West Eighty-Fourth Street. The waiting room is lined with worn sofas. Sarah gives her name to the receptionist, then settles with Busby on the greasy-looking sofa. There are two other people waiting, women with small children. A tall gaunt elderly woman with haunted eyes sits with a plump toddler with full red lips; a heavy young woman with wrecked hair scans her cell phone, sitting by a bored little boy.

Sarah offers them friendly smiles. The gaunt woman meets her eyes but does not respond, the young woman maybe doesn't see her. Her fingernails are bright orange. She flicks rhythmically at the screen.

Busby subsides, leaning against Sarah. The room smells vaguely antiseptic. The receptionist clicks at her keyboard. Sarah wishes she had brought a book for Busby. That's another thing she should be transmitting: book culture.

The door opens and Meg comes in, looking harried. Her hair is tousled, and she's wearing a wrinkled trench coat, carrying her old black shoulder bag. Her belly is evident. Sarah hasn't seen her in weeks: she is now visibly pregnant, at four and a half months.

"Hi, Mum," she says. "What's up, ladybug?" She crouches before Busby, who turns doleful again.

"My ear," she says, rubbing her wrist against it.

"I know, my sweet honey," Meg says. "We're going to take care of it." She puts her hands on Busby's legs, holding the child in her gaze.

"Poor thing," Sarah says, but Meg doesn't reply.

Meg sits on the other side of Busby. "Want to sit in my lap? What's left of it. It's getting smaller." She pats her legs and Busby climbs on, leaning over the visible belly, leaning her face against Meg's chest. Meg rests her chin on Busby's head and puts her arms around her. "It'll be better soon," she says.

"How are you feeling?" Sarah asks.

"Okay," Meg says. "Tired, but okay. I had some of that back pain I had with Nate, but mostly I'm fine."

"And your doctor says everything's going well?"

"Yeah," Meg says. "They're going to induce me."

"Induce you?" Sarah repeats.

With Busby, her first, Meg had considered a midwife. Everyone was doing it—giving birth in bathtubs, squatting on the floor, listening to music, keeping the doctors out. First-time mothers, with nine months to think about it, planned a birth like a wedding, imagining they were in control. I want this, I won't allow that. Without realizing that giving birth was like being run over by a truck, that you had no control, that your body was invaded and then used by foreign forces. Once those big muscles started contracting—which they did without your permission—you were helpless. Things might go well or they might not, your plans had no bearing on it. The way you breathed was irrelevant. Your husband in the room was a liability. Your body, the big deep scarlet unseen part of it, the interior, with those hidden organs and pulsing systems you knew were there but had never felt, took charge. You became an occupied country.

Once you had entered that fierce current you were risking death, both of you. All you could do was close your eyes and endure. Push when you were told. You were not in charge of your body. Your body was in charge of you.

Meg said the midwife was really good. She had great recommendations. And her place was right down the street from the hospital. You'd be only a few minutes away if something went wrong, Meg said. If something went wrong. Sarah imagined Meg strapped onto a gurney in the midst of it, being rolled through the halls to the elevator, waiting for the elevator, seconds ticking by as it went down, being pushed through the front door and out onto the sidewalk. Clattering over the rough pavement down the street to the hospital. Through the doors there, down the corridors, into the elevators to the floor for surgery. How many minutes before you were in the operating room? Brain damage occurred after five minutes without oxygen. She couldn't stand the thought of this. Why would you risk even a single minute of delay?

She'd said nothing, hoping Meg would decide on a doctor instead. Which she had, and thank god, because something had gone wrong: the baby had gotten stuck in the birth canal, her shoulder jammed. Within seconds an alarm had sounded, and within seconds there were five people in the delivery room, oxygen and blood ready, helping to get that baby out safely. When Sarah arrived, urgency was still echoing in the room, there was still a smear of blood on the floor. Though by then Busby was clean and swaddled, silent, with that grave wise blue gaze of the newborn.

Nate's arrival had been hard, too, the labor long, the birth complicated. But it had also been in the hospital, doctors and nurses in attendance. There had been no more talk about midwives. What

Sarah wants to hear now is a plan for the safest of all possible births. She's wary of complication.

"Why induce?" Sarah asks.

"The other two were difficult," says Meg. "She thinks this will make things go more smoothly."

"The new doctor," Sarah observes. Meg's old doctor had moved away. "How does it work, induction?"

"They put you on a drip that starts the contractions," she says. "Then in a few hours, they start. It's all controlled."

Sarah nods. She wonders if it's safe. She wonders if it's just for the convenience of the doctor—aren't most births in the middle of the night? She's wary of interference in the natural process.

The receptionist looks up. "Ms. Thompson?"

Meg sets Busby on her feet. "That's us, ladybug. Let's go."

"Shall I come?" Sarah asks.

"You don't need to," Meg says. "It's a small room. I'll see you after."

Sarah settles back, wishing she'd brought a book. What will it mean, inducement? Or is it induction?

When Meg was four she'd had an ear infection. She'd gotten them often. Sarah would hear the faint, tired cry in the middle of the night. The cry of the sick child. It was always awful, the pain in Meg's face, the fact that there wasn't much she could do about it. Sarah would call the doctor at one in the morning, get the doctor on call, and ask for a prescription. The only all-night pharmacy was in White Plains, forty minutes away. Meg's crumpled pink face, the exhausted wails. Sarah would get dressed, stuffing her bare feet into shoes, yanking on a sweater. She took Meg with her, to comfort her, and to start the medicine as soon as possible. Meg squirmed in her car seat, filling the car with the sound of her pain. Sarah sang, to comfort and distract her, but Meg often cried louder.

Once Meg got an earache on a Saturday night when Sarah and Rob were about to go on a trip. He was doing some business thing in California. He'd made a big deal of it, claiming that she didn't take his business efforts seriously. She didn't, but she wanted to give him support, and she'd agreed to go. It was a conference, he wanted to show her off to the other people. The housekeeper would stay with the children. It was only four days, but seemed alarmingly long to Sarah, the children too little to be without her. But she felt obligated. Rob was right, she never wanted to meet his associates. She was atoning.

She got up in the night, made the call to the doctor, and drove down to the pharmacy. She took Meg, carrying her into the sizzling brightness of the drugstore, overhead lights, the long rows of shelves packed with bright objects, the synthetic smells. Meg was quiet now, knowing that the medicine was coming. Sarah carried her to the counter in back where the prescriptions were filled. Presiding over it was a woman with a long black braid, in a white uniform. Sarah said her name and the woman turned away, coming back with a dark glass bottle.

"Three times a day," the woman said.

"Thank you," Sarah said. Meg began to whimper, relief in sight. Sarah had brought a spoon, and when they were in the car she unscrewed the top and poured out a careful pool of the pink liquid. Amoxycillin. Meg opened her mouth trustingly, like a small bird. She had gone to sleep in the car on the way home. In the morning she'd still been tetchy. Her ear still hurt, she said, but the medicine took twelve hours to work.

They were supposed to leave that afternoon, but that morning Sarah told Rob she wasn't coming with him, that she'd follow him the next day.

"Why?" he said, turning around. They were getting dressed. He was at his bureau, taking out a shirt. It was an expensive one, pale yellow with a windowpane check. He was a bit of a dandy.

"Meg's sick," Sarah said. "I want to be sure she's all right before I leave."

"She's fine," he said. "She's on the medicine. She'll be feeling fine by this afternoon."

"I just want to make sure," she said.

He set the shirt down and put his hands on his hips. He was wearing only his boxers. His chest was narrow, with a sandy patch of hair in the center, like an unexpected beard. "You always do this," he said. "There's always some reason why you won't come to anything to do with my work."

It was true. His projects always seemed dodgy, and she didn't like being around the people involved. All-pork fast-food restaurants, a curved floor mop, some marketing scheme. The people were all enthusiastic and unrealistic. It depressed her to be around them. But she'd agreed to come on this.

It was early in her marriage, when she was trying hard. She was still in love with Rob, and afraid of Rob then. He could be cutting and supercilious. It made her feel bare and unprotected, as though some part of her had no skin and her soft interior was exposed to him. Once, at a dinner party, she said something about politics and he turned to her, smiling for the others, and said, "You know nothing about politics. You should keep your mouth shut." He laughed, and the others had laughed, too. She was too shocked and humiliated to answer. She felt not just silenced but erased, as though she had no place in the world. That night in bed she turned her back on Rob, curling herself into a ball. But Rob put his arms around her and called her Mouse. He didn't apologize. "Don't be cross, Mousie," he said, wrapping himself against her. She ignored him, but after awhile the wash of sex began to move across her. It was something that would be a pleasure, and it would be an end to this rift. But she was afraid of his displeasure. She was afraid he would disenfranchise her as a person. He could do that to her then. In some ways she felt craven, at not standing up to him, but in some ways she felt grown-up. Wasn't that what you did, in a marriage, compromise? Wasn't that what this was?

When she told him she was not going to California, she waited for his anger.

"We have the whole thing planned," he said. "All the wives are coming. Why are you always the one who doesn't turn up?"

"I'm sorry," she said. "I just want to be sure she's all right."

"When has she ever not been all right once she's on the antibiotics?" he asked. "This is an excuse."

He shook the shirt out of its folds and took out the cardboard strip that held the collar stiff. He pulled it on ostentatiously, flapping it open and then closed across his chest. He began buttoning it, closing himself off, turning from a half-naked man with a narrow chest to a man in a starched yellow windowpane check.

But she'd been stubborn. The flapping of the shirt had decided her. "I'll come tomorrow. I'm not coming today."

Rob turned his back then. She was still afraid of him. If he'd stayed facing her, if he'd pressed her, she might have given in.

That night, Sarah put Meg to bed. She took a pill, to get to sleep quickly herself. So she could wake early for her flight. But she was awakened by Meg coming into her room. "Mama," she said, "Mama."

Meg's face was unrecognizable. Her features were bloated and swollen, her eyes were slits.

"Meglet," Sarah said, getting out of bed. "Come on, sweetie, we're going to the hospital."

While Sarah was getting Meg dressed, Meg saw herself in the mirror. She pointed at her reflection. "I don't look like myself."

"Now the sweater, over your head," Sarah said.

In the hospital they put her on an IV with antibiotics. It was an infection in the ethmoid sinus. There was a risk of spreading to the brain. But the antibiotics worked, and by the middle of the next morning the swelling was gone. Meg looked like herself again. Sarah asked the doctor about the timing. The doctor said that in another six or eight hours the danger of brain damage would have been acute. "The ethmoid sinus is right next to the brain."

If she had gone to California then. That memory has never stopped running through her mind, a bad-mother loop, sometimes silent, sometimes loud and insistent. Each time she took a child to the doctor after that, she was countering that narrative.

When they come out, Busby is smiling, her round face lit up.

The doctor is behind them. He's South Asian, with honey-colored skin and thick imperial eyebrows.

"You'll feel better soon, Busby," he says kindly. She doesn't look up but she's cheerful now: the world has taken her into account. Meg brings her over.

"Feeling better?" Sarah asks.

Busby doesn't answer. Meg leans over and helps her into her jacket.

"Thanks so much, Mum," Meg says. "I really appreciate your doing this. I've got to go now, I have a meeting. Can you take her back?"

"Of course," Sarah says. "Buzz, let's go find some ice cream."

She puts out her hand to Busby, who ignores it.

"And Meglet, let's find a time when we can see each other," Sarah says.

Meg tilts her head. "Do you mean lunch, or what?"

"I don't care," Sarah says. "Something."

"I don't really do lunch," Meg says.

"Dinner? I can come in. On the weekend, I could come for the afternoon?"

Meg frowns slightly.

"I feel as though time is passing," Sarah says bravely. "I don't know the last time we talked."

"I don't, either, but it wasn't so long ago." Meg pauses. "I know you feel this way, Mum, but, honestly, my life has no room for anything else. I work full-time. I have two kids, and another on the way. When do you think I have time for lunches? Or dinners? Or even phone calls?"

"No, I know," Sarah says. "I know you're busy." She smiles at her. "I know, you're crazy-busy."

How can there be no time for her in her daughter's life? But she hears in Meg's voice that this is so, and it makes Sarah want to tear her heart out. What she wants is for her daughter to call to complain about the traffic as she's coming home in a cab. Or to tell her something Busby has done. To tell her about a friend's story, or something funny she's heard. It can be just for a moment.

"I know," Sarah says again. "Can I help?" she asks. "Shall I take the kids for the weekend? Why don't I do that?" She loves the kids, of course, but she loves Meg more. It is Meg she wants.

"That would be great," Meg says, but Sarah's not sure she believes the offer. She's not sure she believes it herself, driving them home in rush-hour traffic, amusing them all weekend. She imagines tantrums and boredom, doleful requests for their mother. But it would be lovely, having the children to herself. She should do it. She will do it. She'll tell Warren all this. Maybe he'll want to be there. She wants to introduce him to Meg.

Sarah puts her hand out for Busby. Meg stoops and kisses Busby and whispers into her ear. Sarah watches Busby's face turn radiant.

Meg straightens. "'Bye, Mum. Thanks a lot. I really mean it. I love you." She looks directly at Sarah for the first time. Her narrow face is lean and sharp, her skin sallow. There are brownish smudges beneath her dark eyes. She looks haunted: she's being taken over by pregnancy. She puts a hand behind her back, arching it against the weight of her belly. The ribs have shifted outward to make room. The body declares its priority. The baby is taking precedence, nature is making non-negotiable demands on the mother. Her hair, her teeth, her sleep, all may be sacrificed. And what mother would not sacrifice her hair, her teeth, her sleep, for her child? But Sarah's child is Meg. She is the jealous guardian of this child, not the new one. She gives precedence to her daughter.

"Glad to do it," Sarah says. "I love you." Then she can't help adding, "Are you taking calcium?"

But Meg won't be questioned. She waves her hand dismissively and gives her head a half shake, as if her mother has gone too far.

Chapter 15

JEAN GERSON CALLS THE MEETING TO ORDER. THEY'RE IN THE conference room again. The birch trees outside are in full leaf, but now, late September, the leaves are dulled and dusty. Nancy and Sarah sit beside each other; they're giving a report.

Jean asks them how the exhibition is proceeding.

"Very well," says Nancy. "We've gotten about two-thirds of our first choices—Duncan Grant, Vanessa Bell, Roger Fry, and Dora Carrington are the main ones. A few places are still undecided and we're trying to persuade them. I'll pass around images of the ones we have. Thirty-two pictures. Twenty-three paintings and nine drawings. Plus about twenty photographs, some period, some contemporary, of the artists and their houses."

They pass around the images, black-and-white xeroxes. Sarah watches the faces as they look. Black-and-white doesn't carry the heft of color, and the expressions are noncommittal. Jean asks about the Carrington, Candace about the dates, but mostly they just pass around the pictures without comment. The lack of response makes Sarah wonder if the paintings actually are any good—if they're important. She and Nancy have spent months on this, they've created a critical mass of energy that means the exhibition is important for them. But is something intrinsically important, or is it human effort that makes it so? Maybe this group of painters is just a minor offshoot, a dead end in art history. Duncan Grant's ponderous neoclassical nudes, Vanessa's muted, decorous interiors. Or was there some essential importance about any group of artists who shared an idea? How would you determine intrinsic artistic value? (Fashion changes so drastically: Alma-Tadema was once famously described as the worst painter of the nineteenth century. But he was a master of craft, it was a question of subject matter. Was his work kitschy and vulgar, those collapsing semi-nudes, the archaic scenes, the lush textures and even light? Wasn't everything reducible, though, to this sort of simplistic consideration? Subject, approach, craft—everything was subject to question. Alma-Tadema's work was the height of something—but what was it?)

Nancy talks about the pictures they've secured. "We were turned down flat by the museum in Arizona. We couldn't figure out why. But Sarah knew someone out there who had a friend on the board. She found out that the curator had gotten into an argument with the director, who had urged him to agree to the loan. So we had to find a way to reach the curator but not through the director. So Sarah's friend gave a lunch and asked the curator. Anyway, we now have the picture."

Jean asked about a catalogue. Sarah had asked a well-known scholar, Barbara Schwarzman, to write the essay. Schwarzman had written about this group, but she was being curiously unresponsive. "She takes a long time to answer each time I write," Sarah says, "and she hasn't yet agreed to do it. I don't know if she doesn't want to do it, or if she's ill, or trying to stall, or what. I can't wait too long—if I need to find someone else I need to give them plenty of lead time. Any ideas?"

Shirley Anderson suggests that she ask Schwarzman directly if she'll commit. Jean suggests that she ask other people in the museum world about her—is this something she's known for? Candace Woods asks Sarah if she's certain Schwarzman is the right person for the essay.

"She's written interesting things about artists in the group, I think she'd be good," says Sarah. She can't tell if Candace is still nettled by their disagreement over the exhibitions.

"I just mean, maybe we should find someone less well known, or less obvious," Candace says. "Maybe that would make the whole thing easier." She brushes her blond hair back from her shoulder. Her mouth is set, and Sarah can see what she'll look like in twenty years. The loose blond hair suggests abandon, but she is actually rather prim and disapproving. The mouth will be thin and fixed, little parentheses bracketing it. Though maybe being prim is a good way to manage things. Your life.

"We know another possibility," Nancy says. "A younger curator at the Clark. He's written a couple of pieces on this material, he's just not as well known."

Jean nods. "Have you approached him?"

"It would be awkward to ask if he's interested and then not ask him to write it," says Sarah.

"We're going to give her another week and then ask her to commit," Nancy says. "It feels like there's something going on we don't know about."

"Maybe another exhibition?" Shirley asks. "Is there a competing show?"

"It's possible," Sarah says.

Of course that might be it, Sarah thinks. The absent presence—that moment when you realize the silence that surrounds you is actually the presence of something you didn't know about. A party that everyone else is going to. A girlfriend your boyfriend is seeing. The fact that the director wants you off the board, and has talked to everyone else on it. That terrible moment of realizing that you're on the outside of something, when you thought you were on the inside. She thinks of Warren: but there's nothing she doesn't know about. They are only waiting for the lawyers to agree.

Jean says, "In any case, I think you need to firm it up sometime soon."

"We will," Nancy says. "We're on it. There are a couple of other scholars we've thought of."

"How are you going about finding them?" asks Candace. Her question seems barbed, as though she is looking for something to criticize. "My son works at the Met, if you'd like me to ask him for some names."

Sarah looks at her for a moment. "That's great," she says. "Thank you. What department is he in?"

"Egyptian," Candace says, with satisfaction. "But he'll be able to talk to the scholars in this field." She introduces her son into the conversation with pride and relish, as she might the name of a lover. But it's unlikely that a junior member of the Egyptian Department would be better able to find a scholar of the Bloomsbury group than Nancy and Sarah, who've been working on it for months, and who have been in the art world for decades.

"Thank you," Nancy says. "We'll keep that in mind. We are in touch, actually, with someone at the Met, who works in this field. Mark Henshaw."

Candace nods, tapping her pen on the table. "Good," she says, as though Nancy is following her suggestion.

Candace is new to the community. She and her husband bought a big new Colonial on Bisbee Lane. The place was uninteresting, the earth shaved bare, the house bland. They've done it up with expensive landscaping—big mature trees, a pool and tennis court. All Candace's clothes are brand-new, her narrow leather belts have a pristine glow, her sweaters are perfectly smooth, her skirts perfectly pleated. She looks as though she has never worn anything more than once. And she has a degree in art history. She seems to want to dominate on every level, scholarly, financial, sartorial. Now also maternal. Sarah doesn't admire this impulse, she thinks it's unfair, but of course she, too, would like to boast about her daughter, inject her name into the conversation with pride. My daughter would be able to help with this, she'd like to say. Though her daughter is pregnant, and she wouldn't ask her to do anything. She's due in February.

HE SEES KATRINA'S NAME on his phone and feels a little starburst of joy. It's the first time she's called since this began. He's at his desk in the office, Laurel beside him at hers. As he lifts the phone, he feels Laurel's presence as his ally, a woman, a daughter. He nearly turns to her, to show off what's happened. He's smiling as he clicks on the phone.

"Hi, sweetie," he says. He stands, in case he needs to walk away for privacy.

"I wanted to let you know that I'm getting married," she says, and he feels himself lighten.

THEY'RE IN THE SAME HOTEL, but it's not the same room. Sarah has gotten there first, and is waiting when he arrives. She's brought a book, and is curled up in the armchair, her feet tucked underneath her. It's not the same room, but it's familiar, the same dark wooden bureau, the same wheat-colored curtains. The small stiff boxy sofa, the blurry landscape prints on the wall. Everything in bland colors, a neutral background for any passion the residents supply. The room is cool, and her arms are chilly, but she doesn't bother to get up and turn up the heat. Once he arrives everything will change.

She hears him at the door and lifts her head. When he comes in she is smiling, waiting for the great luxury of his presence, his touch on her, his gaze. But at first he doesn't speak, turning to shut the door. He comes in and takes off his coat. He doesn't look directly at her.

"Hi," she says. There's something wrong. She feels, without knowing it, dread.

He comes over and leans down to kiss her. He puts his palms on either side of her face and holds her gently, pressing his fingers against her temples, her cheeks, as though to record her presence. He smells of the outdoors. He has flown through the glaring skies, driven through the urban landscape, passed by the gatekeepers downstairs, to reach this room. What is it? Dread rises in her chest, as she feels herself clasped in his hands.

"My darling," he says.

"What is it?" she asks.

He steps back and sits down on the edge of the bed, facing her.

"Katrina," he says.

"What?" Something is shifting.

"She's getting married," he says.

"That's what you wanted, right?" she says, trying to make this into good news. She sits up straighter, tucking her legs neatly beneath her. "You like the guy?"

"I do like him," he says. "It's good news that she's getting married. She's going to do it from our house in Maine."

"That's good, too, right?" asks Sarah. Funny that he now has a house in Maine. Which she has never seen.

"She doesn't want me to come to the wedding," he says. "Or to anything else. She's cutting me out of all family events—everything—from now on. Janet agrees."

"The wedding?" Sarah repeats.

"And everything else," Warren says. "Christmas, christenings, birthdays, everything. Her kids, when she has them." He makes a dismissive gesture. "I'm out of the family forever. She never wants to see me again."

He looks up at her.

"Well," Sarah says. She summons reason. "She can't mean it. Forever." She shakes her head. "She'll change her mind. Her kids will want to know you." As she says this she realizes she's talking about decades from now.

Warren looks down at his hands.

On the phone he had felt Katrina's rage like a blast furnace, a big open maw. He has never felt such rage. She would welcome his destruction.

Afterward he'd called Janet, hoping for an ally. Surely she didn't want him excluded from the wedding? Plans for which were well under way, the little church in East Westport already booked, hotel rooms taken for guests.

"This wasn't your idea, was it?" he asked Janet.

"Not my idea," she said, "but it's Kat's wedding. She gets to do what she wants. It's her guest list."

"You can't mean you don't want me there," he said. He realized at once it was a poor start.

"I can mean that," Janet said. "Do you think I want you walking her down the aisle, like the good dad? Sitting next to me in the front pew?"

"We can work all that out," Warren said. "I didn't even know about this. When did she tell you?"

"That," said Janet, "is none of your business anymore. My daughter told me she was getting married and asked me to help plan the wedding. We've got the Fork and Spoon Club for the reception."

"But when is it?" Warren asked.

"Warren, you don't understand. You are not part of this plan. You have chosen to leave our family."

He said nothing. He could feel the power of these women, the implacable nature of their rage, the force of their decree. It was just the two of them, just his daughter and his wife, but they had joined to create a vast force field. It was like a season, this was like fighting against winter. He had been expelled from his family.

For a moment he imagined going anyway. It would be easy enough to learn the date. He imagined coming in quietly and late to the church, sitting way at the back, craning his neck to watch the marriage of his only daughter. Afterward, seeing the faces of his friends as they walked out, seeing them see him. Seeing them register his location in the church, understanding that it signified disgrace, that he was unwanted. Janet and Katrina would have told everyone.

No, he couldn't go to the wedding. Or the reception, though he'd certainly have to pay for it. At the wedding the whole point of the father was the ritual: handing on the promise of protection to her husband. He had loved that idea, the fact that he had protected Kattie, held her sweet presence in his hand, for her whole life, and now he was entrusting her to another man. Apart from feminism, patriarchy, all that (of course she could take care of herself, but she had a father to help), he had loved the idea of protecting her. He would walk Kat up the aisle with her gloved hand on his arm, then she would turn to Chris. But if Warren had no role he'd be an interloper, a jackal skulking around the carcass of his own marriage.

He couldn't go. On that day he'd have to be somewhere else, completely engaged by something else. He thinks of a watercolor class, in someone's studio, listening to instructions, paying close attention to the loaded brush, spreading blurry color across wet paper. Among people who knew him, who didn't know his family. And on all the other days as well, birthdays, Christmas.

His life was being severed from him. The fact of this, the idea that his daughter would now be lost to him, was terrible. That he would no longer know her, that he would be banned from contact, that he could not call and hear her voice, could not feel the warmth in her eyes, could not hold her young body in his arms, that he would not know her children, that he would be an outcast, shunned from the family he had made, was intolerable. Exile from the world he loved. It was a possibility he had not known existed, and the knowledge was frightening. A black curtain would be drawn between himself and his kin. He felt as though the waters were rising around him, up past his chest, to his chin, as though he were drowning. He was a father more than anything, it turned out. He was that first.

This was something he had no power over. He could not control it. The lack of power was confusing; he had never been in this position before, in his family. He had always been the head of the family, he had always felt responsible for their happiness and their safety, in charge. Now this responsibility and power had been taken from him. He was no longer in charge. They were in charge, and they were threatening him; he was humbled and fearful.

He can't, actually, imagine this kind of loss. He can't allow it. Whatever the cost, it can't be greater than this. All right, he had said to Janet.

Now he looks at Sarah.

"What are you saying?" she asks. "Are you breaking this off? With me?"

She says it bluntly, to shock him. To make him hear the words. She knows he won't break it off; she wants him to say so.

He looks at her without speaking.

She draws her knees back up underneath her on the chair. She puts her hand over her bare feet, to protect them.

"You are," she says. "You're breaking this off."

She waits for him to deny it.

"It is breaking my heart," he says.

He feels his whole life with Kat spread out before him. She is knit into him. The sulky teenager who left her shoes scattered in the front hall for them to trip over, her rudeness at the table, the moments of intoxicating sweetness when she surfaced suddenly from the mess of adolescence, throwing her arms around him from behind as he sat at the kitchen table, calling him to celebrate a win. Sitting beside him, rapt and tearful, at *La Bohème*. She is part of him, her whole warm moving life is part of him. He can't sever it from himself, he can't be severed. He can't lose her.

"I can't leave my daughter," he says.

Sarah leans back on the chair. She feels what's happening, that he's shifting. It's like a tide. He is drawing out from her shore.

"What will happen to us?" she asks. Now the room feels strange, the dark wooden bureau, the blurry landscape, the bland tan curtains. This is no longer a place that shelters them; this place is not a refuge.

He has put both hands in his pockets, his face somber. He shakes his head very slightly. Though he is perfectly neat, it seems as though he has just come in from a windstorm: He has been buffeted and blown about. He has been shaken, torn to shreds. She can feel the violence that has passed through him.

"Sarah," he says, as though to record the name.

Sarah shakes her head. "But what?" she asks. "Should I leave now?"

"Please don't." He holds up a hand to stop her. "Please."

She untwines her legs and stands. "I feel as though I've been fired."

"You haven't been fired," he says. "It's me."

She looks at his face, the long furrows and hollows in his cheeks, the irregular lines in his forehead, his bright intent gaze. But they are still here, still together, safe in the room's indifferent clasp. They will have the evening together, the night. None of this has become real.

"I can't stop looking at you," he says. "I can't take my eyes from you."

"Will it mean we will never see each other again?"

"I can't lie to them," he says. "I can't do this if I'm lying to them."

"Does that mean never?"

He shakes his head again. "I can't say the word. But I mean it. I can't ever break my promise again."

"What have you promised?"

"That I will never leave her."

Sarah feels it welling up inside her chest. "I can't say send me a text when you have a moment. I can't just be waiting for your call." She thinks of him coming to her house, standing with her at the edge of the reservoir, blinking and smiling in the wind. "What do you want from me?"

His face is full of sorrow. "I want all of you. I want to marry you. I can't control this." He sits down on the bed and puts his head in his hands. "This is the worst thing I've ever had to do."

"Yes," she says. She sits down again on the sofa. She's not weeping; her body doesn't believe it. He comes over and sits beside her. He takes her in his arms.

Later they leave for the restaurant. Sarah walks through the door first, feeling him right behind her, their bodies touching, jostling, easy. She wonders if this is the last time. She wonders if everything is the last time. They go to a small undistinguished Moroccan place in midtown. No one they know will be there.

At dinner they talk about it, his decision.

By now it has become something they know, the discovery is behind them. Now they own it. Now they know it, now they have met and acknowledged it, now they explore it.

"Do you think Kat talked to Janet about it? Did they agree on it?" Sarah asks.

The restaurant is noisy, with poor service. They have to lean in, close to each other, to hear.

"I think they talked about it," Warren says. Janet's response had been instantaneous and knowing. This felt like collusion, something tightly woven, warp and woof, knitted against him. He puts his hand out, palm up, for Sarah's.

She looks at him. Is he asking her to join him in his acceptance? Does he want her firm clasp of agreement, of partnership? She won't offer support.

A look of intense pain comes over his face. "Please," he says. "Sarah. Give me your hand."

She shakes her head. "How can you ask me?"

He leans closer, but he speaks so quietly she can hardly hear him. "My heart is being torn from my chest," he says. "Please give me your hand."

She puts her hand in his. At once the waiter appears, a thin, harried-looking older man in a long white apron. He stands, waiting irritably with their dinner. They unclasp their hands and he sets down their plates: sloppy tagine, some dark red chicken dish.

"Is this the last dinner we'll have together?" Sarah asks. "I shouldn't have ordered tagine," she adds, and he laughs.

"What would you have ordered instead?" he asks.

"Mrs. Ramsay's boeuf en daube, maybe," she says. "That's the last supper of hers that we know about."

"Do you feel betrayed?" he asks. "Do you think I've betrayed you?"

She thinks for a moment. Another waiter appears, filling up

their water glasses. A white towel is wrapped around his pitcher; he pours water not from the spout but the side.

"Why do they do that?" she asks. "Pour from the side?"

"The ice cubes," he says. "So they won't fall out and splatter."

"I do," she says. "Feel betrayed."

He looks at her, his gaze serious. "I'm sorry."

"You've chosen to give me up," she says. Now that she has said the words she can feel it more.

"I can't give up my family," he says. "What I have now and what's to come. Imagine giving up your grandchildren."

The restaurant is cacophonous, the ceiling dark and low, the tables crowded. Near them is a group of all men, six or seven, shouting with laughter. They are big and hale, powerful, in their forties. They are all wearing suits, all without ties. When one of them speaks, the others all shout answers, drowning out each others' voices.

"They're so loud," Sarah says.

Warren nods.

One of the men stands up from the table, pushing his chair back. He moves around the crowded circle, and as he passes them he stops.

"Warren Jennings!" he says. His voice is congratulatory, as though Warren has achieved something.

Warren leans back, looking up. He smiles. "Henry McCain," he says. It's the man who wants the summer house.

"I thought you had to go back to Boston," says McCain, his gaze not sliding to Sarah, staying carefully on Warren.

"No, I stayed down here," Warren says. "Sarah Watson, Henry McCain. This is the man I met with this afternoon."

Sarah smiles up at him. "Nice to meet you," she says.

McCain is loosened by drink. He nods at Sarah, his shock of hair flopping on his forehead, his pitted face gleaming. "Well, I won't keep you. Talk to you soon." He nods to Sarah again and turns away, not quite steady. He heads across the room, threading his way through the tables.

Warren looks at Sarah. After a moment he says, "Nowhere's safe."

She nods. Who'd have thought they'd see someone they knew, here, in this noisy, midtown place? But it could be anywhere, at an airport, a small Caribbean hotel, on the street in London. They couldn't carry this on.

So it's ending. She would like to hold on to each moment, cradle it in her palm, mark it in some way as it slides past. How can she mark it?

"I wish we'd gone to Bucharest," she says.

He nods.

"I'm glad I didn't sell my house," she says. Though as she says it she wonders if she should have. Would that have made him stay?

He answers, "Me, too."

Everything they say is freighted with the sense of what will happen; as though they are sliding down a mountainside of scree, toward a cliff. They are moving slowly, but there is nowhere to stop, no ledge or sapling, nothing to stay their slide toward the edge.

During the night Sarah wakes often, shifting herself closer to him. She presses her back toward his chest, then turns herself around and presses her front against his. She can't find a comfortable place for her arm, though, and moves again, shifting around so her back is to him again.

He whispers into her hair, "Are you done shifting?" He's laughing, and he tightens his arms around her.

"Sorry," she says. She begins to cry, the tears warm on her cheeks, sliding onto the pillowcase. They must have hundreds of people crying on these pillows, she thinks. She tries not to move, not to allow a sob to shift herself in his arms, tries not to keep him awake, but then she does sob, and she turns around and faces him again, weeping. He puts his arms around her. As long as their bodies are close, as long as they can feel the beating of each other's hearts, it hasn't happened. Yet she can feel the great black chasm below.

Warren holds her against his chest, feeling the heat and softness of her body, the angles and hollows, the awkwardness of her knees against his. They lie like that, drifting, sleeping, and waking, twitching suddenly at some interior fright, then relaxing again, softening into their shared embrace.

In the morning they say little. Warren has to leave early.

"I want to go out first," she says. "I don't want to watch you leave me."

"Whatever you want," he says.

He stands by the bed as she walks to the door. She is carrying her small overnight case: This will bear witness, it has become a part of this. She glances around the room, which has now taken on a nostalgic cast: the stilled, waiting curtains, the glossy chest of drawers, the big square bed, disordered sheets. She will never be here with him again. This place in the universe is now banned to her. She is exiled.

"Okay," she says, flustered. " 'Bye."

His face is stricken by grief, it has worn at his features. She hardly recognizes him. "I love you."

She nods, and goes through the door, pulling it closed behind her. Her knees feel weak. She can't imagine how this can be happening. Outside in the hall, all is ordinary. She carries her bag in one hand, walking past the rows of closed white-paneled doors. The only sound is the susurration of her footsteps on the carpet. She is alone now. She can feel Warren behind her, standing by the big disordered bed. She stands before the elevator and pushes the flat disk. It yields against her pressure, lighting up. The elevator is coming. She stands, waiting. It is astonishing: everything seems so normal in the world.

Driving home, this could be any one of the times that she has driven home after seeing him. The weather has turned grim, the skies leaden. They seem to echo the industrial landscape: the high stiff lamps, the dark wet roadway, the littered shoulder, the grim concrete edging. She is in this place now. She turns up the heater. It blasts hot air in her face, leaving her ankles chilled. Time seems suspended; this is not over. She tells herself it is over. It seems impossible. She thinks of his face during dinner, how they had moved in and out of their shock, sometimes immobilized by it, sometimes outside it. Their eyes had met as they both heard a scrap of conversation in the next booth: a couple complaining about a house they'd rented in Marrakesh. "There was no good cheese," the woman said. "You couldn't find a slice of Brie in the whole country. Morocco." Sarah and Warren had both begun to laugh: the woman's whining, the idea that a country was required to imitate some other country in order to live up to a tourist's expectations; the fact that they were still, at that moment, together in that swift powerful current. They had rocked with laughter. She smiles now, remembering. It's all behind her now, all of the moments.

It begins to rain, or possibly, improbably, to sleet. Is that possible? Something is hitting the windshield in tiny driving pellets as she reaches the turn at the racetrack. No one is on the track now, it stretches bare and brown before the high empty stands. She turns on the windshield wipers. They are still chanting his name. She will have to teach them something new.

At home Bella comes out of the mudroom as Sarah pulls up in the driveway. Bella flattens her ears and licks her mouth discreetly, just a glimpse, a pale, flexible curl, wagging. Sarah begins to cry. She gets out of the car and crouches, weeping, beside the dog. At once Bella turns formal and solemn. She lowers her head next to Sarah's and Sarah puts her arm around Bella. But it's still raining, or sleeting, sluicing onto her face, and Sarah stands up and carries her bag into the house, Bella behind her. In the mudroom she hangs up her coat on the hook. She unlocks the door and goes into the kitchen. The room is dim, the light from the windows is cold and gray. The room is silent and cheerless, the bare counters, the austere cabinets, the rows of black-and-white photographs. She thinks of her children. She has never asked them for solace. She is filled with something, some unbidden emotion. It's not exactly a feeling but an absence: she is surrounded by gray mist. There is nowhere for her to turn. She leans over, then crouches down again to the floor. Bella moves toward her, elegant, intent, her ears cocked. Sarah puts her hands over her face.

She thinks of Tosca, and the aria she sings to her lover

Cavaradossi: of her little house, where they meet, hidden from the world. Don't you long for it, where we stood beneath the stars, and listened to the voices of the night? Don't you remember our love?

Here there is no comfort to be had. There is no place for her in the empty house, no person for her to reach for. The days lie before her, vacant.

PART III

Chapter 16

ON THE SHUTTLE BACK TO BOSTON WARREN FEELS AS THOUGH something has been torn from his body, something visceral. The sense of Sarah is still pulsing through him. He can't understand what he's done. He thinks of Kat, in her wedding dress; he thinks of Janet.

By the time the plane lands it's hot, summer-hot, though it's nearly October now. As he comes out of the airport, under the grimy concrete overhang, looking for a cab, the air presses against him, heavy and dead. His shirt is already sticking to his skin.

At the office the others look up when he comes in. Jack, Laurel, Mason, and Liz are all sitting at their desks, three or four of the others facing them across the open square. It's untenable, he sees it now. They can't sit like this, out in the open, under continual scrutiny, with no respite, no privacy. He should have the office redesigned, or they should move.

"Good morning," he says. He hangs up his coat, comes into the big room, and sits down. He feels himself begin to enter into the world of the office: the beautiful new buildings coming into being, each one freshly imagined, complex, fascinating. He feels the pull of it, the strong smooth current drawing him in. All of it interests him (yet part of him has been torn away from his side), and he sits down between Jack and Laurel. Laurel smiles.

"Welcome back," she says. "How was New York?"

"Good," he says. "McCain likes our plans."

Mason looks up. He's their lawyer. He has a neat ponytail that curls over the back of his collar and a gold stud in one ear. He has a sharp nose and pointed chin, sunken blue eyes. "Do we need to talk about that?" he asks. "Draw up a preliminary contract?"

Warren nods. How easily he sinks into this place, how strong the current is. How interesting these problems. "We do. Shall we go into the conference room and discuss?"

Laurel says, "Can I come?"

Warren nods, and the three of them move into the smaller room. All of them bring yellow legal pads, they all prefer writing by hand.

When they sit down, Warren says, "I was thinking we might reconfigure the space here. No one has any privacy now, and though it's good for projects, it's kind of exhausting. What do you think?"

Laurel looks at him consideringly. She is the most adaptable, always ready to absorb new ideas, not confrontational. "So you mean stay here?"

Mason, who has heard nothing about this, asks, "Is there a question of moving?"

Warren hesitates; he's no longer interested in moving. It had seemed important before, when he was in the grip of a powerful shift himself. But now he will have to move back into the house, back to Janet in her red robe, the gray kitchen. The move back seems monumental, he can't move the office as well.

"We talked about it. The rent is going up. But maybe we should just redesign what we have. Or see if there's extra space we could get on either side."

"Privacy would be good," Mason said. "So I can make a call to my dog without shame."

Warren and Laurel laugh; Mason doesn't have a dog. Warren asks Laurel to find out about more space.

In the evening he calls Janet from his apartment. He's lying on the bed, his stockinged feet crossed. By now the apartment feels normal and familiar. His clothes are in the closet, his books on the shelves, his food in the kitchen cabinets: Swedish flatbread, Uncle Ben's rice, salt. A half loaf of bread, a tin of sardines. He has pulled his life around him like a cloak; now he will dismantle it. He will return to his former life. He will embrace it.

When she answers he says, "Hi."

Her voice is cool and wary. "Hi."

"I thought we'd talk about how to do this."

"How to do what? You're moving back, right?"

"Right. I'm moving back."

"What do we need to talk about?"

"Timing. I've got more here than I can carry. I'm going to get someone with a van. I thought Saturday afternoon, if that's all right with you."

"Saturday's fine." She says this shortly, as if it makes no difference. She sounds faintly irritated, impatient.

There's a pause.

"Janet," he says. "I'm not coming back to be treated like an enemy. We have to agree about this."

There is another pause. "I want you to come back. But you have to want to."

It's impossible for him to answer. He must make it work. He swings his feet to the floor and sits up. He looks out the door, into the little hall. Janet waits. He has wounded and humiliated her. She won't say so, and he admires that. He must revivify whatever it was they had. He feels something inside him collapse, release toward her.

He is knitted into her, all those days and nights in which they were part of each others' lives. One night he'd woken up to hear her sobbing in the bathroom. He'd gone in to find her sitting on the edge of the bathtub, rocking back and forth, her face in her hands. She looked up when he came in, her face red and crumpled, gleaming with tears. He'd sat down beside her and put his arms around her. She sat sobbing helplessly, hunched like a small child. He can't remember what was the matter, only the sight of her face, startled and miserable.

That was part of their lives, and also the time on the river in Jamaica. The time she'd hired a jazz singer on his birthday. The time she'd organized a Mutt Show at their house in Maine, and everyone came. Their dog got into a fight with the neighbor's cocker spaniel and Janet had thrown a pitcher of ice water on them. The time on Nantucket when they'd taken a bike ride at dawn. They'd stopped to watch the sun come up, the fresh wind in their faces. He carries all this inside him, he can feel the weight of it, the size and breadth. Years and years. He can't go back to it while he's harboring resentment. He can't let that poison his life. He draws in a long breath.

He looks into the living room of his apartment, the sofa, the cushions mashed and crumpled. Light from the big windows falls across it. The place is silent. Outside, the city hums to itself. He thinks of this moment as his transition, he is crossing over. He's doing this for his family.

The thing is to do it fully and wholeheartedly, to embrace it without reservation. This is who he is, father and husband. This is his highest calling. This will allow him to be true to himself. It is a vow.

He thinks of Sarah, her unearthly pale blue eyes, her thick short hair. Her steady gaze. He is giving her up. He is putting her out of his life. He thinks of Katrina, sitting beside him on the sofa, shouting at the referee, her pliable limbs, her energy. Grinning at him. Grabbing his shoulders and shaking him when he disagrees. Her dopey glasses. He thinks of her the time when she'd been small, eight or nine, and she'd come into Warren's study one night. Solemn-faced, she stood by Warren's desk, a small spiral notebook in her hands. "I want you to help me do a budget," she said. "For my allowance." The time they'd gone canoeing in Maine and it had rained steadily for three days. They'd eaten dehydrated food poured from packets, crouched under the tarp, soaking wet.

Kat had been twelve then, not yet a teenager, staunch and good-natured. The second night, when they finished their awful meal, she said, "It's actually kind of delicious." They'd come around a bend in the river to see an eagle, flapping low over the surface of the water. He touched down with a splash, then flapped off again, rising, a dark shape twisting in his talons. Kat turned around to him, water dripping from the brim of her hat, to make sure he'd seen it. Her face was alight.

He can't give her up.

"Well, you can't come tonight," Janet says. "I don't have anything for dinner. Will you come tomorrow?"

He hadn't suggested tonight. He is irritated at once; he can't allow himself to be.

"Okay," he says. "See you tomorrow afternoon. Saturday."

He clicks off.

He thinks of Sarah's face. He wants to text her: Missing you.

But where would that end? He will either see her or not. If he's ending things he can't text her. She is closed to him now. She is alive, but he can't find her. He knows where she is, in her house. He pictures the rooms, the polished floors, the big sofas. It's twilight; maybe she's gone to the reservoir with Bella. No, he thinks it's raining. She's inside.

Chapter 17

WHEN HE ARRIVES, JANET IS STANDING IN THE FRONT HALL. He realizes she has been watching for him. As he comes inside, she smiles brightly, her head high. Her hands are in her pockets. She's dressed up, wearing bright green pants and a white blouse, gold earrings. Her eyes are darkened with mascara. He wonders if she's going out, then realizes that this is for him.

He comes inside and sets down his briefcase.

"Hi," he says.

"Hi." Her gaze seems fixed, her eyes wide, as though she's afraid to blink. She takes her hands from her pockets. "I'm glad you're back," she says. She touches the buckle of her narrow belt, nervously tracing the shape of it with one finger.

"Here I am."

He steps toward her. He has planned what he will do.

He must take her in his arms, though he can't bring himself to kiss her: she is not Sarah. He embraces her, holding her against his chest. It's not terrible: It's familiar. She's his wife. It's terrible that it's so familiar. His body knows hers. Holding her, he feels a sinking, dooming sensation, as though he is plunging through the air. This is familiar, and there is no end to it. This will be his life. He closes his eyes, he feels himself plummeting downward, and he tightens his grip. When she feels this—the tightening of his arms—she collapses against him with relief. She hugs him hard, holding him close, and he feels the thick pulse of her sob against his chest. Reflexively he tightens his arms, to comfort her. She is pressed against him, and the feel of her body, so familiar, and her deep sob, move him. Her pain thuds against his heart; he has caused it. The feel of her sobbing is terrible. He feels the heat of her body, the soft pressure of her breasts, the solid ribs, her animal presence. The grief and pain of these past months wash over him: he has caused all this. He feels shame and contrition. He bows his head, leaning in against hers. He moves his hands across her back, stroking and comforting. He is making amends. He is returning to her, he is rejoining his family. That thought breaks him: it's a life sentence. A sob rises in his own chest. They hold each other as though drowning. Now Janet weeps freely against him, deep exhausting shudders, and he moves his hands across her back. He holds her close, feeling the life he wanted dissolve against this urgency and grief and love. Holding her, he can't help himself: he gives his own sob for that lost life.

But now he's aware of the imminence of the movers' arrival. They were right behind him. He steps back, gently disentangling himself—he still can't bring himself to kiss her—and looks at his watch. "The movers will be here any minute." He turns to look out the window, and opens the big inner door. She wipes her eyes carefully, because of the mascara, but now she's smiling and relieved. She crosses her arms on her chest.

"Who'd you get to move you?"

"Some kids," he says. "Laurel found them."

The van pulls up into the driveway. It's white, dirty, and battered, with no lettering on the side. The movers jump out and come up to the door, two dark-skinned young guys in jeans and hoodies. They wear dirty sneakers with the laces undone. The driver has a round cherubic face, his hair cut in a stiff flattop, nearly shaved on the sides. Warren opens the door to greet them.

Yesterday's heat is over. Today is sunny and crisp, the air cool. The trees have begun to turn, the sugar maples to radiant yellow, the ashes to bronzy-mauve. Autumn has moved into the landscape.

"Hey," the driver says, grinning. "We found you."

"Great," Warren says.

They carry the boxes up the walk and into the front hall: a wardrobe, some cartons of books and papers. They carry the wardrobe upstairs, calling to each other, laughing. "More this way!" and "Dude, no!"

Warren goes up with them. In the bedroom he sees them look around: the two bureaus, the two closets. He wonders what they're thinking: Is it obvious, what's happening? Do they know they've brought him back from an attempted breakout? Do they think he's arriving for the first time, the new boyfriend? I'm back home, he tells himself. "Thanks," he says. He won't elucidate.

They jog down the stairs, shoelaces flopping.

Down in the front hall Warren pays, counting out the bills, adding a tip.

"Thanks," the driver says. He's beaming, cheerful. He folds the money and tucks it into his pocket. He looks at Janet, wanting to add something. He nods politely. "Have a good life," he says.

"Thank you," she says. "You, too."

They walk bouncily down the stone path. The driver says something and the other guy doubles up, choking with laughter. They climb into the van, now facing Warren and Janet through the windshield, their faces now sober. The driver lifts his hand before turning around to back out. Warren waves. Janet would have hired a real moving company, with a name and an insurance policy. But he likes these guys, entrepreneurs who need the money. This awareness—his disagreement with Janet—shifts him away from her again.

Warren closes the door and turns to face her. Now his manner is cool. He's not going to talk about it, he won't apologize. By coming back he has canceled any debt he'd acquired by leaving.

He's back, that's all. He won't tolerate recriminations. He nods at Janet and goes upstairs to unpack.

The days fall back into a pattern. They have dinner in the kitchen. He hears about the wedding, about the plans for it. They have moved it from Maine to Boston, from June to February. Janet is in her element, busy and excited, full of opinions—how do women know so much about weddings?—making lists, helping Kat choose the invitations, the dress, the bridesmaids. Menus.

In the morning he leaves before Janet comes down. He gets coffee and a muffin at a stand near the garage where he parks at work.

One day he sends Sarah a text: The Southie in the building department approved their plan. She writes back, Yay! Then she writes, Are we still talking? He writes, I guess not. Sorry. I misspoke.

She writes, I won't answer, then.

Sorry, he writes. But still he writes to her, now and then. He doesn't suggest that they meet. But he sends his thoughts. He can't help it.

One afternoon she is at the museum, meeting with Jean and Nancy. They've hired a designer for the installation and a publisher for the catalogue. They're discussing insurance, which is complicated.

"We may have to pay a higher premium," Jean says. "These are valuable, and they're traveling internationally. I'll need the total value of all of them."

"We'll get you that," says Sarah. She makes a note in her book.

"And what about the essay?" Jean asks.

"It's problematic," says Sarah. "I'd like your advice. The first scholar we asked, Barbara Schwarzman, was so unresponsive we finally just stopped trying to reach her and approached someone else. Now she has come back with a brilliant proposal. The other scholar has said she's interested, but hasn't said what she'd write about."

"What have you said to the second? Do we have a contract?"

asks Jean. "If we have a contract, there's nothing we can do, we have to turn down Schwarzman."

"We don't have a formal contract. We asked the other one—Louisa Hargraves—if she'd be interested and she said yes. It's awkward if we have to tell her now that we're not interested. And Schwarzman is difficult—after the way she behaved, I'm not sure that she'd turn the essay in on time. She's just difficult."

"Did you talk to anyone else who's worked with her?" Jean asks. "This might just be a temporary situation. I'd ask around."

"We did that," Nancy says. "Apparently she's always difficult, often brilliant."

"What's the wording of the letter to Hargraves?" Jean asks.

Sarah looks for it. As she searches, a text arrives from Warren. She reads it quickly and gives a little cough of laughter. Then she looks up, embarrassed.

Jean and Nancy are watching her.

"Sorry," she says, sitting up straighter and frowning. She finds the letter.

" 'We would like to know if you'd be interested in writing an essay for our upcoming show, Bloomsbury and Its Circle. We'd like the text to be between two thousand and three thousand words, and the list of artists is below. We're familiar with your excellent work in this area, and would like to explore the possibility of working with you on this project.' " She looks at Jean.

"And what did she say?"

"She said she'd be very interested. That's where we are. How can I write her now and say, 'Just kidding'?"

"I think we'd better go with Hargraves," Jean says. "That's more or less a contract. We'll just have to tell Schwarzman that since we hadn't heard from her we'd moved ahead elsewhere."

Nancy says, "We may alienate Schwarzman. What if she's had back surgery or something and couldn't respond earlier?"

"We're not responsible for that," Jean says. "We had to move on."

"But her essay sounded fascinating," Sarah says.

"It sounds as though you want her," Jean says.

"It's about a covert, cryptic French influence on the group, one which they didn't acknowledge themselves, since they were English, and insular, and anti-French. I thought it was really interesting."

"Okay, then," Jean says. "If that's what you want, let's figure out a way to make it happen."

"Okay," Sarah says. "I'll come up with the wording and send it to you."

They go on talking about the exhibition. Sarah is thinking of Warren, and his text. Hasn't he said they are finished? Are they finished? She had felt a quicksilver shaft of delight at the sight of his name on the screen.

Afterward she and Nancy walk outside. It's cooler now, though still not cold. The leaves are changing, but languidly, and the air is torpid: the seasons are no longer orderly but random. They stand at the top of the stairs going down to the parking lot. The afternoon sun is slanting through the trees, a hot orange beam against their faces.

Nancy asks, "How's it going with your guy?"

Sarah looks at her. "It's over," she says. "His daughter made him break it off."

Nancy stares at her. "What? How is that possible?"

"It's possible. He's broken it off. Because of her." Saying the words out loud is a shock, like being slit open.

Nancy opens her mouth, then closes it and shakes her head. "I'm so sorry. I'm so sorry."

Sarah nods. "Thank you. That was from him, the text I read. It was nothing. I just couldn't help but read it. I know it was rude, sorry."

"No, I get it," Nancy says. She runs her hand through her short white hair. "I'm so sorry." She looks into Sarah's eyes. "And you—did you think of talking to his kid yourself?"

"Me?" Sarah widens her eyes. "What would that do? She hates the idea of me. What could I say, 'Don't you want your father to be happy?' She wants her mother to be happy."

"But," Nancy says, "how is it her decision?"

Sarah squints into the sun. "I can't control it." She doesn't want to talk about it. "I have to go."

"I'm so sorry," Nancy says, and puts her hand on Sarah's shoulder. "That kid is a shit."

"I don't know if she is," she says. "She's protecting her mother. Would I want my kids to do that, in their place? Probably I would. I have to go," she says again.

Inside her car she closes the door on the world, sealing herself into privacy. She is so used to being by herself, so used to leaving people outside, closing the door on them. It's her way of being safe, but just now she feels alone. She puts on her seat belt, snugging herself against the seat. She feels solitary and adrift.

That night, lying in bed, Sarah thinks, I wouldn't have read it if I hadn't been hoping he wanted to see me. That's what I'm hoping for. She turns over, remembering how it felt to sleep next to him. How he had held her even while he was asleep, his arms tightening around her if she shifted position.

Bella stands up, across the room. She moves quietly to the bed, the metal tags on her collar making a tiny jingling sound. She sets her head on the mattress, near Sarah's face. She presses close. Sarah strokes her head, sleek and warm. She feels the hard skull beneath the silky pelt and begins to cry. It seems unbearable that it should be Bella who offers her this tenderness.

Chapter 18

SARAH AND MEG ARE AT A CROWDED RESTAURANT NEAR MEG'S office. Their table is in the back, and the noise is deafening. All the surfaces are hard—no curtains, no carpeting, no tablecloths—and everyone is shouting. Sarah leans forward, trying to hear. The older she is, the less tolerance she has for noise; a headache flickers at the back of her skull. She has asked Meg to lunch because she wants to tell her about Warren, about the end of Warren. She hasn't told her yet because she still can't really believe it herself. She has kept thinking that Warren will find a way out of this, that he will tell his daughter that she has no right to make this demand. Or something. She keeps thinking of his face when he told her, hollowed by grief. It can't be real, she thinks, over and over, it can't be through. She needs to tell someone about it, though she's not sure it should be her daughter.

Meg sits on the banquette, her swelling belly pressed against the edge of the table. Her face has become full and round, her fine silky hair is lank. Her sweater is unbecoming, a harsh green, with a cowl neck. Her coat is crumpled on the cushion behind her; Sarah's is on her chair. November, and it's finally gotten cold.

"How are you feeling?" Sarah asks. They've ordered soup and sandwich. Meg keeps looking at her watch. She picks up a pretzel stick and takes a bite, crunching noisily.

"Okay, I guess," Meg says. "The way I always feel at six months. I don't throw up in the morning but I can't sleep at night. I feel restless all the time, and my legs twitch at night. Cramp, actually. Already none of my clothes fit but I'm not ready for the back-of-the-bus tent clothes."

"You'll manage," Sarah says. "You look beautiful." And she does, despite the lank hair and harsh green. She is luminous, with that pregnant-woman glow.

Meg looks down at the table. She lifts her spoon and shifts it to one side. "I don't know," she says. "Maybe it was a bad idea."

"Getting pregnant? Of course not," Sarah says. "It won't be long. And you will love this baby."

"I know I will," says Meg. Her face crumples and she raises both hands to cover it. She begins to cry without sound.

Sarah leans across the table, taking hold of her shoulder, rubbing it awkwardly. "Lovey," she says, "don't. Don't. It will be all right."

But Meg is sobbing, her whole body shaking. "I don't know," she says. "I'm afraid it won't."

"What do you mean?" Sarah rubs her shoulder.

Meg shakes her head and takes her hands down from her face, which is red and rumpled. Her eyes are streaming, her mouth contorted. "I have these, I don't know, premonitions," she says. "I'm afraid everything will go wrong." She crumples again, opening her mouth soundlessly. She covers her face.

"Sssh, shhhh," says Sarah, rubbing her shoulder. "Everyone thinks that, everyone has these frightening thoughts. It's normal. It's normal. Don't be scared."

Meg keeps her face down. "No, this isn't the same," she says. "It's really awful."

"I know," Sarah says. "I know."

Meg twists away from her hand. "You have no idea." She shakes her head, looking down. "You have no idea."

Sarah can see the horror in her daughter's trembling body, her shuddering shoulders. She feels the fear in her own body, the visceral tremor. But she wants to be calm.

"This will go away," she says. "This will go away."

"You have no idea," says Meg. She won't raise her eyes.

The waitress arrives, and Meg straightens. The soup is set down before her and she sniffs largely, swiping at her nose.

"Thank you," Sarah says to the waitress, who smiles as she turns away. They must see this all the time, Sarah thinks, tears, arguments, rage, sorrow. Meals are meant for revelations. She takes a spoonful of her soup.

"This is good. Try a little," she says.

"Don't treat me like a child," Meg says, but she picks up her spoon. "There's no salt."

"I'm not," Sarah says. "It's just that food changes things." She leans over to the next table, which has just been vacated. She takes the salt and pepper and puts them in front of Meg.

Meg shakes her head darkly, dismissing the idea that her feelings have anything to do with soup, but she lifts her spoon. Sarah doesn't expect her to talk. She can feel the reverberations in her own body; those fears that are too frightening to speak aloud. They have some superstitious charge. It's dangerous to let them loose in the world.

They're both eating now.

"I'm sorry you're having such a hard time," Sarah says. "But this will go away. I promise."

Meg shakes her head, her face still red and crumpled. She takes a spoonful of the soup, swallows, and sighs largely.

"You think it's hormones," she says, "but it's not. It's something else."

Sarah nods. She does think it's hormones.

"Or I guess it is hormones, too, but it's not just that. It's something huge. I can't describe it."

"I'm sorry," Sarah says. She feels inadequate to this, whatever is taking over her daughter.

"I hate this part of it. When I just get bigger and bigger. I feel like a bus, I can't fit into anything. I feel as though people don't see me. I've become invisible, I'm not a part of the world right now. I'm the body that's wrong, that isn't human. People look right past me, as though I no longer have a face, only a belly." Her voice is full of tears again.

"That's not true," Sarah says. "Or even if it is, it's just that people don't know how to see pregnancy. We've hidden it in this society for so long. It's threatening."

"Thank you, Mom! Now I'm not just invisible, I'm a threat! And don't go all feminist on me."

Sarah shakes her head. She touches Meg's wrist. "You're not a threat. Don't think about what anyone else thinks. Think about Jeff and your kids. That's the center of your world. They love you. I do, too. Everything else is irrelevant."

Meg takes a bite of her sandwich. "I know you're right," she says, "but I don't feel it. I feel as though I'm crosswise to the whole world right now. I'm in outer space somewhere. I'm not connected to anything."

"It will get better, I promise. Just get through this. Hold on to that."

Meg sighs, a long, deep exhalation. She settles against the banquette. "I know. I know. I didn't mean to land all this on you." She looks around, eyes still full of tears, as though to reconnect with the world. "This is an awful table," she says dully. She wipes one eye. "I hate people who ask for better tables."

Sarah nods. "Me, too."

"Sorry. I know you didn't come here to hear all my hormone-induced craziness." Meg gives her a watery smile.

"You're not remotely crazy," Sarah says, though she is still unsettled by the currents of Meg's fear running through her.

"So? How are you doing? What's going on with you and Warren?" Meg asks. She seems shaken but determined. She picks up her sandwich and takes a huge bite.

"Well, yeah," Sarah says. "I did want to tell you something."

"What?" asks Meg, chewing.

"It's over," Sarah says, and it's surprising how the spoken words rouse feeling. She feels her throat close over them. This is what she must say, she has no choice.

"What? Why?" Meg is roused too.

"His daughter told him to," Sarah says.

Meg sets down her sandwich. "How can she do that? She can't do that." She stares at her mother. "How dare she? It's his life. What a disgusting weasel. What happened?"

"His daughter is getting married," Sarah says. "She told him he can't come to the wedding, and she will expel him from her life if he goes through with the divorce."

"It's blackmail," Meg says. "How can it possibly work? If he doesn't want to be married to his wife, how can his daughter make him be happy married to her?"

Sarah shakes her head. She is now crying.

Meg puts her hand on Sarah's wrist. "This is unbelievable," she says. "I can't believe her temerity."

Sarah likes the word temerity; it gives this importance. But she can't speak. She shakes her head, then clears her throat.

"Her name is Katrina. He adores her."

"Well, he shouldn't. She's a horrible weasel."

Sarah looks down at the tablecloth. "The thing is . . ." she begins, but she doesn't know how to go on. Is she speaking as a mother or a friend? The thing is that the older you are, the more important your children are to you. The children become necessary to survival, but saying so sounds like a plea for pity. Does she want to tell Meg? It's so naked, it makes Sarah seem so weak. But the fact is that, at this stage in life, your child can ask you for anything and get it. All those old reasons for standing firm—rules, consistency, judgment, principles—have evaporated. What you want is your child before you.

Once she and Meg had had a shouting argument on the phone, and Meg had screamed at her, "Fuck you! Just fuck you!" The words had entered Sarah's mind like knives. She hadn't replied. She had hung up, shaken. How could she answer that? It was the worst thing in the world.

When Meg called back to apologize, Sarah wouldn't let her discuss it. "It's over," she said. "It's okay." Meg paused, expecting to explain, to apologize further, but Sarah couldn't bear it. She couldn't bear another second of that thought. She wanted all discord in the past. Fighting with her daughter was like walking through the inferno. "It's fine," she said. "It's over. Don't say anything more."

Sarah would have forgiven her anything. Meg had all the power now. As you age, your power dissipates. You understand that a time will come when you need physical support from your child, as well as emotional comfort. When that time comes, will your child set you on the ice floe, or bring you in beside her hearth?

So now she doesn't quite want to tell Meg why Warren's daughter is able to take control.

"I can't believe this," Meg says. She takes another spoonful of soup, watching her mother. "I'm sorry, but he must be a complete weenie if he lets her get away with it. You're better off without him."

"He is not a weenie," Sarah says.

Meg holds both palms up in the air, resting her case.

"He doesn't want to lose his daughter," Sarah says. "His grandchildren. He'd be cut off forever. I can't imagine it."

"I can't imagine doing it," says Meg. "It is unspeakably cruel." Now her energy is directed toward Warren's daughter. "She can't make him feel something he doesn't feel. What will it be like? 'Here's Dad, in handcuffs. Let's take them off so he can carve the turkey.'"

Sarah sighs. "I know. I can't imagine it, either. I think it's breaking his heart."

"Do you hear from him?"

"I get texts every once in a while. Each time I see his name I get excited and I think he's coming back. I can't help it. My little heart goes pitter-pat. But he isn't. Stupid, isn't it?"

"Mom." Meg puts her hand on Sarah's wrist. "This is awful. How can she be so mean?"

"I guess she's just protecting her mother," Sarah says.

"It's not protecting her by bringing a hostage into her house. Does she not notice that he's being blackmailed?"

"He's trying to make the best of it," Sarah says. "He's an honorable man. He's made a promise. I think that's what he's thinking." She nods at the table, then raises her eyes to Meg.

"But how far had you two gotten? I mean, you were talking about moving in together, right?" She shakes her head. "Getting married?"

"Yes," Sarah says. "We had." She laughs. "We'd gotten to the practical part. He has this collection of wooden bird decoys. Ducks and geese and waterbirds. We were trying to figure out where they would go. They take up a lot of room."

"The decoy collection," Meg nods. "How many does he have?"

Sarah shrugs. "I've never seen them. Maybe dozens?" She has imagined them, those still avian forms, rough, dark, or painted and polished, carrying that strange mixed charge of celebration and violence. "Now I'll never see them." This realization wounds her. She will no longer know him, she will have no further portal to his life. She will never see his house in Maine. She'd felt some kind of hope when she raised this subject with Meg, as though Meg might come up with a solution she hadn't thought of. But now she sees there is no solution, she will never see anything more of Warren, his life is closed to her. She lowers her head and gives a little gulp of a sob.

"Mom," Meg says, rubbing her mother's wrist with her thumb. "I'm so sorry."

Sarah nods. "Thank you." She looks up, around the room, at the roaring crowd, the hurrying waiters. Her eyes are still full of tears. "We're a great pair."

Later, from the car, she calls Josh. It always goes to voice mail, and she says, "Just checking in. When can we talk?" It usually takes hours, if not days, to set up a call, but this time he calls her back at once.

"Mom," he says. "What's up?"

Sarah's unprepared, and she begins to cry again. She can't speak for a bit. When she does manage to say it—"That guy I told you about—Warren—it's over"—she's crying harder.

Josh doesn't judge. "I'm really sorry, Mom," he says. "I'm really sorry. This is really hard on you. What happened?"

"His daughter. She made him go back to his wife."

"Whoa. So he was married?" Josh asks.

"Is married. But unhappily. He was getting divorced." She sniffs. "Doesn't that sound absurd? A cliché. Like every story you've ever heard."

But he ignores this. "I'm so sorry, Mom," he says again. "That sucks."

"Thanks, Joshie," she says. It helps, sort of, to hear him say that, but it doesn't help.

Chapter 19

A SATURDAY MORNING IN THE KITCHEN, JANUARY.

Katrina and Chris have come up for the weekend and they are all having breakfast together, and this, right now, is the whole point. This is why he's given up Sarah and come back home to Janet: so he'd see his daughter whenever she turned up. Now he's back in the center of this warm loose drifting core, made by a web of connections, by all the ways in which they have come to know each other over the years. The time they swam in the river in Jamaica. The time Kat fell out of the tree and broke her arm. The time Warren had taken two-year-old Kat into the surf on Long Island and a wave had taken her right out of his arms and he had stood for a second, stunned and terrified, and the next wave had restored her to him, washing her small soft body right onto his chest.

Janet is sitting at one end of the table. She's still in her bathrobe, which is navy-blue with white piping. She holds a half-filled coffee mug, her plate littered with toast crumbs. Before her is an open folder. Katrina sits beside her, wearing a T-shirt, hoodie, and black yoga pants. Her bare feet are hooked over the chair rung, and she and Janet are talking about the wedding. Chris, the reason for all these lists and conversations, sits next to Katrina. He's wearing a V-neck sweater and real pants, which is a plus from Warren's point of view, but his cheeks are covered in stubble, a minus. He's scrolling on his cell phone.

Warren sits at the other end of the table with his laptop. He's looking over the proposal for a new property, half listening to Janet and Kat.

"Bridesmaids," Janet says. "Have you decided about Serena or not?"

"I love Serena," Katrina says. She licks her thumb and presses it onto a toast crumb on her plate. The crumb sticks to her thumb and she licks it off.

"But you don't want her. Which is okay," Janet says. Her pen is poised, ready to cross out Serena.

"I didn't say that," Kat says. "I love Serena. But if I ask her, then I have to ask Kate. And then I'm screwed. It's too many."

"Don't overthink it," Janet says. "They'll understand."

"Mom, they won't," Kat says. "You have no idea. Kate will go nuts. She's paranoid, she always thinks we're leaving her out."

Janet glances up. "And are you?"

"Not exactly," Kat says. "There's no 'we,' anyway. We're not joined at the hip. High school is over. We do things separately." She shakes her head. "But then Kate finds out and she accuses us of leaving her out."

"What do you think?" Warren asks Chris. "Are they leaving her out?"

Chris looks up, startled. He's lean and narrow-shouldered, with very pale skin. His hair is curly and dense. His glasses constantly slide down his nose. He's quiet. Warren doesn't know if he's daunted by their family, or if he's really just quiet.

"What do I think?" Chris repeats.

Warren nods. "Do you know Kate and Alison? Do you know this coven of powerful women?" Warren has known them for years, they are Kat's high school friends.

Chris glances at Kat. He clears his throat. "I've met them all, I think."

Warren prompts him. "And? Impressive, don't you think?"

"Very," says Chris. He pushes his glasses up on his nose. "You definitely want them on your side."

Kat looks at him. "They are on your side," she says bossily. "Because I am on your side."

Chris cocks his head. "I can imagine them making up their own minds. Regardless of your position." He has a mild, deadpan manner.

Kat pauses. She wants to disagree with him, keep control, but she can't actually contradict him. "They do make up their own minds," she allows.

"And what do they think of Chris?" Warren asks her. "I bet they like him."

"Of course they do," Kat says. "They love him. We all spent a long drunken evening talking about how much we loved Chris."

Chris looks at her. "You never told me that."

"Yes, I did," Kat says.

"When was it?"

"Last year sometime. We went to that Thai place. I kept calling you to say I'd be home soon, and each time I called I was drunker."

Chris laughs. "Oh yeah."

Kat imitates herself. "Hi, honey. Just want to let you know, I'm coming back soon, we're just having one more drink. Love you! Mwah!" She kisses the air.

Janet laughs, and says to Chris, "You couldn't have a better confirmation hearing than that!"

Chris shakes his head. "She has no idea what they said. None."

Kat nudges his shoulder with hers. "I do have an idea what they think."

"But no idea what they said that night."

"No," she concedes. "I was hammered."

He looks at his cell, then up at Warren. "I do like them, as a matter of fact. They're all great."

"What about your friends?" asks Janet. She picks up her mug.

"Do they like Kat?" She takes a sip, looking over the rim at Chris. There's only one answer to this question from the mother of the bride.

Chris nods solemnly. "They do."

"Your friends love me," Kat says. "Except for Tim. He hates me."

"He doesn't hate you," Chris says. "He's reserved. He takes a while to warm up."

"Like, a geological age." Kat looks at Janet. "He's never spoken to me."

"Not true," Chris said. "He asked you to open the car door, that time it was locked from the inside."

"You're right. I'd forgotten," she says. "He's a charmer."

"Okay," Janet says. "So I'm assuming he won't be an usher. Groomsman," she corrects herself. "I don't know why you say 'groomsman' now. It sounds like a vaudeville performer."

"It's what you say now, Mom," Kat says. "That's why."

"Oh, because I'm old," Janet says. "That's why."

"Kind of," says Kat.

They've been talking for hours. There is an endless list of things to be decided: parking at the church and at the club, flowers, food, wine. The bridal dinner, the guest lists. It's a subject that energizes them, Warren sees. They are both happy to be making their way through this rich and crowded souk, each new topic complicated and fascinating and important. He's seen a photograph of Kat in the dress, which is lustrous, narrow, slinky. She's beaming and shy, her hair falling down her bare neck. Chris is not allowed to see.

Warren goes back to his screen, looking at building plans. He stops listening until he hears the tenor shift. Kat's voice is rising.

"I don't care," she says to Janet. "I don't want to do it."

"Kat, everyone expects you in the receiving line," Janet says. "It's part of the wedding."

"I'm not going to do it," Kat says.

"But people want to see you personally, it's important to them. All my friends will want to kiss you."

"They can do that another time," Kat says. "Or they can find me on the dance floor."

"Why would you make them do that?"

"I don't know why you don't get this."

"But why don't you want to do it?"

"It's so old-fashioned! I don't want to stand in line for a hundred hours greeting people I hardly know."

"You'll know everyone," Janet says. "If they don't know you well, they know me, which is why they'll be there. Or they'll be friends of Chris's parents."

"I don't want to spend the afternoon saying hello to your friends," Kat says, her voice rising.

"You've been to lots of weddings with reception lines," Janet says. "What is this?"

But something has rattled Kat. She slaps the flat of her hand on the table. Chris looks up, startled. "It's for you, not for me. I'm not doing it," she says. "I feel like a prize chicken, being walked around on a chain. This is my wedding!"

There is a silence. After a moment Chris goes back to scrolling on his phone.

"Chris doesn't want to do it, either, do you?" Kat says.

Chris looks up: everyone is looking at him. "Uh," he says. "I will honestly do whatever Kat wants."

Janet blinks with annoyance. "Kat, this is part of any wedding. You ask everyone to come, you want the community there, to make it real, but you don't want to give them a moment with you? It's rude, Katrina."

"It's not your wedding." Kat stands, shoving her chair back. "I don't want to do it."

Janet sets down her mug. "Of course it's your wedding. But your father and I have a part in it. We're putting it on, as a matter of fact."

"Is this a threat? You won't pay for it if I don't do what you want?"

"Don't act like that!" Janet says. "Of course it's not a threat."

Her own voice is rising. "How can you be like this? Why are you so uncooperative? I've been working on this for months."

"How long do you think I've been working on it?" Kat says. Chris puts his hand on her wrist; she yanks away.

"Kat," Janet says.

"Anyway, I don't even think anyone will come," Kat says. "It's February. People won't even come. And Alison is mad at me."

Warren stands. "Kat," he says, "wait a minute. Of course they'll come."

Kat turns to him. "Don't you get into it. You're still cheating on Mom."

Everyone goes still. They are all looking at Kat.

"What?" Warren says.

"You're still seeing her."

"I am not." He is telling the truth, but somehow his heart has suddenly risen, hammering against his ribs, as though he's lying.

"I looked at your laptop. Your emails. Your texts," Kat says. She folds her arms across her chest. "I know you're still in touch with her."

"What are you talking about?" Warren says. "You spied on me?"

"To make sure you weren't doing again what you'd done before."

"How dare you do that," he says. He's disgusted at the idea of her fingering through his emails. "When did you do it? How?"

"Last night. You left your laptop down here and I know your password."

She does know his password, so does Janet, and he knows theirs. He remembers the conversation, all of them laughing. Janet's was "pigtail," Kat's was "wonderwoman." His was "mountdesert." He's disgusted at the idea that he can't trust his daughter with his password.

"I did it because we can't trust you," Kat says. But she is no longer confident.

"And so now I can't trust you," Warren says. "That is contemptible."

He is disgusted by what she has done, but he is aware, from the behavior of his heart, which is still hammering against his chest, that he is not wholly innocent. Whatever the messages said, they were a means of maintaining contact. They were a silken thread between them.

Kat waits, her arms folded.

Janet says, "Is this true?" She's asking Warren.

"That I sent her some texts? Yes. That's not a crime," Warren says. "Or a betrayal. I haven't seen her again, or suggested it."

"You said you'd stop seeing her," Janet says.

"I have stopped seeing her. I've kept my promise," he says. "And I won't be investigated, Kat."

"Why were you texting her?" asks Kat. She is no longer angry, she's now aggrieved, wounded.

"Friendship," Warren says, but as he says the word he knows it's wrong.

"You aren't supposed to be friendly with her, Dad," Katrina says. "How can you go on doing this?"

Chris has frozen. His eyes are locked on his cell phone, but he is not scrolling. He is waiting for this to be over. He doesn't dare move.

"I can't believe you went through my computer," Warren says. "I don't even know if that's legal."

"It is if you have reason to believe a crime is being committed," Kat says. "In this case, I did. Adultery."

"Adultery is not a crime," Warren says. "It's barely a misdemeanor."

"It is actually a crime in Massachusetts," Kat says. But she's no longer challenging; something else is taking her over. "You've been writing to her." She is near tears. "Why did you do this?" Her face breaks up and she begins to cry, tears flooding her crumpled cheeks. "How can we trust you ever again?"

If he were to be honest, he did harbor some hope of seeing Sarah again. Somewhere he had held that hope out for himself, in some other life, some other galaxy. That's what those texts were for, he knows that. To normalize things, to make correspondence easy, so that sometime in the future when he went to New York he might have lunch with her, perfectly innocently. Was that it? Was he preparing himself to meet her again? What was he planning, deep in the interior of his mind, for his body?

The kitchen is silent. All three of them are looking at him, with that question hanging in the air. How can we trust you again? Janet looks like a schoolchild. She is still and erect in her blue robe, her mug held in both hands. Her face is raised, her eyes search his gaze. Kat, still standing, has crammed her hands into her pockets, her face streaming with tears. Chris is frozen, his fingers stilled. Janet and Kat are looking at Warren: only he can answer this question. The existence of the family depends on his reliability. His integrity.

Now he feels shame about those brief, intimate texts, referring to shared knowledge, a conversation, a book they'd both read. A joke they remembered. Each one a stitch in the long seam of connection. He should have known this. Nausea rises within him.

"I never have seen her again," he says; then he adds, "I won't get in touch with her again."

The three of them are still silent. They are fixed, watching him, waiting for what will come next.

What he'd like to do is take Kat in his arms and comfort her, but he's lost the right to do that. Not even Janet would let him hold her now. He understands that this will take years.

PART IV

Chapter 20

SUNDAY

Meg lies back on the pillows. The upper half of her bed is raised so she can watch TV.

Beside the bed is the metal IV stand, with a transparent bag full of clear liquid. A narrow tube snakes from the bag to a vein in Meg's inner arm, where it vanishes beneath tape. The blue hospital gown covers the huge mound of her belly.

Meg's beauty is voluptuous, like a courtesan's: milky, lustrous skin, wide, pillowy lips, and thick dark glossy hair. But now she's messy and disheveled, her hair tumbled around her shoulders, sheets and pillows aslant. She's wearing skinny glasses instead of contacts. She has quit thinking about her looks. Her body has been completely taken over by pregnancy. Everything else is irrelevant now, compared to the vast swollen hill made by the incipient baby.

Meg, Jeff, and Sarah are watching curling, which none of them had ever seen, in the Olympics.

"I've never seen a sport that's so slow," Sarah says. "It's even slower than golf. Glacial."

"I love the way they sweep the ice in front of the thing as it's sliding," Meg says. "The puck, or whatever it's called."

"Kettle," Jeff says. Of course he knows the name.

"Mm." Meg's voice is faint, as though she's talking from a distance. "I love the idea of guys sweeping."

Meg is in a private room in the maternity ward. It has a long window, two visitors' chairs, and a wide windowsill for books, flowers, cards, piled winter coats.

They are waiting for the delivery, which will happen tomorrow. The countdown began at midday, when Meg was hooked up to the IV. Synthetic hormones began sliding into her veins, sending a complicated series of signals to receptors deep inside her body.

The hospital is taking charge. The doctors are taking over from the body, which hadn't performed so well before. Birth is nature's way of making sure the species survives, but it's a pretty sloppy method. Nature is casual about her resources, running through her supplies with abandon, discarding the mothers. Before antibiotics, childbirth was a common cause of maternal fatality. Mothers bled to death, or died from infections or puerperal fever, as though all nature really cared about was the small morsel of new life, not the shelter for that life. With antibiotics, the maternal fatality rate has dropped: infections and puerperal fever are now easy to treat, though catastrophic hemorrhaging is still a major cause of death.

Everything is going smoothly here, the contractions are on schedule. It's like getting on a train: You'll reach your destination just by sitting in your seat. By tomorrow the baby will be here. It's kind of miraculous.

The Olympics are perfect because of their shared state of idleness, impatience, muted anxiety. Their need for distraction. On the screen are the excited crowds, the tiny, busy figures rushing back and forth. But at any moment this can all be turned off, and the center of the world will return here, to the maternity ward.

"Do you think these guys practice at home?" Meg asks. "'Honey, I need to borrow the broom.'" She stops, frowning.

She has left them. Her eyes are closed, and she draws a long, important breath. Pain has entered the room. No matter how much the doctors are in charge, they can't prevent this. Meg breathes slowly, a faint hissing on the intake, a rushing on the out. Jeff, beside her, takes her hand. Sarah is at the foot of the bed, out of reach.

They watch her, the TV forgotten. Meg has left them. Her face is focused and intent. Her huge belly rises and falls.

When the contraction is over, Meg leans back and opens her eyes. Her dark hair has silver-gray glints: she's old for this, thirty-seven. But healthy.

Meg shakes her head. "That was a big one."

Sarah smiles encouragingly, Jeff rubs her hand. Meg gives them a peaceful, reentry look. They turn again to the TV.

The crowd is noisy: Another team floods onto the ice. A loud official voice makes announcements. Dark figures move across the pale surface. A player crouches, then slides into a static lunge, holding the kettle in front of him, as they both move languidly across the white expanse. When he releases the moving kettle, figures rush forward to sweep in front of it.

"They're not actually doing anything, are they?" Sarah asks. "With the brooms? It looks completely pointless."

"They're probably making some slight changes to the surface," Jeff says, nodding as though he were agreeing, which he is not. "Temperature, smoothness—not much, but enough to matter in the Olympics."

"You must be right," Sarah says. Jeff corrects whatever she says. She thinks he does this out of competitiveness. Meg is at the center of both their worlds: Sarah's only daughter, Jeff's only wife. She thinks he wants supremacy, wants to prove that his world has won. She doesn't think he's aware of this.

A nurse comes in with a tray. Soup and juices: Meg is on a liquid diet, a precaution against the remote possibility of surgery. Everything is so carefully monitored, unfolding in synchrony, like the opening of a flower.

The contractions are becoming more insistent, though still not close. They're halting Meg's sentences. They're driving her, over and over, into that interior place—pain—but it's all leading to the far side, where Meg lies in bed, the new baby, James—he's already been named—cradled in her arms.

Sarah goes home in the early evening to relieve the babysitter. She's spending the night on the sofa. When Jeff gets home she's in her pajamas, under the quilt. Her reading lamp is the only light, the rest of the room is in shadow.

"How was she?" Sarah asks.

"Okay," Jeff says. "The contractions are stronger. But they're still far apart. She's fine." He starts across the room.

"Good," Sarah says. She doesn't know what he's thinking. She doesn't know if she should ask, or respect his privacy. They share a connection to Meg, but their connection to each other is tenuous. She hardly knows him.

At the doorway Jeff stops. Without turning around, he says, "She kept closing her eyes."

Sarah says, "I'm sure she's fine. The contractions hurt, that's all." Surely he must know that?

"Yeah," he says. "Good night."

MONDAY

Jeff asks if Sarah minds if he leaves early for the hospital. She doesn't: he's the husband, he takes precedence. She takes the children to school, then joins him. When she arrives, Jeff is sitting beside the bed. Meg looks different: Pain has entered her face. Under her eyes are brownish rings, and her hair is tangled. The sheets are rumpled, tempestuous.

The pain alters everything. "Hi, my lovely girl," Sarah says. She speaks in a low voice, nearly a whisper, as if in deference. Sarah tells her about the children, dinner, baths. Then Meg sits up.

"I have to pee," she says.

"Shall I call the nurse?" Sarah asks, but Meg shakes her head. She stands clumsily and takes the IV stand, pushing it ahead as she shuffles to the bathroom. When she comes out she pauses, halfway to the bed, for a contraction. She bends over, hissing. When it's over she gets awkwardly back into bed.

"Okay?" asks Sarah.

"Yeah," Meg says.

The nurse comes in. She's in her fifties, wearing white pants and a tunic. She makes eye contact only with Meg. She wraps the blood pressure cuff around her arm and swiftly pumps up the bulb, watching the gauge as the pressure declines.

Meg says, "When I peed I passed a blood clot."

The nurse frowns. "How big?"

Meg makes a circle with finger and thumb. "Like this."

The nurse frowns again. "What color was it?"

Meg shakes her head. "Red."

"No, what color red? Dark or bright?"

"Dark," Meg says.

"You should have called me," the nurse says. "Did you flush it?"

Meg nods. "I didn't know."

"All right," says the nurse. "If it happens again, call me."

When she leaves her rubber clogs squeak on the tile floor.

Meg leans back against the pillow and closes her eyes. Jeff takes her hand and kisses it; she smiles weakly.

"Do you want the TV on?" he asks. "More curling?"

She shakes her head.

Sarah goes down first for lunch. The cafeteria is in a crowded room on the mezzanine, a steam table and refrigerated cabinets. Sarah takes a bowl of thin soup and a huge egg salad sandwich. She carries her tray outside but there is nowhere to sit. She eats standing, leaning against the railing overlooking the lobby. It's noisy, the people around her are talking loudly and laughing. Mostly medical people—maybe it's the reaction to the quiet of the sickroom. She doesn't like the blood clot, the nurse's frown.

In the afternoon Meg is less and less with them. Her face is sweaty now. She's doing the special breathing, the long hissing intakes, the shushing expulsion. When Sarah leaves to pick up the kids she kisses Meg's smooth hot cheek.

"Goodbye, Meglet," she says. "When I next see you, he'll be here. I love you."

Meg smiles faintly. " 'Bye, Mum. I love you, too."

Sarah says to Jeff, "Call me as soon as you have news."

He nods. It's happening now.

At Busby's big bilingual school Sarah signs in with the guard. She writes *Grandmother* in the box marked relationship. Her status is unimpeachable, but she's not quite competent: she's not sure where to find her granddaughter. There's no one in the office and she heads down the hall and through a set of big doors into a gym. She has picked Busby up outside on the playground, but she thinks that's only for good weather.

She crosses to the low bleachers. Classes file in and the room fills with kids, chattering in English and Spanish. It's great that the kids have this access to Spanish, a bilingual public school, but Sarah is always worried that she should be able to speak both languages, like the kids.

Busby's teacher appears in the doorway, a heavyset woman shepherding a wavering line of small children. Busby is taller than the rest. She wears a ruffled red top and dark red jeans. She's looking at the waiting parents, her face sober, dark eyes anxious. She sees Sarah, breaks loose, and runs across the floor.

Sarah hugs the small pliant body, and Busby turns her face up like a flower. She curves backward in Sarah's arms. Her body is light and warm, delicious. Sarah kisses her, but gets only the top of Busby's head, scratchy hair.

"Is Mama home yet?" Busby asks.

"Not yet."

"Did the baby come?"

"Not yet."

At Nate's school he is in his classroom. He's cross-legged on the floor, watching the door. He looks just like Meg, ivory skin, square face, coarse dark hair, and thick eyelashes. He springs up, already speaking, his eyes blazing.

"Is Mama home? Did the baby come?"

"Not yet." Sarah helps him put on his coat. Small children take no responsibility for their limbs; it's like dressing a noodle. Sarah says goodbye to Ms. Fernandez, who is young and beautiful, dark-skinned, with liquid brown eyes and glossy black hair. Ms. Fernandez gives Sarah a special smile: she knows why Sarah is there, what's happening in the hospital.

At home, Sarah starts dinner. It's past five-thirty. She wonders if it's happening now. She stands at the stove, cooking hamburgers. Busby sprawls on the rug, bent over a coloring book. Nate walks in circles, carrying an action figure and making flying noises. At first he walks around the whole room, but the circles become smaller and smaller, centered on Busby. Finally he stops by Busby. He stands over her head, his feet too close to her picture.

Without looking up Busby shouts, "Stop!"

There is no answer. Then Sarah hears him cry, "Busby hit me!"

"That's what you get, Nate," Busby says, not looking up. She is coloring with rapid, slashing strokes.

"Okay, guys, dinner. Right now." Sarah ignores the conflict. Her position is tenuous. She has authority in theory, but not much backing it up. What if she gives Nate a time-out and he refuses to go to his room? Meg and Jeff have very firm rules about everything. "We don't believe in shaming," Meg would say. "We feel strongly about sleep-training." Every generation had new theories, and Sarah wants to be supportive, but she's not sure of all their rules. If Nate defied her, what should she do? She should have asked these questions. She doesn't know what to do about table manners, either. This generation seems to feel strongly that no such things exist.

The birth is constantly on her mind. She is thinking about other things, but it's always happening beside her, clicking along like a train on the tracks.

Chapter 21

AT DINNER THE CHILDREN EAT LIKE WILD ANIMALS, SUCKING noodles noisily into their mouths, grabbing bits of hamburger with their fingers. Sarah doesn't comment. While they wolf down their food, Sarah reads to them.

Busby stands and reaches for the ketchup. Her elbow catches her mug, and apple juice floods across the table. Sarah goes to the sink for the sponge and her phone rings. She leaps back to the table. It's Jeff. The children's eyes are on her, and she turns so they can see her face, smiling.

"Tell us the news," she says; and to the children, "It's your dad." To Jeff she asks, "Is he here?"

"The baby's here," Jeff says, but there's something wrong with his voice.

Sarah nods at the children. Jeff is talking, but she can't quite get what he's saying. She hears the word complications. Something has gone wrong. Is that it? He's saying something that she can't quite understand. He's saying a lot of words, none of which she wants. She wants to brush them aside and get to the real message. The children are motionless, watching. She keeps the smile on her face. They've taken Meg away, is what he'd said. She's bleeding. Sarah pictures an incision on the belly, putting bandages on it. They can always stop bleeding. She is watching the children, Busby's big dark eyes, Nate's square serious face. They are grave and silent. Taken her away to where?

"But she's recovered?" Sarah asks. "She'll be fine?" What were the children hearing?

"Right now I'd settle for breathing," Jeff says.

Everything in Sarah goes silent. The children are watching.

"Let me know when you have any news," Sarah says. Had he said that? The children hadn't heard him.

"Yes," Jeff says, and he hangs up.

She clicks off and looks at the children. "Your mama's had the baby," she says, but her breath is doing something strange. She thinks she's smiling, but can't be sure.

"Yay!" Busby says theatrically, clapping. She's smiling artificially, watching Sarah. Nate slides off his chair and belly flops noisily onto the floor. He pushes himself around on his chest like a fish, swiveling, shouting, trying to outdo his sister. They don't ask when Meg is coming home.

Sarah gets them into the tub, the phone beside her. Their sleek ottery bodies are pale and glistening. They dive and splash, making waves against the tiled walls. Had he said that? What had he meant? "Out, out," she says, impatient. They stand on the bath mat, dripping and shivering. Busby's teeth chatter, and she tucks her hands under her chin like a little animal. Sarah towels them off, the satiny skin, the flat chests, the sweet hollow at the nape of their necks. She wraps them in the big towels. She reads to them on Busby's bed, listening for the phone.

Had he said that? Settle for breathing?

It's not a real sentence. She feels disoriented by the words. The story is long and involved, about underground caverns and dancing princesses. When she finishes, they of course ask for another.

"PleaseNanapleasepleaseNana," Nate says, rolling halfway on top of her, putting his hand over her mouth so she can't say no. Sarah hesitates, feeling his soft fingers over her mouth. She wants to be done. She wants to turn out the light and close the door, turn them off for the night so she can be alone with those words. She wants to spread them out on the floor of her mind, but then what? She wants to examine them but she has a horror of even thinking them. She reads the children another story, listening for the phone.

"Okay, guys, now it's really time," she says finally. Busby lies on her back, gazing with narrowed eyes at Sarah. Sarah kisses her and says, "I love you." Busby says meditatively, "Love you, too." She turns over, shutting them out. Sarah wonders if she's worried. Sarah doesn't want to frighten her. She strokes her shoulder but Busby doesn't respond. Sarah turns out the light. "Good night," she whispers.

In Nate's room Sarah helps him slide into bed, but instead of nestling he suddenly turns rampant, rising up like a sea serpent.

"You can't turn the light out," he commands. "I'm scared." He is serious. Sarah lies down and puts her arms around him. He twists away, supple, frantic.

"Lie still," Sarah says, gently trapping his arms.

"I'm scared, Nana," Nate declares, his voice rising. She can feel the panic inside him. "I'm scared."

"I'm right here," Sarah says. She strokes his plushy hair. He struggles, his limbs hot and lithe, but she holds him. "Sssh," she whispers, "shhhh." She begins to sing: "Hush, little baby, don't say a word, mama's gonna buy you a mockingbird." She feels his body turning quiet. Settle for breathing? What had he meant?

When Nate's breathing turns slow, Sarah sits up. He frowns, then his forehead smoothes: he's asleep.

Sarah goes in to do the dishes. It's half-past eight, the night is closing in. Everything has taken so long: dinner, bath, brushing teeth, reading. It's three hours since he called. When the phone rings, she picks up at once.

"What's happening?" she asks.

"I still don't know," Jeff says. "The baby was born, and everything seemed fine. They put him on her chest. But then they said she was bleeding, and they took him away, and then they took her away. About an hour ago they came out and asked for permission to give her a hysterectomy."

Sarah hears the question in his voice.

"Of course," she says. It's unthinkable to refuse them anything. But she can't seem to understand. Meg's body has been taken over by something, but what is it? Where is Meg herself? "Now what's happening?" she asks.

"They're having trouble stopping the bleeding," Jeff says. "That's all I know."

Sarah looks at the clock: four hours since the birth. She thinks of Meg's pale face, the way she seemed absent. She thinks of the IV, the hormones sending signals, everything coordinated and controlled. The blood clot, the nurse's frown.

"I'll let you know when I know anything more." Jeff clicks off.

The apartment is silent. Sarah cleans up the bathroom, folding the wet towels, hanging the sodden bath mat over the tub. She gathers the flotilla of plastic creatures beached around the drain. Her phone rings.

"I still haven't seen the doctor," Jeff says. "I just wanted to tell you I don't know anything more."

"If this is going to go on much longer, I'll call the babysitter, and I'll come over."

"Why?" Jeff asks.

Because I'm her mother. "Partly for me, because I don't want to be here if something's happening there," Sarah says. "And partly for you. It's not good to wait alone at the hospital."

"I'll let you know," he says.

In the kitchen, Sarah picks up toys from the floor, dolls, action figures, soldiers, airplanes. She piles them in a basket. She opens the broom closet, which is crammed, and a box falls onto her head. She wrangles the broom out, knocking over the vacuum cleaner wand. She sweeps the floor, moving chairs, getting all the grit. The thought of Meg thrums inside her head, but she can do nothing but this: beat back the tide of chaos on the kitchen floor. She thinks of calling Warren. Surely this is an exception? But there is no exception: he has severed her from his life. She doesn't want to call Josh. She doesn't want to say out loud what is happening to his sister.

After half an hour she calls Jeff.

"Nothing yet," he says. "I'll let you know."

"Tell me if I should call the babysitter."

"I'll let you know," he says.

At ten-thirty the doorbell rings, a harsh jarring sound that rips through the silent apartment. Has Jeff forgotten his key? Sarah hurries to the door. The faint light in the hall shines on the head of a young woman, shading her face as she says, "Hi."

In the dimness Sarah recognizes her: a neighbor from downstairs.

Sarah opens the door wider. "Mary Kate."

"Jeff called," Mary Kate says. "He asked if I'd come over so you can go to the hospital."

Sarah's heart contracts. It's that bad. "Thank you."

"I've brought a book," says Mary Kate. "Don's with our kids. I'll just curl up on the sofa. Stay as long as you want."

It was that bad: he had asked a neighbor to come and sleep on the sofa.

"Come in," Sarah says. Why hadn't Jeff told her?

Mary Kate is in her late thirties, with dark red hair and pale freckled skin. Her kids are similar in ages to Meg's, and they share playdates. She and Meg are friends, but not close. He has called in an outsider. It is that bad.

Mary Kate stands by the sofa, holding her book.

"Thanks for coming," Sarah says. "Let me get my coat."

"It's all right." Mary Kate looks into Sarah's eyes. "How are you doing?"

Sarah feels something thickening her throat, panic. Mary Kate has no right to ask this. What has he told her? How bad is it?

"I'm fine," she says, "thanks." But her eyes fill, and she turns away. She won't make this real by crying in front of Mary Kate. Out in the hall she pushes the elevator button hard. On the street she hurries toward the avenue for a cab.

The cab is old and slow, lumbering heavily through the dark streets. Sarah leans forward, urging it on with her body. The driver slows at the sight of a yellow light, coasting to a stop as other cars speed through. Sarah's body is clenched.

At the hospital she pushes through the big glass doors. It's past eleven, and the lobby is nearly empty. Sarah hurries through the serpentine line of stanchions to the visitors' counter.

"ID?" says the woman, not looking up.

Sarah fumbles for her driver's license. The woman taps the keyboard. A sticker inches out of a printer. The woman hands it to Sarah.

"Thank you," Sarah says. Everything seems slow.

"Second floor," says the woman. "Room Eight."

This is new. Sarah sticks the ID onto her coat and heads for the elevators. As she waits, she texts Jeff.

I'm here, she writes, where are you?

Come to the second floor, he answered, you'll see me.

The elevator doors open onto darkness, which fills her with fear.

Ahead is a set of swinging doors, a sliver of light between them. The room itself is dark except for one beam, shining down onto a sofa. On this sits Jeff. He watches her approach.

"Hi," he says.

"Tell me what happened." Sarah sits down beside him. They are in an island of light in a sea of shadow.

"So." Jeff speaks carefully. "The delivery was fine. They put the baby on her chest and she held him. He's fine. But then they took the baby away and a whole lot of people came in and her doctor asked me to leave. Later they asked about the hysterectomy. I haven't heard anything since."

Sarah can't seem to open her chest to breathe.

"We're waiting for the doctor to come out," Jeff says.

"Her ob-gyn?" asks Sarah.

"Any doctor."

It is all around her now, this freighted knowledge. The room is dense with it. The birth was at five-thirty. All these hours are a black hole. She doesn't actually want to know, it's something she can't allow herself to look at.

"What is this floor?" she asks. "Where are we?"

"The ICU," Jeff says.

Behind them a big window gives onto another wing of the hospital, studded with windows. Each holds a patient. She turns away. She can't think about other patients. It's all she can do to protect this one. She is holding Meg safe in her mind.

They sit in silence, looking into the darkness. Now she can see the rest of the room, filled with empty sofas and chairs. Sarah doesn't want to talk to Jeff. She can't bring herself to step outside the sealed capsule of her mind. She holds herself tightly intact. She doesn't want to know what time it is; the later it is, the worse things are.

When the swinging doors open, two men come out. They wear blue scrubs and cloth caps; white masks hang under their chins. Sarah and Jeff stand. Sarah is frightened that there are two of them.

"I'm Dr. Patel," says the taller one, to Sarah. "I'm the intensivist." He has dark eyes and a square handsome face.

"I'm Sarah. I'm the mother." Sarah sort of smiles, but she's not in control of her face. She feels frozen all over. She searches their faces but finds nothing that she wants.

"Let me explain what's going on." Dr. Patel speaks carefully. It seems that at some time during labor, Meg's placenta tore away from the uterus: this is called a placental abruption. The wound began to hemorrhage. The internal bleeding triggered a reaction from proteins in the blood: they became abnormally reactive. At this point Meg had entered the first stage of a condition called DIC, disseminated intravascular coagulation: blood clots were forming and traveling throughout her system. After the birth the uterus had failed to contract entirely. Normally it contracts like a fist. Dr. Patel shows her how this looks, closing his fingers tightly over his palm. The contraction closes off blood vessels that ruptured during birth, and this stanches the bleeding. But Meg's uterus had only contracted partially. The bleeding continued. Then the second phase of DIC began: the proteins that naturally cause clotting had all been used up during the first phase. Now she has no coagulants left and she is still bleeding, in what is called catastrophic hemorrhaging. They have removed the uterus, to stop those particular vessels from bleeding.

Dr. Patel's manner is kind, which chills Sarah. She can't really hear what he is saying. The words keep fading and roaring. She can't bring herself to listen. She watches Dr. Patel make a fist. A hysterectomy is not dangerous. People have hysterectomies all the time.

Dr. Patel continues. The only way this deep internal bleeding can be stopped is through clotting caused by natural coagulants, but Meg has none. Her own coagulants were used up in the first phase of DIC. They are giving her blood transfusions and waiting for the body to recover and to produce more coagulants.

Sarah is only half listening, waiting for the words she wants to hear: stabilize, recovery. Dr. Patel looks at Jeff, who nods. Sarah doesn't want to think of Meg's heart, pumping blood out through her vessels to pool and pool beyond her body. That was not something she could consider, and when her mind came near it her own heart began to race: it is too dangerous.

At last Dr. Patel gives a terminal nod. They have done what they can do. Now they are waiting. She still hasn't heard the words she wanted.

"Can we see her?" Sarah asks.

The surgeon nods again. They go through the swinging doors, and as Sarah enters this new space she feels a chill. At the end of the silent hall is an open space. The nurses' station is on the right, and on the left is a row of open doorways. Except for a mechanical hum, the place is quiet.

The room is narrow, and crammed with equipment. Meg is motionless, her arms and legs spread as though she'd been flung down on the bed. Her face is obscured by a grid of white straps that crisscross her forehead and cheeks, mashing her eyebrows. Her mouth is filled by a ribbed white hose that arches off to a machine. Her face is flattened and crumpled, nearly obliterated.

But the worst is her color: her skin is deathly white. She is the white of a fish on a slab. It is not a living color: it is arctic-white. On the IV stand is a bag of dark red fluid. Tubes are attached to her everywhere, arms and legs, and snaking under the sheet to unknown destinations. Her body has been taken over. High in a corner hangs a bank of monitors, screen after screen jittering hypnotically. Scrolls of data are being inscribed by electronic cursors, rising and falling against the black beyond.

Sarah doesn't want to show her horror. "Hi, Meglet," she says. This is worse than anything she could have imagined, her crumpled, discarded daughter, the deathlike skin.

Meg's eyes flutter, slits beneath her mashed and flattened eyebrows. Her hands are cuffed to the side rails.

"Hi." Jeff comes around to stand beside her.

Meg can't speak because of the tube. Sarah can't make out her eyes. Can she see them? Is she conscious?

"You're doing fine," Sarah half whispers. She pats Meg's bare foot, which is swollen and inert.

"The baby's fine," Jeff says.

"Eleanor and Nate are fine," Sarah says formally, "They all are."

At this Meg gives a horrible jerky nod, and her eyelids flutter. The ribbed tube crowding her mouth is breathing for her. It makes a slow, steady rushing sound, in and out; the compressor gives off a complicated hum. Jeff and Sarah are silent, muted. They listen to the machine gasp and pant. Meg has gone to some inner place, her eyes half-shut.

On the screens the cursors inscribe their jagged mountain ranges, rising straight and zagging down, then rising again. A white electronic dot pulses against a black background, glowing and fading. On the wall is a whole world of information on her daughter. They are recording everything inside her, the most intimate changes, air and blood and brain and heartbeat. Sarah won't cry. She wants to show Meg that things are fine. The compressor gasps.

Suddenly Jeff kneels beside the bed. He takes Meg's hand, chained to the side rail, and presses it against his lips. He closes his eyes. It is a moment so naked that Sarah doesn't know whether to look away or leave. Jeff opens his eyes. He kisses Meg's hand again, then sets it carefully back among the wilderness of tubes and straps. He stands and looks at Sarah.

"Shall we go?" he says, half whispering.

There is nothing they can do. Sarah feels stunned and scalded.

They whisper good night to Meg and Sarah strokes her swollen foot. They walk past the nurses' station and when they reach the outer hallway, Jeff stops and turns, his face set.

"I don't want to arm-wrestle you for this, but I really want to spend the night here."

"The whole night?" Sarah says stupidly. Each new piece of information is a jolt. Is it that bad?

"I've already asked. They'll give me a place."

"Okay," Sarah says. "I'll go back home and relieve Mary Kate. I'll see you in the morning."

He nods and sets off down a different hallway. Sarah heads for the waiting room. He's overreacting. Isn't he? On the way out she meets one of the nurses.

"Meg Thompson's husband wants to spend the night here," Sarah says. "Is that necessary? Should one of us stay?" She waits for the nurse to say no.

"I would," says the nurse.

Sarah feels cold to her bones. Is it that bad?

Sarah goes back to the nurses' station.

"Someone told us there'd be a room for one of us to spend the night," she tells the nurse. "Do you know where it is?"

This nurse shakes her head. "This is the ICU," she says. "We never let people stay. There's nowhere for family members."

Sarah's relieved, the other nurse was wrong, Jeff was wrong. She and Jeff will go home. They'll come back in the morning and Meg will be better.

A man in scrubs is also behind the counter, looking at a computer screen. He looks up at Sarah.

"Is this for Meg Thompson?" he asks, and the nurse nods. "For them, yes. They can stay." The nurse looks at Sarah in silence. Sarah feels cresting terror.

The cab home is fast, hurtling through the dark streets, barely pausing for lights. Sarah texts Josh: She's had the baby. Still in the hospital. Josh texts back a thumbs-up. When she gets home, it's past three. Mary Kate is asleep, curled on the sofa, her hands tucked between her knees. Sarah says her name softly and Mary Kate sits up, blinking.

"I'm back," Sarah says. "Thanks so much for coming."

"How is she?" Mary Kate smooths her hair. "The kids never made a peep."

"She's better," Sarah says. "Jeff is staying."

Mary Kate nods, watching her. She fishes for her shoes with her bare feet.

At the door Mary Kate says, "Let me know how she's doing."

Sarah nods, willing her gone.

Chapter 22

TUESDAY

Warren leaves early for the office. The house is nearly uninhabitable; every room has been taken over by the wedding, which will happen on Saturday. Every table is covered with lists, folders, notebooks, sticky notes. When Warren comes into the kitchen Janet is already there, in her wrapper, making coffee. The table is littered with papers.

"The hotel just canceled the Wadsworths' reservations," she announces. "And the Converses'."

"What do you mean?" He takes a banana from the bowl on the counter. "They can't do that."

"Apparently they can. They're doing renovations and thought the rooms would be ready, but they're not. They have no ideas about where to put their guests."

"That's awful," Warren says, "but you're not responsible. For finding people rooms. This is Boston, people are grown-ups."

"They're coming from California," Janet says. "I do feel responsible."

"You do, but you're not," Warren says. He holds the banana, its skins bright and smooth, like plastic.

"How's everything else?" he asks. Every morning there are new crises. Chris's parents have turned out to be surprisingly difficult. They live in Minnesota, and have requirements: Chris's mother, Luanne, has a huge cohort of cousins that must be invited, though Kat had wanted to keep the wedding small. His father, Fred, is a diabetic, and uses a cane, sometimes a walker. They're pleasant, but they travel in a cloud of need. The bridesmaids are a continuing source of drama: Serena and Kate are at odds with each other. Each day there is bickering. A wedding seems to create its own weather. Everyone is anxious to have their needs met, though, of all events, a wedding is only about two people.

"That's all for the moment. Coffee's almost ready."

"It will be fine," he says. "You've hired Wendy, ask her to find other rooms."

Wendy is the wedding planner, a small brisk woman with curly blond hair. She's highly organized, and carries a red notebook. Warren admires her; he's a little afraid of her. Wendy knows everything, including how Janet feels about the diabetic and his walker. Wendy knows where he should be seated in the church, and how to get him there most easily. She told Janet she'd dealt with a blind man with a seeing-eye dog, nursing mothers with screaming babies, dogs who carry the rings and lose them, and ex-spouses who fought over the seating.

"A wedding is a microcosm of society," she'd told them. "Everything is an amplified version of itself. And no matter how we try, it will never be quite perfect!"

Janet didn't smile. She wants it to be perfect.

Warren feels tenderness for Janet's wish for perfection, though it makes it sort of hell for everyone else. The wedding is her apotheosis as a mother, her value to the world. She has produced the bride, demonstrating her genetic worth, and she is producing the wedding, demonstrating her social worth, her worldly skills. Now girls get married later, and Kat is making many of the decisions, but when Warren and Janet were married, her mother had presided over everything like a great sybil, all-knowing, all-powerful.

She had been the holder of the arcane knowledge: whose names came first on the engraved invitation, what font to choose, the order of the bridesmaids, all of it. Now those rules have vanished, and you can have any kind of wedding you like. But Janet likes tradition. She thinks the knowledge itself is sacred: Knowing to say "dinner jacket" instead of the vulgar "tuxedo." Knowing to call a coming-out party "a small dance," no matter how big it is. The knowledge meant you are not an outsider. Janet is a snob, though she would deny it. She has created a little fenced-in area, like the Royal Enclosure at Ascot.

Warren holds up his banana to her, to signify breakfast. "I'm leaving. I'll get coffee at the office. Good luck with all this."

In the car he feels released, as though the cloud of tension has drifted past. He thinks of Sarah; he tries not to do that when he's at home, as though his thoughts have a geographical boundary. He wonders what she's doing, where she is. He'd written her a last letter, which he mailed himself. He told her why she wouldn't hear from him again. If she ever needed him, he said, she should write to him this way, to his office. But what had he meant by that? What would she need him for? Under what circumstances would he break his word to Janet and Kat? Life-and-death? He can't think of a situation that would allow him to go to her. Not her life, not his death. He's made his choice. He can't break his word again.

He's in the thick of the traffic, the lanes sliding in curves toward downtown Boston. When might she need him? He feels this in his chest, the fact that he has excised himself from her life. He has made it impossible for her to need him. When he thinks of it this way it is intolerable, and instead he thinks of Kat, her energy, her bright presence in the house, how he loves having her there. Sometimes she goes shoeless, in leggings and big thick socks. Coming into the kitchen, she takes a little run and then slides on the smooth floor, skidding to the table, sliding to a stop. Strands of her long dark hair lift around her shoulders. He calls her the Pony Express, because she moves at a gallop. Because she slides in, grinning, to the table. So that's what he thinks about, instead of Sarah.

SARAH CALLS JEFF at seven, though she's been awake since five. "How is she?"

"The same," he says. "Come over when you've gotten the kids to school."

Sarah wakes the kids. When she says Nate's name, at once his eyes spring open, bright and liquid as a bird's. He's completely awake, as though he's been waiting all night for this moment.

"Is Mama home?"

She smooths his hair, cupping his warm head.

"Not yet," she says. "She's still in the hospital. She's getting better."

The children droop over breakfast. Nate leans sideways. Busby eats with her head propped in one hand. Sarah fills their lunch boxes, thinking of the hospital, where the world is standing still. The motionless body, the electronic cursors inscribing their endless news. Sarah pours soup into thermoses, slices apples. Meg's corpse-white face, beneath the broad tight straps.

She gets the children into their jackets. Busby won't look at her. Below her eyes there are dark circles, like bruises. Sarah wonders if she'd really gone to sleep so quickly.

She takes Nate first, and by the time she reaches Busby's classroom, two flights up wide wooden stairs, they are late, and Busby is anxious. She race-walks down the hall, sneakers squeaking on the tiled floor.

"Hurry up, Sassy," she says sternly, using her private name for Sarah, but then at the door she waits, shy. Sarah turns the handle quietly, as though they can sneak inside unnoticed.

Ms. Gonzalez is sitting in a chair, holding a book. The children sit cross-legged on the floor. Ms. Gonzalez beams.

"Come in!" she says. "Tell us the news!" She beckons. "Tell us, how is the baby, and how is the mama?"

The children have turned their faces up, like a circle of flowers. Everyone waits for Sarah's answer.

"Everyone is fine." Sarah makes a smile with her mouth. She thinks of Meg's bloodless face, the hideous sounds of her breathing. "Everyone is fine," she says. "Busby has a baby brother named James."

"Congratulations!" The teacher claps her hands. "Class, can you say 'congratulations' to Busby?" She looks at the children. "Can you say, 'congratulaciones'?"

"Congratulaciones!" the children say in wavering voices, and one little girl, the class show-off, with two perky ponytails, comes over with a wide artificial smile and kisses Sarah loudly on the cheek. Ms. Gonzalez beams. Sarah says thank you. She keeps the smile on her own face.

At the hospital Sarah presses the button for the second floor. In the waiting room the other sofas are now occupied by a family group, two heavy middle-aged women in suits and heels, and a lean man in suit and tie. Their faces are solemn. Sarah strides past them toward the swinging doors.

In the room, everything is the same. Meg lies flat and motionless, her face, between the straps, still chalk. Her mouth is still engulfed by the monstrous hose. Up in the corner are the monitors, scrolling and pulsing.

Jeff nods hello.

Sarah speaks to Meg. "Hi, lovey," she says, nearly whispering. "How are you feeling?"

Meg's head twitches. The ventilator gasps. Her eyes are nearly shut. Her body doesn't move.

Sarah turns to Jeff. "How are you? Where did you sleep?"

"Down the hall," he says. "On a sort of pallet."

"I'm glad they gave you that. Did you get some rest?"

"A bit." His eyes are hollowed. The beard-shadow on his cheek is like a dark stain. He looks exhausted.

"I should have brought your things," she says. "Toothbrush and stuff." Tomorrow she'll bring them, if there is a tomorrow.

Jeff shakes his head. "I can buy things downstairs."

"What's going on?" Sarah asks.

"Still critical but stable," he says. "They're monitoring everything. That's all they'll say."

Sarah nods. She doesn't dare ask what this means. She's surrounded by a galaxy of information too frightening to consider.

"Have you had breakfast?" she asks. "Do you want to go get some, and I'll stay?"

"Great." He stands. "Can I bring you anything?"

Jeff is courteous, remote. She has no idea what he's thinking. It would be intrusive to ask him, and she is too frightened herself to offer comfort. She is afraid her daughter will die. She doesn't dare speak of what they are facing.

"No, thanks," she says.

But he doesn't move: he's frightened, too, she thinks.

"She lost a lot of blood," he says. "They keep saying that."

Each new message is a blow against her heart. She can't bear this terrible news.

When he leaves, Sarah puts a chair at the bottom of the bed and hangs her coat on it. There is no room for coats, books, flowers. Sarah watches her daughter's chest rise and fall, each breath made by the ventilator.

Meg's body is so colonized by equipment and pain that all Sarah dares touch is her foot. Sarah strokes one bare foot, then she stands and puts both her hands on both of them. Meg's feet are pale and swollen, heavy in an awful way. Sarah begins to massage them, pushing hard into the arches, stroking the insteps, squeezing the toes. Meg's eyes are closed; Sarah doesn't know if she can feel this. But Sarah is sending her a message: That Meg's alive, that her body is working. That her mother is there. She presses against the arch, squeezes the toes.

When Jeff comes back he looks better. He sits down by Meg's head.

"Thanks," he says.

"How's the baby?" Sarah has braced herself to ask, though she can hardly bear to think of the child who has dealt this blow to her daughter. She can't bring herself to say his name. She can't consider him as a separate person, one who might go on alone.

"He's fine," Jeff says. "He's in the nursery. I'm going to visit him later."

Sarah says nothing. It's not his fault. But she can't bring herself to see him.

"Only one family member is allowed," Jeff says.

Relieved, she nods. "It should be you."

The day seems not to move. The cursors describe their mountain ranges, the pale star of the heartbeat pulses on the black page, the ventilator gasps. Jeff reads a professional journal. Sarah has brought a book, a memoir about a crazy childhood that's supposed to be hilarious. "My mother never changed her socks, she had some idea about beneficial flora." She reads that sentence over and over; it's never funny. Everything seems irrelevant.

"I'm going to get some coffee," she says to Jeff. "Would you like anything?" He shakes his head.

Sarah stops at the nurses' station. The woman there is in her forties, small, with narrow black-framed glasses. She stares at her computer screen.

"Good morning." Sarah smiles. The nurse is the connective point. The nurses oversee Meg's charts, they check her vitals. They'll know if something's wrong and will press a button, broadcast a code, get help. Sarah needs the nurses as friends and allies. "I'm Meg Thompson's mother. Could you tell me how she's doing?" She smiles. She's naked, here, vulnerable.

The nurse looks up. "Thompson?" she says. "Critical. She's in critical condition."

Sarah waits, but the nurse says nothing more.

"Critical," Sarah repeats.

That wasn't the word she wanted. And she'd hoped for a smile, sympathy. Nurses are trained to do this, withhold themselves emotionally. Still, it feels like a slap in the face. She's asking for succor. She doesn't want that word *critical*.

The nurse says, "She lost her blood volume, twice."

Sarah nods. What does that mean?

"She's received eleven units of blood." The nurse says this severely, like a rebuke, as though Sarah, or Meg, is to blame. It's the tone that hurts her, since Sarah doesn't know what it means. Each of these announcements is another blow.

The nurse repeats it. "Eleven units."

"Yes." Sarah would be happy to take the blame if it would only be over.

The nurse looks down again at her screen.

All that day Sarah and Jeff sit in the room. Sarah's afraid to look at the monitors. She's afraid that if she looks she will see the lines sink down and flatten. That's what happens in the movies. The tiny white star, pulsing against an infinity of black, emits a steady electronic beep which Sarah believes is the heartbeat. She is terrified that it might stop while she is listening. Flatlining.

Periodically a nurse appears to look at the screens, record numbers, check the IV. Meg's belly is still huge, as though she has not yet given birth. Along the edge of the gown the hysterectomy incision is visible, horrible black staples against the pearly skin. Meg's legs are wrapped in thick pneumatic pads that slowly inflate and deflate. They are for circulation, because Meg is not moving. Her body is entirely still. Her face is still white. Sarah has never seen skin so frighteningly white. Her lips, stretched open by the hose, are the same color as her cheeks.

In the afternoon the doctor arrives. He checks the monitors, then they follow him outside to talk.

"How is she?" Sarah asks.

"She's in critical condition," he says. "But stable."

No change. Sarah nods. She's keeping herself on the surface of a lake of unbearable knowledge. She can't allow herself to slip into the darkness of that world: learning the truth about those lips the color of chalk.

When Sarah arrives at Nate's classroom he is waiting for her.

As soon as he sees her he asks, "Is Mama home?" His bright eyes are fixed on her face.

"Not yet." She kneels to help him on with his jacket.

"But when is she coming?" he asks. The question is so full of yearning that she feels her throat close. She puts her arms around him for a moment, before she can answer.

"When she's better," she says. "We don't know exactly."

At Busby's school, Sarah and Nate are in the gym when Busby appears. Busby runs across the room, not smiling.

"Is Mama home?" she asks.

"Not yet," Sarah says.

Busby says nothing. She stands at the chasm that lies between what adults know and what they tell children. Sarah can feel the heaviness she carries, at her mother's absence. It's inside her, too. She wonders: If Meg dies, should she take the kids home with her? In her kitchen, looking out the window, slumped and listless, waiting for dinner to be over, waiting for the day to be done, waiting for their mother to return, in that flat endless place of afterward.

That night she is slow, slow to make dinner, slow to get them in bed. She doesn't give them baths: Why should they bathe?

Jeff calls during dinner to talk to them.

"How is Mama?" Busby asks politely. She looks out the window as she talks.

"What did your dadda say?" Sarah asks, when they've hung up.

"He said she's getting stronger," Busby says.

"That's right," Sarah says, though she has seen no evidence of this. She puts her arms around Busby, who pulls away. Sarah can feel the pulse of fear. She can't tell her everything is all right. What are the rules? Should you lie to children, to comfort them? What if you promise them that everything would be all right and then it isn't?

She texts Josh that Meg is still in the hospital.

She wishes she could tell Warren. She has his letter in her wallet, folded small. *My darling Sarah*, it begins. *I can't write to you anymore. As it turns out, it has become a choice between you and them. I can't lose them. I can't lose my daughter.*

She may have her own loss; she can't let herself think of it.

WEDNESDAY

At breakfast, Janet sits at the table, frowning at her laptop. Kat sits beside her, face gleaming from the shower. Her hair hangs over her shoulders, wet and black, like seaweed. Warren sits at the far end of the table at his laptop. He's working here for a bit: He likes being in the thick of things. It is fascinating how fraught all these details are. In themselves they are small—hotel rooms, the cars, the flowers—but the event itself is monumental. It's the conjunction of the family and the world. It's the place where private life becomes public. The young couple is entering the world of adults. And the families are presenting themselves. Kat and her husband will take their place within the generations. But the mechanism that will effect this enormous shift is made up of tiny inconsequential pieces.

Janet raises her hands. "Yes! We've got hotel rooms! Wendy found them."

"Go, Wendy," Warren says.

"Does the florist know where to put the flowers in the church?" Kat asks.

Janet nods. "They've done it hundreds of times."

"I'd like to go over there and look at it," Kat says.

"Want me to go with you?" Janet asks. "When are we doing the baskets?"

The dining room has been taken over by the baskets, small bags of presents to go in the hotel room of every guest. He can't remember what they finally decided to put in them. It's mostly food—candy and pilot biscuits, postcards, something to drink, all local. Why offer snacks and trinkets to people who can buy their own stuff? But it seems to be a part of the wedding culture.

A hairdresser is coming to the house on Saturday morning, to do Kat's and Janet's hair. That had been a struggle: Kat never went to a hairdresser, and wanted to do her own. Janet had overridden her: What if her hair didn't look good that day? Kat had capitulated. The hairdresser would work in Kat's room. Wendy was orchestrating it all: the rooms, the cars, the baskets. It was like a military campaign.

Once the ceremony begins, it's inexorable. It has its own life, unfolding into being. Once the bride starts up the aisle, through the expectant crowd, toward the waiting husband, nothing can halt it. He remembers standing at the altar, worrying about the ring, loose in his pocket. Janet was coming toward him with an odd fixed smile, hand tucked under her father's arm. Was the ring still there? He couldn't remember the order of the service, when to say I do and I will. The room had expanded around him, into a vast soundless space. He kept his eyes fixed on Janet.

He stepped forward as Janet came near. When she reached him she gave a tiny conspiratorial smile, just the corners of her mouth, with that pirate glint in her eyes.

Today, Janet is brisk and certain. This is a performance. She wants it perfect. Her eyes have no pirate gleam.

It's different from a military campaign because it's charged with joy. Joy is beneath all this: he can see it on Kat's face. Joy buoys the whole event. Joy and fear—it is unthinkably brave and thrilling. Kat and Chris are declaring themselves: he finds this moving.

Kat looks at her cell phone, scrolling through emails.

"Oh my god," she says. "Holly may not be able to come."

"What's happened?"

"Her brother was in a car accident." Kat frowns, reading. "They don't know how bad it is."

"How awful," Janet says. "I hope he's all right. Is he older or younger?"

"Younger," Kat says. "Tuffy. He's in college somewhere."

Tuffy's spectral presence hovers, evoking a rush of provisional sympathy. Though he may actually be fine. Right now he is merely a complication. Kat types her response. One unintended consequence of cell phones is ambidexterity. Warren uses only one hand to type onto his phone, another example of what separates his generation from his daughter's. He wonders if the difference had been so marked for his parents. Had they been overwhelmed by the onslaught of the new? He remembers trying to show them how to turn on the TV set, when they were still living at home. He wrote out instructions, explaining which device to use, in what sequence. He left it beside the TV. He thought they never used it, never even saw it. Later they lived in assisted living, where the TV was always on in the lounge. They didn't have to learn how to work it. They're both dead now. He's been thinking of them a lot recently, maybe because he's been sealed off from Sarah, as he's been sealed off from them.

When Warren was a child his father had seemed large and threatening. He'd been bulky and loud, in command of everything, the car, the meals, the vacation. But at the end of his life he'd become shrunken, tottery, and uncertain. The flesh had fallen away from his bones. His eyes were pale and watery, his white hair thin and flyaway. Then it seemed that the world provided an endless series of shocks. His mouth hung slightly open, a fine white line of saliva in the corners, like salt on a stone. He was so different from the earlier father. Warren feels an ache for him now.

His father had been bemused by Kat; she was too headstrong. He'd have preferred a pretty little mouse who curled up with a book, instead of a hoyden who played Frisbee with her cousins. It was his mother who loved Kat, smiling through the window as she pounded about. His mother tapped on the pane. "Lovely," his mother said, no matter what Kat did. "You're a wonder."

Kat and Janet discuss the flowers, the brother, the hotel rooms, while he reads plans on his screen. He wants to be part of this, but he wants to be part of something else as well. He slips on his headphones. He always listens to opera this way; Janet doesn't like the music taking over her airwaves. He puts on *Figaro*, which is beautiful but not compelling. Some operas take him over completely: he can focus on nothing else while he's playing *Norma*, or *Don Giovanni*. The greatest operas are tragedies, stories of passion and sorrow, in which death comes at the end. It's the music that makes the stories so powerful; music is emotion made audible. But *Figaro* is an opera buffa, a comedy. A tragedy ends with a death, a comedy with a wedding. Figaro and Susanna will outwit the scheming Count and marry each other. He can think about other things while the plot unscrolls. The overture begins, glittering with brass.

He finishes reviewing the proposal for a new house before the opera is over. He takes off his headphones. Everyone has left. The refrigerator makes its sudden loud industrial drone. The house feels empty. He wonders where Sarah is. It's now five months since he wrote to her, by hand, a real letter, the only way he could communicate without detection.

> *My darling Sarah,*
> *I can't write to you anymore. As it turns out, this has become a choice between you and them, and I can't lose them. I can't lose my daughter. Kat has asked me to stop all communication with you.*
>
> *She has said that if I don't she will cut me off forever, starting with the wedding, from which I'll be banned, and including all contact with her and her future children. I simply can't do it. I can't resign from the family I've been part of, which I started, thirty-four years ago. I was ready to lose Janet, but I can't lose Kat, and all the children to come. So I have promised that I will cease all communication with you, forever. This is my promise to her, and now that I've made it I must keep it, as a matter of honor.*
>
> *I can't bear doing this. My heart wants to be with you. This is tearing my heart out. You must know how much I love you.*
>
> *You won't hear from me again.*
> *My heart is still yours.*
> *W.*

Chapter 23

WEDNESDAY, NEW YORK

Sarah and Jeff sit all day in the room. Meg is still white and silent. Sarah and Jeff don't speak, except about meals. They are too miserable to speak. When the doctor comes, they follow him outside. There is no change. Still critical, but stable.

At lunchtime Sarah checks at the nurses' station.

"Any news on my daughter, Meg Thompson?" she asks.

The nurse looks up. "Still critical." She says it like a challenge.

Sarah nods, hoping for something better.

"Organ failure is the risk now," the nurse says. "If that happens, there's nothing we can do."

Sarah nods again, panic rising.

"Okay," she says. She won't say thanks.

She walks away, holding herself very straight. All the rest of the day she concentrates on not allowing the words near her. Back in Meg's room, she rubs her feet, over and over.

That evening, when the children are in bed, Sarah opens her laptop. She hasn't been able to read emails before this; the outside world has seemed entirely irrelevant. Now she reads them: Messages from Nancy about the exhibition. From tennis friends about games. She can't imagine playing tennis. She can't imagine going anywhere but the hospital. Nancy sends a message titled, Baby: How's Meg? What did she have?

She can't write down the words. She answers Nancy's questions about the exhibition—Try dealing directly with the registrar, she suggests. See if the dealer has a good photograph, if the collector doesn't.

She answers Carey, the dog walker taking care of Bella. Every day Carey reports: Walked to the reservoir. Bella inspected a dead tree very carefully, I wonder if someone is asleep in there.

Lastly she texts Josh. She doesn't want to talk to him, doesn't want to say the words out loud. She's still in the hospital. The baby, James, is fine. I'll call when I can.

She makes up her bed on the sofa. If Meg dies will she stay here, like that man on NPR whose daughter died? His grandson asked when he was leaving and he said, "Never." Will she give up her life and take on this one? Would Jeff want her? She couldn't live on the sofa. She'd have to get an apartment. She'd have to sell her house. What about Bella? She wishes she could explain to the dog why she is away for so long.

She pulls the sheet up. Each night she takes a sleeping pill, but before it kicks in she lies in the dark, willing herself not to think about Meg.

She recites a poem in her mind, the one about the lake isle, and peace, and the linnets' wings—the linnets' wings. She is usually asleep when Jeff arrives, though she hears him come in, moving cautiously past.

THURSDAY, BOSTON

Warren is ready to leave for work, but a problem has arisen: the liquor store has delivered the wrong order to the Corinthian Club, where the reception will be held.

"How can they not know what we ordered?" Janet says, on the phone to Wendy. "Can you please have them pick it up and deliver the right one? I'll go over this afternoon and check that it's right. Oh no, I can't." She looks at him. "Warr, could you go and make sure they have the right stuff?"

"I can't now. I have meetings all day. I'm playing squash at six. I can go after that. Is that too late to be useful?"

"Yes. I'll get someone else." She turns back to Wendy. When she clicks off she looks up again. "What else are you doing?"

She means what is he doing for the wedding, for which he has a good answer. "Tomorrow I'm taking Chris out to lunch at the Corinthian."

"Oh good," she says.

He feels a flash of irritation at her assumption that she is in charge of everything, his schedule, his relationship with his son-in-law-to-be. But they both want Chris to become part of the family. And she wants to know that Warren is back and can be trusted. Warren knows he can be trusted. It pains him that Janet's not sure. This is the hardest thing he's ever done, the crushing of his heart.

He has four meetings that day, and never leaves the conference room. At the end of the last one, people stand to talk to each other, gradually dispersing.

Warren remembers coming here to call Sarah, wishing for his own space. He'd thought of reconfiguring the whole office, or finding new quarters. Now it seems unthinkable, but that wild current had threatened to overturn his world, ending his marriage, throwing his company into confusion. It had erupted like a volcano, flaming lava pouring across his landscape. That had been his world. Now the lava has cooled into cold stone. It's everywhere, covering the terrain.

Laurel says to Jack, "The Suttons, the ones who want an outdoor shower. They want something unconventional, they say. What if we made the house out of cork?"

"Or popcorn," says Jack. It is a habit, in the office, to float impossible ideas.

"I love popcorn," Laurel says. "Think how it would look at sunrise!"

"And in the rain," says Jack, and they both laugh. No one ever considers the way a new house will look in the rain, it is a running joke.

"The inevitable metamorphosis, beauty into despair," says Laurel. She is gathering the detritus of the meeting, crumpled paper (everyone still uses pads and pencils) the empty coffee cups, clearing it all away.

Warren thinks of metamorphosis, how we think of it as a single seismic spasm, Gregor Samsa becoming a cockroach, but actually everything is always in a state of metamorphosis: plant into dirt, cloud into rain, sea into mist. He doesn't want to think of his own, how his life has changed. He wants to drain the emotion from the picture of his own world, because if he lets himself feel, he might not survive the pain. It is like a needle in his heart.

Warren heads off for the racquet club downtown. It's in an old nineteenth century brick building. It's bland and modern inside, but retains the dignity of solid walls and good proportions. It has a dress code—no baseball hats, no denim—but it's not exclusive. He likes this, that it's not made up of people who all went to the same three colleges. The members come from everywhere. He's playing today with an Indian friend, Ravi.

The aisles in the locker room are narrow, with wooden benches down the middle. He changes clothes and sits down to lace up his shoes. He likes the physical change from work to workout, shedding the office, entering the game. Ravi appears at the end of the aisle, racquet in hand.

Ravi is in his fifties, tall and fit, with honey-colored skin and heavy eyebrows. He's from Calcutta, and though he's lived in Boston for decades, he still has a slight, lilting accent. He's calm and easygoing, fun to play with. He and Warren met here, and they've been playing together for years. They're friends, but they don't see each other elsewhere, and they don't talk about personal things. Warren stands up and closes his locker. He wonders what it would be like to tell Ravi about Sarah. They don't have mutual friends, it would still be a secret. He's read that keeping a longtime secret is physically damaging, a burden on the system. He can't tell. It would be disloyal to Janet. The two walk out to the court. They talk about the news, the new president.

"I wish he'd be a bit more collegial," Ravi says. "I don't think he's winning over the Republicans." They're walking down the long corridor to the courts. "He's a bit stiff-necked," Ravi says. "A bit superior. It's not a good way to make friends out of your enemies."

"I kind of like his manner," says Warren. "It is a bit grand—but he is the leader of the free world. And he gets humble when he needs to."

"But never with McConnell. He never gets folksy with them."

"I don't think it would matter," Warren says. "I think the Republicans would hate him no matter what he did."

Warren opens the door for Ravi. The court is a high narrow box, white walls, and a gleaming wooden floor. Everything echoes. The players stand side by side, trading shots, hitting a small hard rubber ball onto the wall. The game is fast and violent, and because of the cramped quarters, the players often collide.

They stand at the back of the court; Warren wonders if Ravi holds Obama to a higher standard because of the color of his skin. He's never talked to Ravi about race. It seems offensive to raise the subject. If their positions were reversed, he wouldn't expect Ravi to raise it.

They start warming up. The ball must hit the wall dozens of times before it's soft enough to play with. They trade strokes, sending each other easy hits, up and back. The space echoes with the sound of the smacking against the walls. It's a relief to be here, focused on the flying ball, the empty court. He feels light, poised, ready to swing hard.

During the game he thinks of nothing but this, smashing the ball into the corner, lunging low, reaching high. They play for an hour. Ravi beats him, as he often does. But it's close, it always is.

On their way back to the locker room they walk loosely, their limbs now at ease. Warren wipes his face with a towel.

Ravi says, "I worry about him."

He's been thinking about Obama the whole time.

"He's doing a great job," Warren says. "A great job."

He wonders if Ravi has a different feeling about government, coming from India. Maybe Ravi doesn't trust democracy to hold fast against this kind of opposition. Maybe he thinks race will split things apart. Warren knows democracy will hold. It's good to think about politics and not the wedding. It feels good to be hot and sweaty. Even his head is sweating, he can feel it through his hair.

ON THURSDAY MORNING Sarah stops at the nurses' station. Because of the changing shifts, the nurses are often unfamiliar. Sarah always smiles, but they act as though they have never seen her before.

"Good morning," Sarah says. "How's Meg today?"

The nurse is looking at her computer screen.

"Meg Thompson, Room Eight," Sarah adds. She waits, deferential, and finally the nurse looks up.

"She hasn't turned the corner yet. She's not out of the woods."

Has not. Sarah nods and turns away, her heart pinched and tight. Inside the room her daughter lies flat, eyes closed, the machine still gasping. Sarah sits down and puts her hand on Meg's foot. Meg's eyes flicker. Sarah smiles at her.

"Hi, lovey," she says. "You look better today. You're getting better, I can see that."

Meg blinks again. She looks no different.

But that afternoon two nurses arrive with a cart full of equipment and ask Sarah and Jeff to step outside. They are going to take Meg off the ventilator.

"Really!" Jeff says, and the nurse nods. "That's very good news, right?"

The nurse won't admit much. "It means she's improving."

"I'll take that," Jeff says. "I'm happy with improving."

The other nurse says, "She has a strong young heart."

At the thought of this, her daughter's strong young heart, tears spring into Sarah's eyes.

"When should we come back?" Jeff asks.

"Fifteen minutes, we should be good," the nurse says.

Sarah and Jeff go out to the waiting room.

"How are the kids doing?" he asks.

"They're scared," Sarah says. "I tell them she's getting better, but I'm not sure they believe me." The presence of fear is heavy in the apartment, it presses against her as well.

"But this is good news," Jeff says.

Sarah nods.

That dressed-up family is back. They are silent, upright. One woman nods stiffly at Sarah, who nods back. She wonders who they are there for, and what happened. But she doesn't want to connect. It seems like bad luck to enter someone else's world of pain and dread.

Inside the room, Meg has been freed from the white straps. The ribbed hose no longer fills her mouth. She is there: her face is back, pale, but her. She now has a pillow under her head. Her eyes are open. Sarah and Jeff beam at her. She is still hooked up to the monitors, which are blinking, the mountains rising and falling, but the ventilator, with its horrible gasp and wheeze, is gone.

"Hey," Jeff says. "Congratulations."

Sarah takes hold of Meg's feet and presses against the instep. The pneumatic pads are still strapped to her legs.

Meg speaks. Her voice is raspy and diminished, a harsh whisper. "Thanks, Mum," she says, "that feels good."

Sarah's throat closes, and tears well into her eyes. She has not heard Meg's voice for four days.

That afternoon Sarah and Jeff begin to talk. They talk about books—about Kazuo Ishiguro.

Jeff says, "I liked *Never Let Me Go*."

"But didn't you love *Remains of the Day*?"

"Not as much," he says. "I'm not so interested in politics."

"Politics?" Sarah repeats. "I didn't think it was about politics. It was about the butler and the maid. It was about love."

Jeff laughs. "Well, that's another way to look at it."

Sarah wonders if she should reread it: Had she missed the whole point? "What about *Never Let Me Go*, then? Did you think that was political?"

"In a big way, yes," he says. "You know, the government and the individual. Individual freedoms."

"It was terrifying," Sarah says. "And also about love."

A nurse comes in and they stop talking. Sarah goes back to the crossword, Jeff to Sudoku.

When the nurse has left, Meg speaks with her eyes closed. "Keep talking," she says. "I like hearing you." It's an effort for her to speak.

When the nurse comes in again she asks Sarah and Jeff to leave, and they go to the cafeteria for lunch. When they are settled at the table, Jeff looks at her.

"I went to see the baby," Jeff says.

"And? How is he?" Sarah wants to sound encouraging.

"He's fine," Jeff says. "Big, actually. Nine pounds. The nurses were really nice."

Sarah nods: Of course they were. Everyone here knows their family. They all know what nearly happened on Monday night.

"Did you hold him?"

Jeff nods. He knows how to hold a newborn, carefully supporting the head, the fragile neck.

"I'm glad you've seen him," Sarah says. Jeff is more magnanimous than she is.

Jeff nods, but he seems silent and distant. Abruptly he looks up.

"I have to tell you something," he says. "I found a scrap of paper in Meg's bag, with the things she'd brought to the hospital. It's something she wrote while she was in surgery."

"What did it say?" It frightens her to ask.

"She'd been intubated," he says. "So she couldn't speak."

She waits.

"*Am I going to die?* She wrote it to the surgeon."

She can't answer. She can't allow that sentence into her mind. She didn't die, she tells herself, she didn't die.

"Also, I want to say thank you for being here. I love you."

She is unprepared for this. Is he saying it because he thinks their vigil is over?

Around them is the metallic bustle of the cafeteria, loud voices, cutlery. They are at a small table next to the wall. Beyond Jeff she can see other groups, eating and talking loudly. This offers a release from the silence and intensity of the sickroom: here people can laugh and interrupt each other. A young man in scrubs points at the man beside him, shouting. Everyone at their table is laughing.

But Jeff is silent, waiting for her response. He is frozen because of Meg, who lies motionless in Room 8. Micro-clots still sliding through her bloodstream. They are clinging together like people holding on to a floating log. Though they are nearly strangers.

"Thank you," she says. "I love you."

His hand rests on the table, and she puts her hand over his. She hopes this is not the beginning of the end. He turns his hand over and grips hers, hard, as though they are close, and love each other, and at that warm pressure she begins to cry.

FRIDAY, BOSTON

Warren has asked Chris to lunch at the Corinthians Club, a neo-classical mansion built by a nineteenth century tycoon. It has elegant interiors, a friendly staff, and an uninspired menu. Warren likes it, and wants to offer it to Chris. He wants to welcome Chris to the family.

Before Warren's own wedding he'd been taken to lunch by Janet's father. Paul Cartwright had blue eyes and scoured red cheeks, and was friendly but impersonal. At lunch he'd told golf jokes and made political comments which Warren ignored. He invited Warren to call him by his nickname, "Quacky." Warren liked him, though he could never bring himself to call him Quacky. They'd never become close. Warren would never have asked his advice. He wanted to do things differently with Chris.

Warren arrives first, and watches Chris as he is shown into the dining room by the maître d'.

"Welcome," Warren says, standing up.

"Thank you," Chris says. "This is great."

They sit down; neither wants wine, and Warren orders Perrier. They fill their glasses and Warren raises his.

"To you and Kat," he says, "welcome to the family."

"Thank you," Chris says, raising his own glass. They drink the lively water.

"Now," Warren says, "remind me of where you grew up."

"Minneapolis," says Chris. "My father's a financial planner. My mom's a secretary." His response is quick and self-assured.

"And I know you went to Berkeley," says Warren.

"Where I met Kat."

"And what a good thing that was," Warren says. "Remind me of how it happened?"

"She picked me up, actually," Chris says. "At a convenience store. It was late at night, and we were in line, waiting to buy food. She was ahead of me, and she turned around and started talking." He grins as he remembers. "She was so cool."

Warren laughs, delighted. "What did she say?"

"They announced that the store was about to close," Chris says. "Kat said that this was when robberies happened. She said if one happened, would I be on her team?"

"And you said?"

"I said yes." Chris's face is animated, remembering.

"Then, after we'd bought our stuff—and there was no robbery—we went out on the sidewalk and she asked if I wanted to go hiking the next day. I said yes again."

"She is cool, our Kat. And you went?"

"Yeah," says Chris. "We went on a trail neither of us had taken before and we got lost. We didn't get back until after dark. It was fun."

"How did Kat take that, getting lost?"

"She didn't like it," Chris says. "At one point she got upset. But I knew we were heading south down the mountain, and that eventually we'd hit the road, which ran east-west."

"Did you have a compass?"

"Yeah. But also the sun was out," says Chris. "So we knew where east and west were."

"Of course you did," says Warren. He's impressed: Maybe Chris is a good match for Kat. He's not just quiet and good-natured, he's also smart and resourceful. "Well, we're glad she started that conversation."

"Thank you," Chris says. "I appreciate that."

The waiter appears and sets down their plates, sole for Warren, hamburger for Chris. The atmosphere becomes more confidential.

"Can I ask you something?" Chris says.

"Of course," Warren says, pleased.

"Was Kat always like this?" Chris asks. "I mean, as a little girl, was she, like, stubborn, and brave?"

"She was," Warren says. "Anything she took on, she would finish. I remember her when she was learning to skate, falling again and again, getting up again and again. She wouldn't cry, she'd just get up." That tiny little bundle in her snowsuit, skidding and sliding, faster skaters sizzling past as she fell over and over. Each time, she got up again, face bright, arms out for balance. "She was always stubborn and brave. She doesn't really compromise." During an argument she would lock herself into some impossible position. At times he'd felt sorry for her: Intransigence was isolating. It would be hard on Chris. It was hard on Warren. "You may want to help talk her down from her position sometimes. She won't get down on her own."

"Yeah," Chris says, though Warren isn't sure Chris understands what he means.

"What do you and Kat like to do together?" Warren asks. "After dinner. Do you read? Watch TV? Play games? Janet and I used to play backgammon. She was very good, actually." She had been very good, good on the odds, good at knowing when to double and when to quit. He shouldn't have said "actually."

"Sometimes we watch the same show, sometimes we watch different things on our laptops. Or play different games. Sometimes we both read. And then we both like to hike, though we don't do that much from Brooklyn."

"And you both like basketball," Warren says.

"Actually, I'm not as big a fan as Kat is," Chris says. "I told her at the beginning. Full disclosure."

Warren laughs. He likes Chris more and more. "That was brave."

"It was hard for her, but she accepted it," Chris takes a drink of Perrier. "She's actually very forgiving. She just needs encouragement."

Warren nods, but Chris seems uncomfortable at what he's just said. Warren thinks he's thinking of Kat's intransigence toward her father. He wants to raise this subject anyway, so he dives in.

"You know that Janet and I were separated for a while," he says. "I'm sure Kat told you. It was hard on everyone."

Chris nods nervously, with that anxious look of someone young listening hard to someone older, unsure of how to listen or what they mean.

"I don't want to go into what happened, but I take all the blame," Warren says. "Just so you know. It was no one else's fault." Chris nods again. "Marriage is hard and complicated. But it's worthwhile."

As he says these words, Warren feels suddenly physically disoriented, as though he's falling. What is he saying? Why is he offering these bromides? Would he have married Janet, if he could do it over? For an instant he is in a kind of hell. He has only returned to his marriage because of Kat.

He looks up at Chris. He'd meant to ask for his help with Kat, to urge her to forgive him. But he can't bring himself to beg. And Kat would be furious if she found out.

He looks at Chris, but says nothing more. The thought of Sarah pierces his heart.

FRIDAY, NEW YORK

Sarah asks the nurse how Meg is.

"Not out of the woods yet," says the nurse.

Meg is still pale, though her lips are no longer the color of her cheeks. She is still swollen, her beautiful tapering fingers gross. There is a strange smell in the room.

"I've been throwing up," Meg says.

They have taken her off the Dilaudid, which was wreaking havoc in her GI system. She has been vomiting a horrible black bean soup; the smell is fierce. Meg lies still, her eyes closed, face clenched. Sarah massages first one foot, then the other.

The heavy sliding glass door is always open, though sometimes they close the curtains for privacy. This morning the door is open when the nurse comes in to check the IV. Sarah watches her face for clues. Suddenly from down the hall they hear voices.

"Oh Jesus!" someone wails. "No, no, no, no!"

"He's gone! He's gone!" another voice cries, high and plangent. "Oh sweet lord!"

"No, lord!"

The nurse glances at Sarah, then strides to the heavy door and slides it shut.

"Lot of things going on around here," she says.

Sarah doesn't look at her. She won't acknowledge this. There is a risk in saying a single word. To say the word gives it power. All this is balanced on a knife point, it will tip one way or another. She says nothing, as though she hasn't heard the cries, as though she has no idea of what the nurse is talking about.

Later the family walks past: the women in their good wool dresses, the man in his suit and tie. They walk single file, their eyes cast down as if in shame. Their faces are stiff and wretched. That's how it happens, Sarah thinks. It could happen right here, in the ICU, as they are trying to save you. The shame of losing.

That afternoon the doctor tells them that he'd hoped to transfer Meg to maternity that day, but he can't. She hasn't turned the corner yet.

Sarah and Jeff nod.

Still, one by one, the machines are being disconnected. The staples are removed from her stomach, and the pneumatic pads from her legs. The electrodes are taken from her chest with a horrid ripping sound. She is constipated, and told to walk. Meg sits up, and Sarah helps her out of bed. She sets down her feet as though they are inanimate objects. Jeff takes one arm, Sarah the other. Meg shuffles painfully, wincing at each step.

"Fuck," she says.

"Keep going," Sarah says. "It will get better."

Jeff puts his arm around Meg. Her face is pinched with pain.

That afternoon, Busby waits to speak until she is outside. She doesn't want the class to hear. "Is Mama home?"

"Not yet."

Busby seems all right on the way home, but at dinner she suddenly folds herself down over her plate. Her head goes straight down in despair, her silky hair fanning out over her hamburger. She's crying.

Sarah takes her onto her lap. "What is it, my lovey?" Busby is sobbing. "What is it?" She speaks against Busby's hair.

"I don't think Mama is coming home," Busby whispers. Nate looks at her, and his face clouds over.

"She is coming home," Sarah says. "She is. She's much better today. She has her phone now. Let's call her."

Meg answers in a faint breathy whisper. "Hello?"

Sarah says, "I have someone who wants to talk to you."

Busby takes the phone carefully in both hands. She sets it at her ear and cocks her head, diffident.

"Mama?" Busby asks. Her face is fearful.

At Meg's voice her face lights up. Listening, she nods, over and over. Her fingers twist at the ruffle on her smock.

"Yes," she says. "I love you, too." She hands the phone back to Sarah. Sarah gives it to Nate, who presses it against his head.

"Mama? Are you coming home?" He looks at the ceiling.

"I love you, too, Mama," he says at last, and hands the phone back. He slides off his chair and begins to gallop in circles, bent over, his arms out. He's shouting. "Yah! Yah! Yah!"

SATURDAY, BOSTON

Warren is in his wedding clothes: his best suit, very fine wool, very dark navy with a faint pinstripe, a white Egyptian cotton shirt, very crisp, and a heavy silk tie, dull blue with a fleur-de-lys print. The suit is only for ceremonial occasions. The same for the black leather shoes, polished to a discreet glow. The left shoe pinches a bit, which might be somehow appropriate. Maybe a ceremony requires a certain mortification of the flesh. A humbling. Monks kneeling on stone floors, hair shirts. Though Warren doesn't believe in deliberate mortification. He celebrates the mortal coil. He enjoys being alive, in this world full of delights, people with unexpected ideas, views through trees and past walls, cloudscapes, glimpses of paradise. He relishes being human. And he likes ceremony, costumes, ritual. He doesn't mind the pinch of the shoe. Celebration is the point.

Kat is still in her room, getting dressed, with Alison and Kate. Janet is already ready, majestic in electric blue. As he is ready to leave the room Warren says, "See you downstairs."

Janet turns from the full-length mirror. Her face is flawless and radiant, her eyes are darkened, her lips glisten. Her glossy blond hair is set in waves. She's wearing the diamond earrings he gave her, and the diamond brooch. The gold birthday bangles. He has given her jewelry for years. He'd enjoyed it, dealing with a pleasant woman at Shreve, Crump & Low. He'd enjoyed being a trusted client. He'd enjoyed feeling generous, seeing Janet's face light up. He'd enjoyed seeing her wear the jewelry. None of that had happened since the hiatus. He'd lost the impulse. He can't bring himself to pretend.

Janet meets his gaze, her own steady. The earrings glitter, the brooch gleams against the blue silk.

"You look wonderful," he says. She looks powerful, accomplished, polished. She looked like a successful matron—a species supreme in its evolutionary niche.

"Thank you." She speaks regally, as though accepting her due. For a moment they stand still, and she holds his gaze. She has triumphed. This is her moment. She's made him return for this day.

She tucks her bag, matching blue, under her arm and walks past him, heading for Kat's room. Down the hall she opens the door into the sanctum sanctorum.

Warren goes downstairs, feeling the little pinch on his toe. He hears voices from the kitchen. The house is full of people. Wendy will be back there, a wire hanging from her ear, talking briskly into space. Warren sees Chris standing in the dining room, and he goes in.

"You all set?" Warren asks.

"I think so," Chris says. He stands stiffly upright, as though imprisoned by his clothes. Warren wonders if he's bought his dark suit just for this. No one in tech wears suits to the office; what was a uniform for Warren's generation is an awkward throwback for Chris's.

"Have you got the ring?" Warren asks.

Chris nods. "In my pocket."

"That's all you need. Wendy will tell you everything else. And the minister. When are you leaving for the church?"

Chris shakes his head. "Don't know."

"Wendy will tell you. Don't worry," says Warren. "It will all go all right."

Chris nods slowly. "So why am I so nervous?"

His face is solemn. He has chosen to make this intimate vow in the presence of the community. It's part of being a grown-up: Warren believes this; Sarah comes into his mind and he feels a deep stab of grief.

"Because it's so important," Warren says. "But it will go all right. I'm glad you're marrying Kat."

Chris nods. "Thank you. Me, too."

The house is filled with tension and excitement. A strange woman is in the kitchen with Wendy, who's talking on her wire. The bridal bouquets and the boutonnieres are missing. The delivery van is stuck in traffic. Wendy talks in a low fast voice, working out where they are, how fast they could get here on foot. Or should they go straight to the church?

The wedding will happen no matter what, it will happen without the flowers, even without the ring. He thinks of Anna Karenina, and Levin's missing shirt. He'd once gone to a wedding where everyone waited in the church and finally the bride marched up to the altar, but the groom was missing. He'd gotten the time wrong, and was watching the game. The bride laughed and marched back down the aisle; someone went to fetch him. This wedding will roll on, in the hands of Wendy and the minister, who will be standing at the altar in his black robes, waiting for Warren and Kat to make their slow, rhythmic approach up the aisle.

Finally Warren and Kat sit in the limo, parked outside the church, until it's time to go in. Janet has gone in already. Warren sits beside his daughter, her dress foaming over his leg. She holds the bouquet on her lap, a frozen waterfall of lilies and roses. He pats her gloved forearm.

"You okay?" he asks.

"I'm so nervous," she says. "I just want it to start. My heart is hammering. When will it start?"

"Soon," Warren says. "It's almost begun."

Kat won't look at him. She looks straight ahead.

"Your mother and I kept doing the wrong thing with the ring," he says.

Then Kat turns with a sweet smile. "Dad, you've told me that." The smile is so unexpected, it's like a warm breeze against his heart. "Many times," she says.

"I have?" He is helpless with love for her.

"Many times." She is still smiling, her funny mischievous smile, mouth pursed, eyes alight.

"Sorry," he says, besotted.

Her cell phone buzzes, and she looks down.

"It's Wendy," she says. "It's time." Her eyelids flutter nervously.

Warren nods. "Good luck."

Kat opens the door onto the sounds of the street, traffic and people. She steps out, and Warren slides after her. On the sidewalk, against the bustle of the city she seems fragile and vulnerable, the cloud of tulle massing around her head. Her face is fresh and pure. He offers her his arm, and they cross the sidewalk and step inside the church.

Wendy is in the front hall. The organist is playing riffs of Purcell. The little church is full, the air charged with anticipation. The congregation is expectant. Jewelry glitters on the women; the men are in dark suits, their hair sleek.

When they assemble, Wendy gives the signal. Alison and Kate, in their long blue dresses, set off with stiff, unnatural strides, their bouquets held close. At the altar they turn and face the congregation. Warren and Kat wait. Wendy nods, and Warren squeezes Kat's hand against his side.

"Okay," he whispers, and they begin the walk. This child is his, she will always be his.

Kat seems in a dream, though he only glimpses her elegant profile. Her neck rises from the heavy white satin, her throat creamy. Her beautiful curved mouth is still. Her gaze is mysterious, inward. She is matching her steps to his. Her hand is on his forearm. He remembers how she slipped her six-year-old hand into his, the day they left the summer house. Now he puts his left hand over hers, covering her gloved fingers with his. Chris is waiting, his face solemn. Janet is in the front pew, her blue back perfectly upright. The organist plays a trumpet voluntary, not perfectly, but well enough, the notes rippling through the high spaces of the church.

IN MATERNITY, Meg is allowed to see James. Sarah sees him, too. He is brought in a little rolling metal cart, like laundry. He's yellowish pink, with squinty eyes and wispy dark hair. In Meg's arms he twists and squirms. Meg cradles him as he arches his back and fusses. "Oh, oh, oh," she says. "I know, I know." Finally he lies still and fixes his gaze on her face. Her milk has come in.

On Monday they come home. Sarah waits in the apartment with the children. Meg walks slowly and gingerly. James is a tiny pink scrap, wrapped in flannel, cradled in the carrier.

Sarah still can't bring herself to hold him. She will, but not yet. He is so close to something she can't bring herself to know.

"Mama," Busby says, clasping her hands beneath her chin, like an Edwardian child.

"Mama," Nate says, opening his arms wide.

Meg carefully crouches. "My loveys," she says, then grimaces at something inside her. She hugs them, carefully, for a long time.

WARREN AND JANET have dinner in the kitchen. Frozen pot pies. She is still talking about the wedding.

"I thought Chris's parents were adorable, actually," she says.

"I liked them," he says. "I liked hearing about her day trading." Chris's mother, Luanne, bought penny stocks. She had explained her rules: If the stock went down two points within six hours, she sold. If it went up within four hours she bought more. Once she'd made a certain profit, she sold. She was quite funny about it, lively and enthusiastic. Warren enjoyed hearing about it; he liked eccentric hobbies. He liked smart women.

"Oh, the day-trading," Janet said disapprovingly, shaking her head. "That was crazy."

At moments he felt nothing but despair.

AFTERWARD Sarah could not think of any part of that black week without feeling sickened and faint.

"When I was in the operating room," Meg said later, "I came out of the anesthetic while they were working on me. The ventilator was in my mouth. I couldn't speak and I tried to write on my leg. I wrote the letter D but they thought it was P. They brought me a pad and a pencil. I was writing Die. I asked if I was going to die. The doctor wouldn't answer. He said it was a good sign that I was awake and asking. I was there, but I could feel how easy it would be to slip away. I could feel that possibility, just letting go and slipping away. But then I thought of the kids, and Jeff. And I held on."

Chapter 24

ONE OF THE PLEASURES OF BEING A PARENT, WARREN HAD always thought, was being able to help your children. To protect them from the hot stove, from illness, from penury. And to celebrate them.

It had given him great pleasure to put on Kat's wedding, to provide that constellation of food and drink and bloom, the solemn and the convivial, sacred and secular. It was a joy to present Kat to the world, to show how greatly she was valued, how precious she was. All money spent on children contained evolutionary contradictions—it will diminish your financial worth, and so lessen your chances for survival, but it will increase your children's societal worth, expanding their chances: They will be safer, better educated, more likely to thrive. Or anyway that is what you hope. Warren had been more than happy to pay for the wedding.

He had also offered to help Kat get a bigger apartment. Chris was moving in and her apartment was small. But she had dismissed his offer.

"No, we're good," she said. The apartment was near the subway and near the park where they biked on weekends. Plus she couldn't be bothered to move. "I've just gotten married, that's enough for a while." As if marrying and moving were favors that he had asked her for.

The response felt like a rebuff. Not the fact of it but her manner, which was offhand and dismissive. And reflexive, as if she'd set herself to reject anything he suggested.

As a parent you were always the object of your children's anger. When Kat was eight she had left a note: *I have run away because you won't let me watch televison. Goodby. Love Kat.* All family relationships contained fury, but weren't they set on a foundation of love? That was established when you first held that tender body in your arms, when you first met that calm otherworldly gaze, when you felt that deep visceral connection. So that later, when you had arguments, that foundation lay below. You could trust each other. Wasn't that how it was meant to work?

When Warren made the apartment offer he was still in a sort of exile. He had been technically forgiven, but it seemed that Kat felt he was still on probation. He had moved back in with Janet, but he was not yet allowed back inside the family. Kat maintained a distance from him, treating him with chilly courtesy.

He wondered if part of this was because of her marriage, that she had chosen another male. Maybe it was normal to reject your father when you cleaved to your husband. Maybe Kat felt she had to choose between them. But Warren hadn't asked her to choose; he'd thought she'd add Chris, not that she'd subtract him. And Chris, who was good-natured but clearly uneasy about Kat's anger, didn't want to get into it. He smiled pacifically at Warren and avoided conversation.

After Kat's smile in the limo before the wedding, Warren had thought things had righted themselves. But it hadn't happened; after the wedding Kat was still remote.

It seemed that some internal balance had shifted, some switch had been flipped. In the next few years Kat and Chris stopped coming to the house in Maine for vacations. They began taking biking trips in exotic places: Colorado, British Columbia, Puglia. Of course they should spend their vacations wherever they wanted, but it was disappointing. Warren had added on to the house; he'd envisioned his daughter coming there with her husband and children. But Kat could no longer find the time. She also stopped coming up to Boston to visit them: she was so busy. If Warren and Janet wanted to see her and Chris they must travel to Brooklyn.

He doesn't mind the travel, but he misses the intimacy. There isn't room for them in the apartment, so Janet and Warren stay in a hotel. This means they don't drift easily in and out of each others' presences, as they would have at home in Boston. It means that he and Janet are either there, in Kat's apartment, sitting on the sofa in the living room (the kitchen is too small), or they are back at the hotel, alone with each other. They all go together to museums and restaurants and the theater, but these are group expeditions, public and impersonal.

Warren knows that their house is the parents' domain. It feels natural to him and Janet to have their daughter return, but maybe it feels claustrophobic to be in the place where she is always the child. It's natural for her to establish her own realm, where she chooses the furniture, what time she gets up.

On that first visit, during the spring following the wedding, Warren learns things about her that surprised him: Kat doesn't like bread, for example. Warren had always assumed this was necessary for life, but there was none in the fridge, though there were bagels and tortillas. Also that Chris likes to cook Mexican food. On Saturday afternoon, after the museum trip, Janet and Warren sit on the sofa in the living room while Chris and Kat are in the kitchen, chopping and stirring. They speak a culinary language together—tomatillos, jalapenos, chicharrones—that Warren doesn't recognize. Warren takes pleasure in learning these things, he admires everything Kat does. He loves the expanding of her world, but the fact is that Kat and Chris live in another country, where he is only a visitor. It's not the discoveries that make him feel excluded, it's the way she treats them. Each of her responses reminds him of the distance between them. If she'd told him she liked Mexican food, he'd have learned that language with her: but she hadn't told him.

That afternoon when she comes out of the kitchen he and Janet are sitting on the sofa. Janet is doing something on her cell phone and Warren is reading the actual newspaper. He'd bought it that morning on the way over.

"I forgot something," Kat says. "I need more cheese. I have to run out to the store. I'll be right back."

Warren folds the paper. "I'll come with you."

"Okay," she says neutrally.

Warren puts his arm around her shoulders. "I don't want to waste a moment. I don't get to see you enough."

Within the circle of his arm he feels her body go still: She's waiting for release. It sends a chill through him. He lets her go and they head downstairs without speaking. Out on the sidewalk they walk side by side, and Warren looks around at her neighborhood. He wants to connect to the place she's chosen. Brooklyn had been farmland until the mid–nineteenth century. Since then it had grown in fits and starts, gentrifying, fading, shifting commercially and socially. Now it is in an upswing, as young people move there in droves. Her neighborhood is pleasant, low three- and four-story houses lining the street, a few struggling plane trees putting out their jagged leaves. The houses are untouched since the 1950s, with aluminum window frames and ugly railings. But the atmosphere is friendly, busy, safe. He wants to compliment her.

"I never realized how low the buildings are here," he says. "It means you have a big sky. You have so much more light here than in Manhattan."

"Yeah," Kat says. "We do."

She's polite but distant. Between them is a gap he can't close.

Anything Warren says seems artificial, and anything she says seems condescending. He can't remember how they used to talk. What did they say? What did they laugh about? He can't find his way back to the ease they once shared. He can't make her laugh. If he thought Kat's coolness were permanent it would break his heart. But he's sure it will change.

He doesn't say anything about this to Janet.

When he moved back, Janet had been purely grateful, but over time her gratitude has become less pure. Now there are small barbs embedded in it, like toast crumbs in honey. She makes sarcastic comments about his absence, or men's vagaries. She makes veiled references to Sarah. He ignores the comments about himself, but he won't permit any mention of Sarah. And he doesn't want commiseration over Kat's behavior. He doesn't want Janet's sympathy, or a tacit acknowledgment that he's done something unforgivable. Because he doesn't believe he has; he believes he's been honorable. He keeps his feelings about Kat to himself. He's patient. He believes that Kat will come around again to being her loving self. What choice does he have?

He has one means of escape. During the weekend he puts on his headphones, turns on an opera, and enters another world. He spends long hours alone in his study, while the opera gathers inside him, filling him with the rising drama of the story, the complicated patterns of the music. He listens to the famous ones—*Don Giovanni*, *Norma*, *Turandot*—which he has seen—and the less famous ones, the ones he has never seen—*Elektra*, and *Dialogues of the Carmelites*. The Met has put them on, but he's missed many of their productions, and now he will never go to the Met again. The music takes him up. Also he begins going up to the house in Maine, off-season, to hike. Janet doesn't come with him; she doesn't like hiking, and their friends don't go up off-season. Warren goes alone. He drives up after work on Friday and leaves early on Monday morning. He has two full days of solitude, walking the trails of Acadia. The wide stone terraces of the summits, the cool green tunnels of the forest paths.

He rarely permits himself to think about Sarah. He made this decision early. Thinking about her at all is a form of betrayal. His feeling is like an addiction, and the only way to quit is to quit. He doesn't permit himself to wonder what she's doing right then, or wish he could tell her something funny, or imagine that she's walking down the street toward him. He doesn't permit himself any of this. He's promised not to see her again. He's promised to stay with Janet. These are moral obligations; this is a matter of honor. He has renounced Sarah.

But he does, as solace, allow himself the fantasy of a parallel life with Sarah. He doesn't allow himself to furnish it with details, doesn't spend time imagining it, but he allows himself to believe in that other existence continually scrolling along beside this one. He'd heard of a man who could hear different symphonies simultaneously inside his head. At any moment he would know exactly where he was in each one, which notes were being played, though all the time he'd been walking around and talking to people. At every moment Warren is aware that there is a parallel life with Sarah. He feels it running silently alongside this one, humming with an inaudible vibration. Though he is a dutiful husband, a good father.

FOUR YEARS LATER Kat becomes pregnant, and then she does need help getting a new apartment. She doesn't ask Warren, though, she asks Janet. Janet asks Warren.

They are in their bedroom, getting dressed to go out for dinner. Janet stands before the opened closet door, looking in the full-length mirror. She wears a brightly patterned tunic top over black pants. Her feet and ankles are bare, bright white against the black pants and high black heels.

She smoothes the tunic over her hips, then turns sideways. "Does this make me look fat?" She has begun to thicken through the waistline. "God. Am I fat?" The tunic catches lightly at the thickest points.

"No," Warren says. "You aren't." He smiles at her in the mirror. He is at his bureau, putting on his tie.

"I think I am," she says, frowning. "I'm going to have to do something."

He watches his hands in the mirror as he does the magic trick, setting the silk band around his neck, twisting it, looping it over and under. He slides the knot into the white cleft of the collar, the neat sartorial finish to every male of his generation. Though the new billionaires, tech moguls, don't wear suits and ties. Gates likes sweaters; Zuckerberg, hoodies. Everything loose, drawstringed, zippered, nothing shaped or ironed or buttoned. Maybe in another generation the suit and tie will be gone. Warren likes them. He doesn't want to move fast and break things. He wants to move carefully and make things work. He feels like a steward, not an invader.

He is putting on his jacket when Janet speaks again. She is still looking at herself sideways, smoothing the fabric over her hips as though she could smooth away the flesh.

"Do you think we could help Kat get a bigger apartment? They'll need one now, with the baby. I told her I thought we could."

He looks at her in the mirror. "She asked you?" He can't help putting a faint emphasis on "you."

Janet meets his eyes and nods.

It's another rebuff, a needle prick. Why had she not asked him? He'd have liked to say yes. It would have given him pleasure.

He turns away, buttoning his jacket. "Yes, of course."

It appeared he'd have to wait to be rehabilitated.

Kat has already found the new place: two floors of a brownstone. The rooms had high ceilings and ornate moldings and tall windows that shuddered in their cases, but Kat and Chris ignored the Victorian detail. When they moved in they furnish it in a modernist style, no carpets or curtains, everything bright and hard-edged. The coffee table is made of wire grid, like a long metal cage.

Later Janet says to Warren, "It's all so rigid. There's no comfort in it. It's so barren."

"It's her generation," he says. "You didn't want what your mother had in her house."

"Of course not," Janet says. "All those hunting prints and leather chairs. Why do you always take her side?"

The baby was due in late March. Janet went down four days early, but the due date came and went. Every night Janet called Warren to say that it hadn't happened. She tried to think of things to take Kat's mind off it.

Kat and Chris had chosen not to learn the baby's gender. Kat had chosen green for all the baby things. She wouldn't tell Janet the names they were considering.

"I'm afraid they'll choose something ridiculous," Janet tells Warren.

"Like what?" he asks.

She pauses. "Jellybean," she says. "They joke about it. At least I think they're joking. What if they aren't?"

"Then we'll learn to love Jellybean," Warren says.

"Suddenly I get why the name is important," Janet says. "I always thought it was silly, grandparents getting upset over them. Didn't your grandmother have a stroke when she heard about your brother?"

"She did. She limped for the rest of her life, because my parents didn't name him after his grandfather," he says. "Don't have a stroke."

"No," Janet says. "But I hope they don't call it Jellybean."

"Me, too," Warren says.

"Have you stopped taking her side?" she asks.

"No," he says.

On the sixth day Janet says, "She's so depressed. I feel so bad for her. Today at lunch she set down her sandwich and put her face in her hands. She wasn't crying. I asked if she was having contractions and she shook her head. 'What is it?' I asked, and she said, 'Don't even ask me. You have no idea.'"

"But what was it?" Warren asks.

"Hormones, I guess, but frightening," Janet says.

"Poor Kat," he says.

"She thinks the baby will literally never come. I mean, she knows that can't be true. But she's kind of in despair."

"Isn't there something they can give her to make it happen?" Warren asks. "Some shot?"

"Her doctor wanted to induce her but she refused. She read it may cause hemorrhaging." Janet sighs. "I hate seeing her so unhappy."

Maybe this is the worst of being a parent, being unable to help your child in distress. He is helpless here.

"What did Chris say?" he asks. "How's he doing?"

"He's being great," Janet says. "Earnest and kind. Maybe a little scared."

"Have you talked to him?" Warren asks.

"I tell them both it will all be fine," says Janet. "And it will be."

On the eighth day she says, "Today I took her shopping for some new things for the baby. We brought them over to the counter and the salesgirl said, 'When are you due?' Kat said, 'Eight days ago.' The girl froze and then she glanced down at the counter. I could see she was thinking Kat might give birth right there," Janet says. "And actually I think Kat may have started then. On the way home she said she was feeling twinges. I think it's begun."

"Shall I come down?" Warren asks.

"I'll call you in a bit," Janet says. "Her doctor said not to come in yet."

She calls him later. Everything's fine, she says, and it's happening. Kat's in early labor, and she and Chris are taking her in. Warren should come down. But by then it's too late for him to come that night, and he books an early morning flight. When he wakes at six he calls Janet: Kat's still in the labor room. By the time he boards the plane, she has not delivered.

As soon as he lands at LaGuardia, while the plane is bumping across the tarmac, he calls Janet. He's on the aisle, and as he waits for her to answer, he leans forward to look out the window, past his seatmate. The man is large, his body spills over the shared armrest. He wears a dark zip-up jacket and aviator glasses. His creosote-colored hair is slicked back from his forehead. He's staring at his cell phone as Warren looks past him.

Janet's nearly shouting. "He's here! Everyone's fine!" she says. "They're both fine. He's enormous! Quite yellow at the moment, but that's nothing."

They're both fine: At these words Warren feels his body undo some invisible knot. The sky is clearing, the clouds open. He'd had no idea that knot was there. "Yellow?"

"Jaundice," Janet says. "They use a sunlamp. Where are you? Come straight to her room."

When he clicks off, Warren turns to his seatmate. He never talks to strangers on planes, but now he says, "My daughter just had a baby. My first grandchild."

The man turns. His nose is broad and flat, and his wide face is mottled with red patches. He breaks into a beaming smile.

"Congratulations!" He puts out his hand and Warren takes it. It's large and humid, the grasp firm. The man pumps Warren's hand, submerging it. "You're a lucky man!" he says. "I never had kids. Boy or girl?"

"Boy," says Warren.

"So the family will survive," the man says. "That's what my grandmother would say. La famiglia sopravvive. Congratulations!" He's still pumping.

"Thanks," Warren says.

"Will they name him after you?"

Jellybean, thinks Warren. "I don't know."

In the sudden spotlight of the man's attention, and in the turbulence of his own joy, Warren feels something move in his chest. He feels a pinch inside his nose: he's almost weeping. The membrane between him and the world has become diaphanous. There is nothing protecting him from a terrifying union with all things.

"Thank you," he says, smiling. He takes back his hand. The plane jolts heavily, making a cumbersome turn toward the terminal.

In the taxi, rattling and bouncing down the Long Island Expressway, he stares out the window again, thinking of Kat. He thinks of her as she'd been, lithe and muscular, beside him on the sofa, shouting at the referee. Now that it's over he's aware of the reservoir of fear he had carried inside. He is emptied of it now. His lithe, powerful daughter: He has been frightened for her. This is a strange passage, in which death and birth ride side by side through the body, paired antagonists. Only one will win. There's no way to reach birth without passing death. But now it's over. He thinks of the baby. He imagines it bright yellow, like a banana. It's fine. He can deal with yellow, which will be mysteriously treated with a sunlamp. Though wouldn't that make him more yellow?

He remembers Kat at the peak of her rage. Standing at the dining room table, suffused with fury, hands on hips, strands of her hair sticking to her bare shoulder. He no longer thinks of how it felt to be the object of her rage, but of how strong she was, how righteous. How she had defended her mother, his warrior daughter. How she had made a moral claim on him.

He's thought of this moment often. He doesn't let himself consider what he might have done, how he might have opposed Kat. What she doesn't know is that it wasn't fear of her retribution that had changed his mind. It was a moral reckoning with himself. He had to commit himself to this vow, leave Kat or Sarah forever. He'd left Sarah.

The taxi slows—is there ever a moment in which the traffic on these highways doesn't slow to a crawl? Warren watches the row of houses beyond the service road. The closer they come to the city, the closer the houses are to each other. Stained roofs, faded asphalt siding, small windows, and bleak front stoops facing directly onto the service road, then the highway. He can't imagine living under the assault of the noise. Whatever you're used to seems normal, and whoever lives in those houses is used to it. But right now he's aware of those people, whoever they are, and the lives they lead along this roaring artery. He feels the current of the underclass, the people below the poverty line, who can't reach the middle. The whole tribe who can't ever send their kids to college, who can't break the cycle.

As Warren bumps along the roadway, this seems crucially important. He's on the board of an organization that addresses underserved communities in Boston. It's run by dedicated people, and it produces results. But in the great scale of things the progress seems so slow, so incremental.

Warren wonders if the people in these houses are safer now, closer to stability, house ownership, health insurance, all that, after four years of this Democratic president. When he'd been elected it had seemed like the start of a new liberal era, but now it's not clear how much has improved. Obama was hamstrung by Republicans and racism.

History moves in pendulum swings: each side thinks each shift is final, evidence of a new era, but the shaft always inclines toward the middle. And now the middle has shifted, though, and Republicans have moved further to the right. It's a mystery to him how they can ignore the needs of the people who elect them. He watches the houses as they pass. One has rusting metal awnings over the windows, a sad effort at gentrification. But what could you do to improve those places? He looks in the mirror at the cabdriver, a grizzled older man with a fierce expression. He wears a turban: a Sikh. Warren wonders what his journey to New York has been like. If he is lifting his children into the middle class. He feels respect for him, living on this alien continent, among strangers who can't speak his language. What if you never heard your own language around you?

The traffic has picked up speed, and they now are hurtling along the highway. Warren feels raw, exposed, as though a layer of himself has been peeled away. He's moved closer to something, something beating and alive. He remembers seeing Janet in the hospital, after she'd had Kat. She'd looked exhausted and ravaged, but indomitable. Her body had survived something he would never know. Now Kat has made this same journey. It gives him an odd sense of himself, his genetic identity. He is no longer in control, it will go on without him, carried out through others, down the generations. He is like a cell in the ocean, awash in the vast marine world. He feels part of something endless and exhilarating, something that encompasses and engulfs him.

When they reach the hospital he gives the cabdriver a big tip. "Thank you!" he says. He's not sure if the man speaks English or can hear him through the glass. He shouts, "My first grandchild!" Beneath his turban the driver's face wears a watchful frown, which doesn't change at Warren's shout. He nods, then looks away.

Warren doesn't care. He raps the car roof lightly with his knuckles, to signal his joy. The world is light around him.

Getting his visitors' pass, he beams at the man behind the desk. He suppresses the urge to say why he's here. On the eighth floor he makes his way through the maze of hallways. Everything seems important: the polished tile floors, the framed photographs on the walls, pictures of western scenery. Yes, he thinks, the Grand Canyon. Yes, the Half Dome. Good choice. He passes a man in blue scrubs pushing a cart full of clinking equipment. Everything seems evidence of the excellence of this place. In maternity the nurse at the desk is on the phone. He smiles at her as he asks for Kat's room. He can't help himself, the world seems radiant. She gives him a friendly look and tells him Kat's room number, 821. He walks down the hall, hearing his footsteps on the polished floor, looking for her name. It's on a little plaque, white incised letters on a black background. It gives him a little thrill. He feels this mounting inside him, the importance of everything, shimmering around him. He feels the imminence of this encounter. He is approaching the summit.

The bed is beside the window. Kat's lying back with her eyes closed. Janet sits on the windowsill, talking quietly on her phone. She blinks her eyes in greeting, still talking. She turns away as Warren reaches the bed and leans over Kat.

She is shockingly plain. Her skin is sallow and drained. Her hair lies in flat hanks about her head. There are deep greenish circles below her eyes, and her nose seems sharper. Without her bold, dark liquid gaze, she's absent. Her eyelids are frail violet membranes over the swell of her eyes. They tremble: beneath the lids her eyes move. A few strands of hair are stuck to her cheek. The hospital gown gapes open over her shoulder, showing her pale skin. Her clavicle seems shockingly near the surface, the bone pressing against the skin. She is pared down to the core. How has she come through this? She is so slight.

His chest swells again, and he feels a great rising wash of tenderness for his daughter. He's moved by his connection to her, humbled by her accomplishment. He's awed by her fragility and her courage, the determination of her body to withstand such travail. And she is his, she is his own brave marvelous girl. Not that he takes credit for her, he does not, but by some remarkable chance he is her father. This is miraculous. His body unknots itself again, shedding fear, accepting glory, and another wave of emotion passes through him. There is nothing like this moment, looking down at his lovely, resting daughter. His throat closes, he blinks back what must be tears.

He leans over and smooths the hair off Kat's cheek. Her eyelids flutter and she opens her eyes. He smiles down at her. Bliss unspools through him. Bliss and pride.

"Hi, sweetie" he says. "Congratulations." He's nearly whispering, so as not to wake her up if she's asleep, but to let her know that he's arrived if she's dozing.

She opens her eyes and looks directly up into his. For a moment she looks full at him. He's leaning over, his face right over hers. He's ready to kiss her cheek, but Kat closes her eyes. She lies motionless. Her eyelids are now still, her eyes unmoving. She has refused. She is waiting for him to move away.

It comes to him that he will never see Sarah again. There is no parallel life. This is the only life.

He draws away. Janet clicks off her call.

"Hi, there," she says.

He stands and puts his arms around her, to avoid speaking. Humiliation floods through him like fever. She draws away and says to Kat, "Wake up, sweetie. Your dad's here."

Kat opens her eyes again. She meets his without smiling. He smiles at her but doesn't move.

"Congratulations," he said. "I'm proud of you."

"Thanks." She gives a challenging little smile.

He feels charged and distant. He puts his hands in his pockets.

He spends the morning with them. Chris, who had been there all night, has gone home to sleep. Janet calls people to tell them while Kat dozes. Warren goes out for the paper. He spends the morning reading it, then doing the crossword. He goes out to make calls to his office; when he comes back Chris is there. He looks exhausted.

"Congratulations," Warren says.

Chris smooths his hair back nervously. "Thanks," he says. "It was amazing." He looks completely undone.

"Glad you came through it all right," Warren says, and Chris laughs.

"Yeah," he said. "I had to leave a couple of times."

"No shame in that," Warren says. He wonders if Kat will ever turn her implacable judgment on her husband.

The nurse wheels in the baby. Warren peers down at the swaddled bundle, the creased and mottled face.

"What's his name?" Warren asks Kat.

She looks at the baby instead of at him. "Connor."

"Connor?" Janet repeats. "That's not what you said before."

"That's what it is," Kat says.

"Why?" Janet asks irritably.

"Why not?" Kat says.

"It's Irish," Janet says. "We're not Irish."

Kat shakes her head. "All names have ethnic antecedents. We like it. We like the name, Mom."

Janet looks at Warren, then back at Kat. "Right," she says. "Just, you said before that it was William Cartwright. You and Chris both said so."

"It's Connor," Kat says. "We talked again. Anyway, Chris's family has Irish blood. If you go back."

Janet takes a breath, but says nothing.

"Connor," Warren says. "I like it."

Kat doesn't look at him.

The nurse hands the baby to Kat and helps get him settled on her nipple. Her milk hasn't come in, this is the thick yellow colostrum. The baby is barely able to connect, he opens and closes his tiny grasping lips like a fish. Kat snugs him against her chest, singing a little cracked lullabye. Later she feeds him with the tiny bottle. He is still lean from the womb, his face wrinkled like a little old man's. He grimaces and smacks his lips, his tiny red starfish fingers opening and closing in the air. He doesn't know what air is. He doesn't understand this space. Kat whispers to him. "Connor," she says, "Connor."

Warren and Janet go out to get lunch, leaving Chris and Kat alone together.

As soon as they are at a distance Janet begins to talk. "We aren't Irish," she says. "Not that there's anything wrong with being Irish, but why would you choose a name that is explicitly something you are not?"

Warren says, "Mmm."

She turns to look at him. "You're still taking her side."

He puts his arm around her. "It doesn't matter what we think, it's not our baby. It's theirs."

"But he's part of our family," she says. "His name should show that. His last name will always be another family's. His first name should connect with us. I feel like she's trying to keep us out."

Warren says nothing. He keeps his hand on her shoulder as they walk past the nurses' desk. He nods to the nurse. Kat has chosen to name the baby away from them. She won't make the linguistic connection Janet had hoped for, she won't declare her allegiance. But names are only one way for a family to survive. Your family will continue in unexpected ways: a hand gesture, the shape of an eyebrow, musical talent, stubbornness or compassion, a tendency to ear infections. This tiny Connor will be his own man. Kat doesn't want him burdened by her family; it's her choice to make.

And she doesn't want him in her life. She has turned away from him. It has been four years. This is his future. There is no Sarah; he's bound by his vow.

Chapter 25

SOMETIMES SARAH TYPES HIS NAME INTO A SEARCH ENGINE. She wants proof that he's there in the world. And she enjoys writing out the letters, summoning up lexicographical evidence of his presence. Sometimes he is quoted in an article about modern architects. Once she found a photograph of him in a group, standing in front of a glass-and-steel building. When she enlarged it on her screen his face was blurred. He was smiling, but she couldn't make out his eyes. She looked at it for some time.

She had seen the notice of his daughter's wedding. She pictured him, distinguished in his dark suit, walking her down the aisle: how handsome he was. She wondered what the bride had worn—wiry, athletic Kat. Not a hoodie and yoga pants. Probably a long white dress, why would you not choose to be a princess on that one day?

Sarah will never know what Kat wore or how Warren looked: She is banned from that family's life forever. She can never again look in at it through Warren's gaze. In that family's life she is anathema.

She actually had been anathema to them. Because of her the family had nearly split apart. But she doesn't think she's bad or immoral. She's read that convicted murderers think of themselves as good. It's true that her presence had nearly split the family, but surely it was Warren who bore the moral responsibility for the family, not her. Was it her fault that Warren had fallen in love with her? What were her moral obligations toward his marriage? Though she doesn't quite trust this line of reasoning: she had always refused to go out with other married men, on principle. What was the principle? She wouldn't be involved in someone else's ethical landscape. But in Warren's case she had allowed that principle to bend. How did she justify that?

She had no justification.

The other woman was always blamed for adultery. Because women are the vessels of morality? Are they expected to have higher moral standards than men? Maybe she should have turned away because he was married, and in fact she had always done that before. But she had known Warren from before, that was why this was different. She wasn't starting a new relationship, she was continuing an unfinished one. She'd been wrong to end it as she had; she'd felt an obligation to set things right. And there was also the intoxicating current of his presence, the depth of his gaze. The power of his attention. She'd do it again.

Though it is terrible to be responsible for the end of a marriage. And there is something that she owes another woman, some loyalty. Men are loyal to each other, they all acknowledge the universal will to stray, they cover for each other. So what does she owe Janet?

She owes Janet nothing, but she has betrayed herself. She doesn't want to be the person who has destroyed a marriage. And it's Warren who has restored it, not she.

She doesn't know what his life is like now, but she thinks he's trapped. He's honor-bound to lead that life now. He must smile at Janet when he comes home, he must hold her at night. She knows he can do those things again because he's always done them. She's afraid he can't breathe.

It's painful to think of him, both because he's gone and because she thinks he's leading a life of arid unhappiness. Though maybe she's assuming too much. He was happy before all this, happy enough, anyway. Maybe he's happy enough now, though she can't bear thinking that, either. This is a life sentence. What if keeping his promise will drain his world of joy? If he'd held fast, she's sure that Kat would have relented. She would have softened.

But leaving Janet would have been selfish and cruel.

The justification for leaving a marriage was that you were increasing the sum of happiness in the world. You were ending your own unhappiness, and your spouse's (if you weren't happy, your spouse couldn't really be happy, either), and he or she would find real happiness elsewhere. The children had only known an unhappy marriage. Now they would learn what happy parents are like, and they would become happier, and able to create happy marriages themselves. But actually all this is false and self-serving. The only person whose happiness is increased is the departing spouse. There are no moral grounds for leaving a marriage. You are breaking your vow and causing pain to others. It is selfish, cruel, and dishonorable. How could he have lived with that?

Every day she wakes to the loss; each morning it's a new blow. The day lies ahead, flat and empty. Sometimes the first thing she does is weep, the tears spilling sideways into her hair. A photograph of him stands on her bedside table. He's sitting on the sofa downstairs; she took it the first time he came here. He's looking up at her and smiling, his arms open wide. It is unbearable to look at— he was right downstairs, wearing that blue sweater—but she can't bring herself to put it away.

It is pointless to cry, over and over, because he's gone. Yet the tears come. Sometimes, at night, she goes into her bathroom and closes the door behind her. She sits on the edge of the tub, and cries with the loud ugly wails of a child. She can't seem to stop this.

In the evening, walking to the reservoir with Bella, she thinks of that first time he was here. When he arrived he'd set his hands on his hips as he looked around, admiring the half-timbered walls, the steep roofs. The long-legged dog walking toward him, aloof but courteous.

"Is she a Standard?" he asked, and Sarah nodded. She's pleased that he knows the breed, doesn't name it. Poodle.

"Hello," he said quietly. He'd dropped down to crouch on his heels. Bella extended her nose toward him. She sniffed lightly, then shook her head. It was a gesture of friendship; Bella, who doesn't like everyone, had liked him. She'll never see him again, either, though she doesn't know this.

They'd walked down together to the reservoir. He'd held the creaky gate open for her, he'd stood beside her at the edge of the bluff. They'd watched the sunset spilling red across the light-filled surface of the water.

Sarah stands alone at the bluff. The sky is overcast, and along the horizon, above the dark line of trees, the muffled sun gives off a dark reddish glow. The evening breeze has picked up, and the surface of the water is pricked and rippled. The wind moves across it in sudden patches of scintillation, darkening the water now here, now there, like a creature hunting.

She remembers Tosca's song to her lover Cavaradossi, begging him to come to their little house. It was about the moon and the stars shining down, the whole night murmuring of love. She hears herself make a sound; she is crying again. Bella looks up. Sarah touches her head.

"It's all right," she says, but she can't stop.

She goes back across the field as the light is leaving the sky. By the time she reaches the house the landscape has darkened, and when she steps inside she turns on the lights. The windows are black, the landscape has vanished. Night has entered the world.

The thing about absence is that it is always there. He is always absent from her life. Each time she faces this thought, accepts it and moves on, it reappears. He is always absent, from every plan she makes, every thought, every idea, every room. From her future. He is always absent. She can never reach him.

The days are gray now.

She can't help but go on with things. His absence is the largest thing in her life; she has to live around it.

In the spring Josh had flown back East to meet Meg's new baby, and he came out to stay with Sarah for a few days. She was surprised at what a relief it was to have him at home, what a comfort to find his tall, lanky, familiar figure moving through the rooms. She hadn't realized that she was missing this—someone she loved and trusted in the house. Josh helped her with some planting. She was putting in trees beyond the hedge, as higher barriers against the road. Three *Cladastris luteas*, yellowwoods, beautiful native trees. With smooth silvery gray bark, and creamy hanging blooms like wisteria. Josh dug the holes, big generous pits, tossing up shovelful after shovelful of rust-colored soil. Sarah wheeled the trees out in the wheelbarrow. She dragged the hose; they both shoveled dirt in around the root balls.

She remembered going to see a friend in the maternity room, after the birth of her second child, a boy. Sheila held the little tiny red-faced scrap in her arms and said, "Now I have a son to take care of me!" Sarah had laughed at the time, but now understood.

She and Josh had dinner in the kitchen, at the long table. He sat across from her, so tall! His long arms moving and gesticulating— he'd always used his hands when he talked. He had a sort of beard, coarse dusting on his chin and cheeks.

He set his elbows on the table to talk. He brushed his hair back from his forehead, he had always done that.

"What about the girlfriend?" Sarah asked. They had eaten the pasta-and-sausage casserole, they were on to the salad. She was tossing the frail green leaves, watching him as she lifted and turned them. He pushed his hair back.

"Over," he said. "A thing of the past."

"Sorry," Sarah said.

"All good," he said.

"What happened?"

"I don't know. She said it wasn't working. She doesn't like hiking, she doesn't like surfing, she doesn't like the stuff I like. We weren't a good match."

"Did you think you were a good match?"

Josh picked a slick black olive from the little blue ceramic bowl. He tossed it up in the air, lunged forward, and caught it in his mouth. "I did, yes."

"Then I'm sorry," Sarah said. "Also, she's an idiot."

He gave a snort. "She's not, but thanks." He looked at her. "What happened with your guy?"

"Went back to his wife," Sarah said.

"I'm sorry," he said.

"Such a cliché," she said. "A married man who says he's leaving but then goes back. How trite is that?"

"But?" Josh said. He took another olive, not throwing it this time.

"It was more complicated than that. He was someone I'd known years ago, in college. I was in love with him. So this was a part of an earlier story."

"Why did you break up in college?"

Sarah looked down at the bowl. "I don't exactly know," she said. "Mostly because other things intervened, our colleges were quite far apart—he was in Maine—and then I met your father. But the first thing"—she hesitated—"the proximal cause, was something he said to me. It changed my feelings."

Josh took a drink of wine, waiting.

"He asked me to go on a trip, around Europe, and then behind the Iron Curtain."

"Why did that change your feelings?"

"I didn't understand it. It frightened me, it was so reckless. As though the KGB were a joke. You really couldn't go to Communist countries then. People were arrested and put in prison as spies. It wasn't a joke." She paused. "It seemed so dangerous and so foolish that I just . . . pulled back from him. I withdrew. I didn't want to argue and I didn't want to end up in a dangerous situation. I thought this was part of his character. Also I thought he'd been fired for bad behavior from a job. I thought he was someone I couldn't trust."

Josh nodded. "And then you started seeing him again, later, and what did you think?"

It was hard to admit. "First of all I found out that he hadn't been fired, he'd resigned in protest at the way someone else was being treated. And I'd misunderstood him. I'd gotten it all wrong."

"I'm sorry," Josh said kindly.

Sarah nodded. "As it turned out, he was someone I could have trusted."

THEY HAD finally gotten Barbara Schwarzman to write the essay, but she had turned it in late. Sarah was disappointed.

"I think it's really unoriginal," she'd told Nancy. "The whole point of getting Schwarzman was that she had new things to say about this subject. But this is just a series of biographical sketches. Really! Where are the searing insights about Carrington? What about Vanessa's rise and fall? This is just warmed-up hash. We paid her good money for this! She had that idea that they were the direct descendants of the Pre-Raphaelites."

"But no one will actually read the catalogue," Nancy said. "They'll flip through it and look at the reproductions. Scholars don't do groundbreaking work in an exhibition catalogue."

Sarah sighed. "They could. This is a perfectly legitimate place to publish."

"We're still only a small regional museum," Nancy said, "despite being distinguished. The groundbreaking work will be published in an academic venue. This is as good as we can expect."

"Well, I am disappointed," Sarah said. "All that fuss about her schedule, and not being able to meet the deadline, and she turns in something straight from Wikipedia. I could have written this."

"We wanted the name," Nancy said. "We got it. The *New York Times* will mention the essay by Barbara Schwarzman. And it's not a bad one. I think it's fine."

Sarah had shaken her head. "Well, it's done. We can't send it back for revision. But it's disheartening."

While she'd been planning the show she'd been buoyed up by her feelings for Warren—all that time she'd been up in the empyrean. Everything had been exciting. She had told him about everything—which pictures they'd been promised, the problems with lenders, the essay, the design. He'd been her colleague, her partner.

After Warren had left her, the project no longer held the delight for her that it had. After that it seemed insignificant: a group of relatively minor artists. She has always thought art was important; her whole career had been based on that idea. But now she wonders, to what end? How does it better the world?

In the fall after it closed—the Bloomsbury exhibition had been a success, though not the blockbuster they had hoped—the Exhibitions Committee met. It was cold that day, and she kept her coat on. The big windows were behind her, and she could feel the chill against her back.

They were discussing an exhibition about the environment. Jean Gerson asked the committee what they thought.

"The news is always too dire," Candace Woods said. "No one will come and see it."

"Some people will come," Shirley Anderson said. "Even if they don't see it, people will know about it. It will raise the level of awareness. That's how change happens."

"We're an art museum," Nancy said. "We shouldn't be putting on political shows."

"Everything is political," said Shirley. "Whatever we choose, we're looking through a political lens. The Bloomsbury show is about a small group of elite white artists and writers. It ignores people of color."

"Anything we do is de facto exclusionary," Jean Gerson said. "It excludes everyone but the group we've chosen. We need to balance the exhibitions, not try to include everyone in each one."

Sarah said nothing: everyone seemed to be standing on an island of self-righteous political awareness, competing for first place in wokeness. All this mattered less to her now. She has lost some sense of competitiveness, or communal responsibility. She didn't care so much about it.

On some mornings she wakes up happy: during the night she's forgotten. She wakes up thinking of something to tell him, or of something he said, and then she remembers. She is alone again.

It's odd, she thinks, how you can be alone in a room but not feel alone, or be alone in bed and suddenly feel it, cascading over you. She will be alone from him forever, but she can't believe that. Over and over she wonders if there might be some reversal. What if Janet died? Or Kat?

One morning, walking into the kitchen, Sarah looks around and says, "Where are you? Where are you?" Bella cocks her head, watching. The room is silent. He's not here, he's never here. He's chosen to be somewhere else.

Nancy comes to her house for coffee. They sit in the kitchen. The birds—goldfinches, now in their summer splendor, tossing radiance around—cluster on the feeder.

Nancy asks, "So, how are things going for you?"

"Good," Sarah says. "Everything's fine. Meg and the kids are fine. The baby's three now. He's a holy terror, but at least he's sleeping through the night."

"I read that in the first year of a baby's life the parents lose seven hundred hours of sleep," Nancy says.

Sarah laughs. "I'm so glad I never have to lose seven hundred hours of sleep again."

"I know, right?" Nancy says. "One of the many many benefits of getting older." After a moment she asks, "What about your guy?" Sarah had told her it was over. "Do you ever hear from him?"

Sarah shakes her head. "Never."

"Not even a text?"

"No," Sarah says. "He took a vow."

"Jesus," Nancy says. "Really, a vow?"

"Something like that," Sarah says. "I'll never hear from him again." As she says the words she realizes that some part of her hopes it's not true. Though she knows it to be true, and in that moment she feels a wave of excruciating grief. It is like a cliff breaking off a mountain, the whole side of the mountain sliding off in a cloud, gone. She has lost this part of herself. She takes a breath to keep from crying.

Nancy looks at her. "I remember when he sent you those flowers in London."

"Me, too." She still has the florist's card in her wallet.

One night Meg calls. Sarah knows what her evenings are like, struggling to get three kids down for the night, when they kept popping up again, crying or restless; doing one last load of laundry, sending late-night emails for work; but here she is, on the phone.

"Mum?" she says.

"Hi, what is it?" Sarah asks. Something must be wrong: anxiety is part of her body's response to her daughter.

"Nothing," says Meg, "nothing's wrong."

"How are the kids? How's the baby?"

"They're all fine. He's a dream, actually, he sleeps much better than the others."

"I'm so glad," Sarah says. She waits for the reason for the call. "How's work?"

"It's okay," Meg says. "It's good. I have a new manuscript in that I love."

"And the boss?"

"Is okay. I don't know. I can't tell. It's okay right now."

"Good," Sarah says. She's waiting.

"I wanted to know how you are," Meg says.

"How I am?" Sarah says. "I'm fine."

"I know that that guy breaking things off was hard for you," says Meg. "I never got to talk about it with you, after. The baby came along and everything was chaos. But I've been thinking about you, and wondering how you were."

Sarah says nothing for a moment. This is so unexpected, it upsets the balance between them so completely, that she feels uncertain of what to say. Who is she, if she is not the invincible mother, who does not feel fear when the airplane shudders, when the house creaks, when the snowstorm closes in? She is not that invincible person, and Meg's question shatters something in her. She can't pretend to be. Her throat closes.

"Mum?" Meg says.

But she can't speak.

"I wanted to say I'm so sorry," Meg says. "It must be so hard for you."

Sarah takes a breath. "Thank you," she says.

"Would you like me to come up and see you?"

"I'm fine," Sarah says. "That's sweet of you."

"We're going to come up this weekend," Meg says, "on Sunday. I'll bring lunch."

The feeling comes flooding through her, partly gratitude, partly loneliness.

PART V

Chapter 26

WARREN HAS GONE OVER ALL THE CURRENT PROJECTS, MAKing sure that each has a manager and a path forward. He hand-writes a memo, undated, stating how the company should work in the event of his absence. He'd made Jack the head, but with equal shares going to Mason and Laurel. The memo won't have any legal authority, but it's a guideline. He asks his lawyer to add Connor to his will, and sets up a small trust fund for him. This would surprise no one.

Now it's like watching an hourglass as it empties: The finish is in sight. These days are like the beat of a drum.

One Thursday in late September he comes home from work to find Janet in the kitchen. He can see her through the window before he comes in. She's talking on her cell, and when he comes in she waves and points to the phone. "But when did she tell you this?" she says into it.

He waves back and heads upstairs to shower and change. On this night he is aware of every detail. Mounting the stairs, he's aware of the carpet underfoot, narrow stripes of gray and black and brown. The pile is wearing down in the center; it must be old, though he remembers when it was installed. Ten years ago? Twenty? The years telescope, the decades collapse into each other. The years behind pile up, the years ahead diminish. This is the difference, he could now tell Sarah, this is what's new about being this age. The horizon line has moved closer. There are far fewer possibilities. Now he knows there are trips he will never take, books he will never read. When he was younger the possibilities had been endless: someday he would visit Antarctica, Bhutan. Maybe Alaska. Now he knows he will never see any of them. Now the future has shortened, the past stretches endlessly behind. The moments that make it up are chronologically indeterminate. There are so many times—encounters, conversations, books, movies—he remembers but which he can't connect to any date. All these moments lie scattered on the great plain of the past.

Walking up through the stairwell, he sees the upstairs hall, hung with family photographs. There are his parents in their wedding portrait, side by side, faces in profile, gazes meditative. There are Janet's parents in black tie at some anniversary, dazzling white shirtfront, bouffant hair and glittery earrings. There is Kat, birthdays and graduations. There are the family trips: the camp on the Masai Mara, where the cheetah climbed on top of their van. Luxor, with Kat posing as the hawk-headed god. The villa in Tuscany, where Kat fell off the balcony and they thought she had died. On the porch in Maine, the low, gray-shingled house set among the pines. The wedding picture of Kat and Chris, a swirl of white veil around her head, both of them beaming. Kat standing at the door of the Museum of Bacon—or was it Corn?—from the time she'd driven across the country with a college roommate. These moments are all evidence of lives lived, though right now they seem meaningless. He turns away from the picture of Kat.

He'd written her a letter, so that he could put down everything he felt. He told her how much he loved her, and how glad he has always been to be a part of her life.

> *I've done something to damage our relationship, but as you know I have done everything in my power to atone for what I've done. I've done what you've asked, and now I'm asking you to accept my response. This is how we*

> *grow, as adults, not only by taking a stand on principle, but by recognizing how humans function. By accepting their faults and failings, by accepting their apologies, and by seeing them as the full, whole, flawed, and enterprising people that they all are. We accept each others' failings and when they atone for them we forgive each other. That's something we must do, or we are stuck forever in judgment. That's not where you want to live, I hope, dearest Kat. If you won't allow me to mend the break between us it will break my heart. I'm asking you to return to me. I love you.*

Kat had not replied.

Some switch inside her had been turned. This was to be his life: to be allowed inside the family circle, but not into the center. This was his future, the torture of false intimacy.

Now he mounts the steps slowly.

He's trying to see everything and take it inside himself, as though it's his responsibility to keep it. As though he is the keeper of this place. He has a sudden impulse to tell his father what he is doing, explain himself.

After his shower, he dries himself carefully, running the towel over his arms, his legs. He can still feel the packed mass of muscle, but the muscles are ropy now, less solid, and the flesh is beginning to hang loose from the bone. He is aging. He is memorizing each moment: steam has taken over the mirror, soundless and complete, blotting out the world with its silvery presence. This is how the bathroom smells, shampoo and flowery soap. This is how he looks, blurred by steam, wild-haired, blue-chinned.

For dinner that night Janet has heated up frozen chicken pot pies.

"I hope you don't mind," Janet says, when he comes down. She's standing at the stove. The pies rest on a blackened cookie sheet. She pushes one onto a plate with her finger. "Ow," she says, and puts the burnt finger into her mouth.

"I don't mind," Warren says. Why should he mind that she uses technology to make her life easier? Why should she cook when she has so little interest in it? He spends his day doing something he loves. She has run the household dutifully for over forty years, made sure the place is clean, the beds are changed, and food is on the table. For all this time she has contrived to please him. He can't ask for more.

They sit down and Janet spreads her napkin on her lap and takes a sip of wine. She is ready to talk, humming with something. "That was Meredith on the phone. She has a title for our next book club meeting."

"What is it?" he asks.

"She says it's great," Janet says. "All the book clubs are choosing it. It's about a family secret. It's called *Family Secrets*. I know, it sounds kind of cliché. But she says it's really good, we'll love it."

Warren nods. "Sounds good," he says. "Has she read it?"

She leans forward. Her hair is still glossy, blond. It falls around her face like a mane. Her turquoise earrings catch the glint from her eyes. She doesn't usually wear earrings when they're home alone—she's dressed up for him. In conciliation for the frozen pot pies.

"That's the thing," she says, confidential. "She hasn't read it. But she's telling us we'll love it! How does she know?" She laughs, tilting her head. "It's not great literature," she goes on. "You wouldn't like any of these books. They're entertainment. All they do is give you a little escape from the world around you." She takes a bite, then gasps, the pie is so hot. Her gasp is quick and energetic. She opens her mouth and fans it with her hand: She's laughing at herself. Her hair swings forward.

She's performing for him, with her glittering earrings, her glossy hair, her comic turn. He admires her vitality, her energetic response to the world. Her humility. Her generosity: he has benefited from all of this. But her conversation—her conversation he cannot endure.

"That's what a book should do," he says. "Take you away from your world."

She waits, still smiling, but he doesn't go on. So she does.

"The last one we read had the craziest plot," she says. She lifts off the whole crust of the pie with her fork, releasing a cloud of steam. She begins to explain the plot, which is complicated and, as she's said, kind of crazy, about a patrician family with a genetic trait that had entered the clan through an illicit affair a century earlier.

"So it was sort of a love story and a detective story. That one was Meredith's, too, come to think of it," she says. "And it was terrible! So complicated and so stupid! We all complained. Now she's got another one."

She laughs again, her raucous machine-gun laugh. He watches her face, lit up by the delight she takes in the world. He's grateful for all the dinners she's cooked, all the plots she's described. All the gossip, the stories about her friends, her groups, her committees. All the love she has showered on their child. The way she laughs. Her good nature. She has given him everything she has. It's not enough.

"The one I wanted was about a family in California," Janet says. "They'd lived there for five generations, so, very connected. And rich." She nods chattily. "But the grandfather is about to die and he hasn't written a will. The granddaughter is his favorite, but her brother works in the business, which was lumber but now has diversified." She's proud of the word. "So the brother would be just as sensible a choice. But he's kind of conniving, and he tries to edge out his sister. And he does, and the grandfather says he's going to write a will leaving him everything, but then the brother is in a horrible car accident and is in the hospital and he regrets everything he's done. Then he dies before the grandfather does change his will. So the daughter inherits in the end, and she also falls in love with a really great guy, so you know she'll have a happy life, but it's really sad."

"It sounds it," says Warren.

"It's like one of your operas," she says.

He says again, "It sounds really sad."

"No, really, it is like one of your operas. It's a tragedy."

He doesn't answer and she says, teasing, "You don't agree. But why isn't it a tragedy? Like an opera?"

After a moment he replies. "So, in an opera, the tragedy involves passion and honor. Some deep passion drives the character, and then there's a crisis, and then honor demands death. Rather than leading a life of dishonor. It has to include passion and honor."

"'Passion and honor,'" Janet says. "That's just the kind of thing you like to say, Warren." She laughs at him. "What do you mean, though? What do you really mean by honor?"

He smiles back. "A moral code. Holding yourself to a certain standard. You make a commitment. In a tragedy the characters will die rather than break a promise. A promise to themselves. Sometimes it's a promise to love. Tosca commits suicide because her lover is executed. She refuses to conceive of a life without him."

Janet shakes her head. "She'd get over it! Killing yourself because someone else has died—it's romantic, but, really, no. Stupid."

"She gives up her life for love. She gives up the world without him. She doesn't want that world. She's being true to herself. To her idea of love."

"Okay, then, this isn't a tragedy like an opera," says Janet briskly. She moves on. "But it's really sad. They all love each other. And they forgive each other when the brother is dying. He apologizes and they forgive him. Doesn't forgiveness count?"

"It counts," Warren says. "But it doesn't change the tragic path." He smiles again, to temper this.

"'The tragic path,'" she says. "Okay, well, this book doesn't have a 'tragic path.' But you should read it. You'd like it."

He nods. He will never read one of her books.

He can't breathe; this is not enough.

That night he turns to her in bed, sliding his hands beneath her silky nightgown. Their bodies are familiar to each other, this is a duet they have played many times. She turns to him at once, lying back on the pillow. He knows her body, the thickened layer of flesh over her ribs, the heft of her breasts. She knows how to move under his hands, they have pleased each other for years. Warren begins this out of a sense of obligation, but halfway through he begins to fail. He can no longer summon up the certainty he needs. He's afraid that she'll stop and try to help him, which will end everything. He labors on with his task, now heavy and lumbering, a load of flesh instead of a spear. His body has lost its intention; he can't remember how it used to feel. But he keeps going—he owes her this—and in the end he manages it, though not the way it used to be, which was a mindless, effortless pleasure. She hasn't come, though, and he shifts to attend to her. When she has finished he moves up to face her, and strokes her hair. He can't bring himself to say he loves her.

"I'm glad you're back," she says. He strokes her hair again.

Chapter 27

SARAH HAD RENTED A HOUSE FOR A WEEK, FOR MEG AND HER family, out at the eastern end of Long Island. It's on a quiet street in Sag Harbor. The house has big willow trees around it, trailing their long hanks onto the lawn, and a hammock in the backyard. There are four bedrooms (the two boys share). James is now eight; Nate, twelve.

Sarah has made good on her own promise: on Thursdays she has been driving in to see James. She took him to the park in his stroller, sleepy, cheery, fretful. Pink-cheeked in the cold, sweating in the summer heat. She took him to music classes, where they sat on mats and swayed to drums and piccolos. She took him to coffee shops and climbing walls, libraries and gymnastics, judo and art classes. She knows him, his quick lovely spirit. His naughtiness, his self-deprecation. He's the baby, so everyone adores him. He's the baby, so he's always last. "I have no idea what you're talking about," he offers, when the others talk about a book or a movie he doesn't know, secure in the knowledge that this is not a risk, he doesn't need to keep up. He'll be taken care of. Sarah finds this endearing.

All that week they basked in the sun, the weather has held, miraculously, now that climate change has interrupted the familiar patterns. Summer is no longer a long celebration of blue skies, but a scattery patchwork of cloudy days, fitful rains, sudden cold spells, staggering heat. But this week has been old-fashioned in its genial blue and gold. They have gone to the great wide white beaches, carrying the stuff of summer: beach umbrella, cooler, towels, the lunch hamper. Sand got into everything, and James stubbed his toe on a rock, which was the cause of some anguish and a good deal of noise—he's apt to consider himself fragile. They picked blueberries in the fields, and had a scavenger hunt in the backyard. They've had a good week. Sarah wondered if it would be the last. At some point Meg will want to have her own family vacation, one that doesn't include her mother.

Their last night, Friday, they had corn and tomatoes and hot dogs, and sat outside at the picnic table. The boys were playing some game, counting under their breath and chortling secretly, doubling over. Busby was beyond them now, and won't play with them, she was too sophisticated.

"Corn on the cob may be the best food in the world," Sarah says. She has it all over her chin.

"Arguably," said Jeff. "Though sea urchins are a close second."

"Have you ever had one?" Sarah asked.

He nodded. "I went to a conference once in Tokyo. They're actually delicious."

"You are braver than I am," Sarah said. "But we knew that." Though they never did have a conversation about it, the stay in the hospital, the watch they kept over Meg, has made them closer. They now trust each other.

"I have a French friend who doesn't like corn," said Meg.

"She's never had fresh corn," said Sarah.

"No, he has," Meg said. "It's a he. He says he's had it straight from the field and it's overrated."

Sarah said nothing. She has curbed her habit of making brash responses.

Meg went on about the Frenchman—he was an editor at her house, but had left to become a literary agent, specializing in Indian writers.

"He was so bossy," Meg said. She licked her mouth. "But wonderful. I liked him."

"Mom," Busby said meaningfully. She raised her napkin ostentatiously to her lips. She was an adolescent, her features soft and undetermined. Her hair was long and shiny, her gestures awkward. She was alternately shy and arrogant. She was like a young animal, not yet what she'll become, full of unknown promise.

"Thanks," Meg said. She grinned and wiped her own mouth. Busby gave her a mock-stern nod, as though she'd be watching.

How easy they were with each other. Sarah thought of her own mother: She would never have corrected Carola's table manners. How sealed off from each other they had been, and why? It was a lifetime ago now. All that silence and reticence—no one acts like that anymore. But in her family, in her childhood, intimacy had seemed beyond their reach. It hurts Sarah to remember the distance between herself and her parents, the things they had never said. What had her father thought, marrying into such a dominant tribe? Had it been hard for him? She had never dared ask. Such simple questions, so utterly out of reach. And whatever caused her mother pain, Sarah had never heard it. Carola had held herself always separate. When she was dying, in the hospital, Sarah had sat beside her. She lifted her mother's hand; it was shockingly heavy. She had kissed it and cried. I know it wasn't you. I know it was Dad who made you make that trip, when I was a baby, she thought. I know you loved me.

Her mother had already been gone.

Now Sarah has determined that she will listen: to her daughter, to her grandchildren, to her son-in-law. The greatest failure in her life—at this age she confronts this kind of awful milestone—had been her failure to listen, her failure at intimacy. The time, when they'd been young, when she had not opened herself to Warren. She had not asked him to reveal himself, to step into the beam of her awareness. She had not asked him what he had meant, or who he was. She had judged him and turned away. That failure was always with her.

"Sassy, I want to show you a magic trick," James said. He called her Sassy, as Busby does, though Nate called her Nana. She was closer to James than to the others, because of all those hours together. He held her gaze, excited. "Watch my fingers." He held up his hand, grimy and dark with summer. "And listen to exactly what I say."

"Okay," Sarah said. "Listening."

Chapter 28

THAT FRIDAY AFTERNOON WARREN LEAVES STRAIGHT FROM the office. Heading out of Boston the traffic is slow, inching along. Warren has the radio on low, but drifts in and out of attentiveness: the news is always dire. He thinks about work, about the house on Nantucket. About the problem of the windows, though he won't be the one to solve it. He won't think about Kat, about Janet. About Sarah. Finally he crosses the bridge at Kittery, and he is in Maine. Past Portland the highway is empty, but he doesn't reach the house on Mount Desert until nearly midnight. It's dark. The woods come right up to the house, and there is no moon. He stands by the car and waits for a moment, letting his eyes adjust, then moves, feeling his way through the dimness, across the driveway to the front door.

On Saturday he wakes early. The house is low, one story, with a long swooping roof and big chimneys at each end. The bedroom faces west, so the morning light is dim, the window a blurred pale rectangle. For a moment he lies still, listening to the silence.

The house stands near the edge of Somes Sound. Below it the ground is covered in low shrubs as it slopes down toward the water. At the shore are soft, scythe-edged grasses, and the long, rounded shapes of pink granite that stretch along the water like prehistoric creatures. Woods surround the rest of the house: white pine, balsam fir, maple, oak, beech. The trees are beginning to turn now, striking bright fiery notes among the dark conifers. Birdsong still ripples through the trees: a wood thrush scatters his jeweled notes into the air.

Warren gets up. He wants to be on the mountain before anyone else. Much of the point of climbing is solitude. A certain deep joy derives from being alone at the summit, where you stand turning, slowly, turning and turning, taking in the wild circular view, your face brushed by the clean silent wind that touches nothing else. You must be alone, not among garrulous strangers asking if you had done this before, or if you were ever scared along the sheer parts.

The trail he's taking today is closed for much of the summer because of nesting peregrine falcons. He's always glad when it reopens, when that piece of wildness is available again.

He dresses quickly, pulling on hiking pants, long-sleeved T-shirt, sweater, fleece. His hiking boots are by the back door. Also his backpack: thermos of water, cell phone, trail mix, a banana, rain jacket. Bandages. What he always carries.

He eats breakfast standing, waiting for the coffee to brew. He chews quickly: breakfast is an obstacle to the day. He wants to get on with it. His father had eaten breakfast at the table in the dining room, and then he'd settled in with the paper on the train to Philadelphia. His father had worn a hat. That leisurely passage, feeling in charge of the world, or anyway that you were the recipient of vital information about the world, folding the big sheets back into the correct quadrant, front page first, then moving on to the odd interesting article on something you'd never heard of, is history.

Warren had read the paper on the subway in his early working days, but now he scans the headlines on his cell phone. Often he doesn't even look past the front page. The nature of the endeavor has changed: opening the physical paper was a commitment of time and space, but on a cell phone everything is fast and temporary, provisional. No one wants to settle down and read anything on it. What it offers is vast but superficial.

Today he doesn't even look at the headlines. Today he's not in that world.

He sets his bowl in the dishwasher. Last night he'd made himself scrambled eggs, those dishes are in there too. He pours powder into the little cup, slides the top shut and closes the door. He presses Start and the machine responds with its discreet hum. Strange to start something he will not see the end of.

He has spent many summers here with Janet, but since his return to the marriage he has come here many times alone. At first he came to hike, but after awhile—he felt faintly guilty about this, as he had on his honeymoon when he talked to the fisherman—he had begun simply to spend time here alone. Sometimes he doesn't go hiking at all, even if the weather is good. Sometimes he spends the day reading and listening to opera. Or he goes for an easy walk along a carriage trail, those wide soft dirt pathways that lead over the arched stone bridges, across steep ravines and rushing streams. Through the trees that rise straight and lofty overhead, creating their own shadowy green twilight. All this gives him solace. Janet has never asked to come with him.

At the back door he laces up his hiking boots, rough-side leather, heavy-soled, comfortable. He's worn them all over the island. He's hiked these mountains many times: Dorr, Cadillac, Sargent, Parkman, Pemetic, Champlain, Norumbega, Beech. He knows the shapes of the mountains, the way they rise and fall in lordly cascades, high above the surrounding sea. He knows the great stone amphitheaters opening onto the deep blue sky and the steep forested slopes, or onto the trim dark islands—the Porcupines to the east in Frenchman's Bay, Sutton, Greening, and the Cranberries to the south, the sea glittering beyond. He knows the exhilaration of those views.

He pours the rest of his coffee into a plastic mug for the car. He pulls on a light jacket.

All this is familiar, but something is rising inside him, marking time like the ticking of a clock.

Arriving at the summit is itself a reward. Arrival was like reaching Valhalla.

In the car, he heads east, across the island. The roads are empty.

He passes a field with two horses grazing in it. He always wonders about them: who owns them? He has never seen them ridden, they are always just moseying about the field, grazing or swishing flies. They are a mystery. There were these things that you kept track of, questions outside your life but not outside your range of curiosity, things you would never know the answers to. You thought you might someday learn them, but you would not. You would not.

He takes the Park Loop Road, then turns into the parking lot for Champlain. The lot is empty, he's the first.

He gets out and puts on his backpack. He locks the car with a little chirp, then changes his mind. He unlocks it and drops the key on the floor mat on the driver's side. He crosses the parking lot, his boots crunching loudly in the early silence. The air is cool and light, the breeze uplifting. It is like an overture.

At the trailhead is a stern sign, warning hikers that this is a difficult trail. No children, no dogs, no one scared of heights. No climbing in wet weather. The trail—Precipice—contains real risk. Warren has seen this sign many times; he feels a certain modest satisfaction, having met these challenges. He knows them well.

It begins with wide granite steps, a shallow staircase leading to the trail. As Warren starts up he feels the pleasure of familiarity, the way the place folds about him, the journey unrolling ahead. And he feels the ticking clock within him. The ground rises quickly and soon he is picking his way through boulders. Then boulders become the trail, a motionless avalanche of hurled shapes that must be clambered over. Small blue blazes discreetly mark the way. They are painted on boulders and trees, in places where you find yourself uncertain. As he climbs over the granite shapes his heartbeat quickens: his body is preparing.

Beyond the boulders the trail enters a grove of trees, with their tall solemn shapes, the faint spicy whiff of balsam. The trail climbs steadily and rapidly, steeper and steeper. He can feel his heart within his chest. A staircase for giants, huge steps made of squared-off boulders, rises ahead. He moves steadily upward to an internal beat. He can hear his own breathing. Is it loud? He has nothing to compare it to. He wonders if fear and exertion register as the same thing in the body. He is breathing hard. The trail steepens, twisting, and the iron rungs appear. Here begins the challenge. Taking the smooth iron bars above in both hands, setting his feet carefully onto the ones below, he pulls himself up the steep face. The physics of climbing: three points of contact at all times, both hands and a foot, both feet and a hand, holding fast and letting go, raising your body up and up and up. Trusting the iron rungs, driven into the granite a century ago. They're for climbers, but they're puzzling, set at odd angles: a corporeal jigsaw. You must solve the puzzle with your body, twisting here, reaching there. His body struggles upward, step by step. He feels it in his upper arms, his calves. His boots pushing against the iron rungs. Step by step he climbs up the sheer face.

It is exhilarating to conquer the mountainside. Thrilling.

The trail turns and twists against the cliff, insolent, fiddling its way up. In some places it goes along a ledge, the cliff face on one side, a sheer drop on the other. The space below is like a dream, opening up and drawing him into it. Rapture of the heights. He is careful never to look at it, never to look down. It's like thinking of Sarah.

The iron rungs beckon upward and he follows, hand over hand, foot over foot. He climbs farther and farther; he knows what is coming. His heart is pounding now, he can feel the big open hammering throughout his body. He can't think. He is only setting his hand in a safe place, pulling himself upward, his boot on a safe place, pushing himself up. He is coming to the narrow ledge along the flat steep face of the cliff, the place where it all converges.

Rung after rung, then a steep clamber up, following the blue dashes. His pulse is thudding in his ears now. His body knows what is coming, whether he is thinking of it or not. He is not thinking, he keeps himself from thinking, though he knows it.

He has known this was coming, he has planned what he will do and he will not pause, because if he pauses he will stop, and he will not stop. He will not take off his backpack, which for some reason seemed right, because that would be a signal and he is not sending a signal.

Here along the ledge the trail is not difficult. It's flat and safe, a narrow stone walkway jutting out from the mountain. On the outer edge of the path are low iron rungs, railings that lean inward against which you may brace your feet so you can press yourself against the mountain and safely pass the drop.

Warren reaches the narrow passage. Above him the mountain rises sheer and implacable, and below is the abyss: hundreds of ringing feet of nothingness, blue air, the soft, clean wind. Roaring emptiness. He walks at the same hiker's pace he began with, steadily, step by step. He is under a spell, and when he reaches the place where the narrow ledge curves tight around the face of the cliff he steps over the low railing and balances there for a moment, steadying himself, then takes the next easy step out into the singing emptiness that will hold him forever. He is looking down.

Acknowledgments

I'd like to thank my incomparable agent, Lynn Nesbit, for her brilliant insights and unflagging support of this book, also her assistant, Mina Hamedi, for her thoughtful comments; my first readers, Maggie Simmons and Susan Burden, for their thoughts and support. My great thanks, too, to writer and doctor Daley Walker, for his advice and counsel regarding medical issues in the text. I'd also like to thank my wonderful editor, Jill Bialosky, her assistant Drew Weitman, and the team at Norton; also my extraordinary publicist, Paul Bogaards, all of whom have helped this book find its place in the world. And always, thanks to my dear husband, Tony, and to our children, Gardner, Victoria, and Roxana, for sharing with me my life as a writer, and for making it possible.

ROXANA ROBINSON is the author of seven novels, three collections of short stories, and a biography of Georgia O'Keeffe. Her books have been chosen as *New York Times* Notable Books and as *New York Times* Editors' Choices. Her books have been published in England, France, Germany, Holland, and Spain. Her fiction has appeared in *The New Yorker*, *The Atlantic*, *Harper's* and elsewhere. She is the recipient of many awards, including the Barnes & Noble "Writers for Writers" Award. Roxana Robinson has received fellowships from the National Education Association, the MacDowell Colony, and the Guggenheim Foundation, and she was named a Literary Lion by the New York Public Library. Robinson has served on the Boards of PEN and the Authors Guild, and was the president of the Authors Guild from 2013 to 2017. She teaches in the MFA Program at Hunter College. She lives in Connecticut.